TUNIN
ROVE

ENGINES

TUNING ROVER V8 ENGINES

How to get the
best performance
for road and
competition use

David Hardcastle

Foulis

Haynes

First published in 1993
Reprinted 1994 and 1996

British Library Cataloguing-in-Publication Data
A catalogue record for this book
is available from the British Library.

ISBN 0 85429 933 5

Library of Congress catalog card no. 93-79166

G. T. Foulis & Company is an imprint of
Haynes Publishing,
Sparkford, Nr. Yeovil, Somerset,
BA22 7JJ, England

Printed in Great Britain by J. H. Haynes & Co. Ltd.

Contents

Introduction

When my book *The Rover V8 Engine* was published in 1990, it was never intended as a technical handbook for those wishing to tune the engine for road or race track, but rather as a celebration of a venerable and versatile power unit with an interesting and illustrious history that is appreciated and enjoyed by enthusiasts all over the world.

Admittedly that first book did contain a chapter which gave some broad tuning advice, and briefly examined the multitude of options available. However, it was obvious from the response I received from many readers of the original book that a second book devoted entirely to tuning the Rover V8 would not go amiss.

The theory and practice of engine tuning will always be subjective, and the Rover V8 engine with its multitude of options and specialists is no exception. Ask half a dozen engine builders their opinion on a specific aspect of building a Rover V8, and you will get at least half a dozen different answers!

For the enthusiast wanting to build him or herself an engine for a road car or competition vehicle, the options can be many and therefore possibly perceived as confusing, but this should not be considered a disadvantage. On the contrary, the Rover V8 cannot be bettered for providing abundant power at a realistic price in such a compact and versatile package.

At the end of the day the choices open to anyone contemplating an engine build are confined within the budget available, but trying to do something with limited resources should be no excuse for not doing the job properly. Engine building is about details. Yes, you can literally bolt on a certain amount of additional horsepower, but why settle for that when additional work and attention to those details will take that horsepower gain and increase it further? Also, what good is additional power if the engine has not been assembled properly and suddenly breaks in a very expensive manner, ruining valuable parts and involving the builder in expense that could have been better invested in making horsepower?

I have intentionally avoided quoting specific brake horsepower or torque figures for certain modifications or parts because the sheer variety of engine specifications, capacities, camshafts and induction systems available to the builder means that the power gains from a particular modification can vary enormously depending on the actual engine involved. I am also sceptical by nature, and so I have only quoted power figures in cases where I am as sure as I can be that they are accurate. Building an engine and installing it on a dyno (dynamometer) is the only real way to know the truth, and to have backed up the information in this book with dyno figures for every part and modification was just not practical.

I have tried to assemble all of the available knowledge on tuning this engine, although there is much that continues to remain clouded in secrecy. Some individuals were more forthcoming and willing to divulge information about how things are done. I have also tried to avoid expressing rigid opinions on how things should be done. You learn quickly with this engine that there are many differing views and most are worth listening too, but there is nothing wrong with arriving at your own solutions to problems or finding your own ways of doing things. Even the professionals do not have all the answers, and there is still plenty of scope for further innovation.

ROVER V8

I would recommend anyone who has the knack with things mechanical to have a go at building their own engine. It is a fascinating subject and immensely rewarding. Specific power outputs are of only academic interest when you turn the ignition key on that beautiful Rover V8 and it bursts into life with a deep burble, and revs smoothly and cleanly to 6,500 rpm, powering your vehicle forward with astonishing ease. A V8 engine makes one of the most beautiful sounds in the automotive world, and the Rover V8 has a certain silky refinement about it that is quite unique. Enjoy.

ACKNOWLEDGEMENTS

For the majority of the time writing this book was simply an indulgence of my spare time, investigating a fascinating subject and, most importantly, meeting some very pleasant and interesting people, all of whom had one thing in common: the Rover V8 engine.

I am not an engineer, nor actively involved in motor sport, although I have much worthwhile experience in working on cars, and an avid interest in engines which for one reason or another has often focused on the Rover V8. In order to write this book I have had to depend on the help and co-operation of a number of companies, and the openness and generosity of many individuals within those companies. The profile given to these companies within the book was not asked for, but I am delighted to be able to give credit where credit is due.

I would therefore like to thank John Eales of J. E. Developments, whose support, extraordinary knowledge and involvement made writing this book possible; everyone at J. E. Engineering who has supported both of my Rover V8 books with patience, considerable time and genuine interest; Simon Law at Rovercraft; Charles Pinion, Peter Pinion and John Watson of Real Steel; Kev Jenkins; Reg and Ray Woodcock; Roger Parker, whose collaboration on the fuel injection chapter was invaluable; Peter Burgess and the lads at Automotive Performance Engineering; Mick Richards for the most amazing car ride; Geoff Lee for building a mean engine; Robert Thornton in Adelaide; Mark Grinnall; and Mark Johnson.

Chapter One
The story so far

The Buick/Oldsmobile 215 cu. in. aluminium V8 engine, from which the Rover V8 has descended, was first put into production over 30 years ago, and its design goes back even further than that. Of course this is by no means a record for a successful automobile engine, but it does make this engine one of the industry's historically significant products.

The principle aim of designing and building this engine in aluminum was to reduce its weight, because the excessive weight of contemporary cast iron engines was perceived as a major obstacle in the building of "compact" American automobiles. Compared with many other notable American V8 engines, the Buick/Oldsmobile engine was not exceptionally powerful at 155–185 bhp, but its weight was exceptional. Buick declared their version of the aluminium engine weighed 144 kg (318 lb), while Oldsmobile admitted to approximately 159 kg (350 lb).

It is interesting to look at the weight and power outputs of some of the more significant engines produced by the industry during the period when it was dominated by a wide variety of V8 powerplants. The Chevrolet small-block is probably the most outstanding large-scale production engine to emerge from the United States, certainly in terms of versatility, length of service, and sheer production numbers. Introduced in 1955, a 265 cu. in. unit with a short-stroke, oversquare design, it achieved 1 bhp per cu. in. by 1957 (as a production unit) and had grown to 400 cu. in. by the late 1970s. Chevrolet engineers tried building an all-aluminium block of 283 cu. in. (3.875 x 3.00) and then tried an aluminium 327 cu. in. version (4.001 x 3.25) with steel cylinder liners to overcome porosity problems, but neither engine was produced in significant numbers. A regular cast iron Chevy small block weighed around 261 kg (575 lb), or 204 kg (450 lb) with aluminium heads.

The Chevrolet big-block which appeared in 1965 as a 396 cu. in. monster weighed in at an equally monstrous 313 kg (690 lb), which could be bought down to 272 kg (600 lb) with aluminium heads or 209 kg (460 lb) with an aluminium block. Power, of course, was prodigious in any form.

The Windsor Ford small-block appeared in 1962 as a 221 cu. in. engine, but quickly evolved through 260 cu. in. into the famous Ford 289 Hi-Po of 289 Cobra and Shelby Mustang fame (amongst others). It weighed around 222 kg (490 lb), as did the equally legendary Boss 302 engine which appeared in 1969, rated as 290 bhp at 5,800 rpm.

The famous Ford FE big-block, the 427 "side-oiler" version of which powered the mighty 427 Cobra, carried a massive 318 kg (700 lb) weight penalty, and while its power made the Cobra a legend, its weight did nothing for the car's handling and agility.

Engine weight is a significant proportion of total vehicle weight, and in the early 1960s was an important issue. Lighter engines enabled manufacturers to build lighter, better handling, more compact automobiles with better fuel consumption, and the giant General Motors, through their Buick, Oldsmobile and Pontiac divisions, wanted to be leading other US manufacturers in producing cars for the emerging compact market sector. The result was the aluminium Fireball V8.

There were two distinct variations of the same Buick/Oldsmobile design (Pontiac used the Buick version), differing in small but important details. For instance, the Oldsmobile version of the engine differed from its Buick

ROVER V8

brother by having the combustion chambers cast into the head (the Buick's were machined into the head) and six cylinder head bolts around each cylinder instead of the Buick's five. There were also differences in the rocker gear arrangement, inlet manifold, and exhaust manifolds. It was the Buick version that was adopted by Rover.

Oldsmobile introduced the new Rockette engine (their version of the Fireball) in their compact F-85 model. There was a two-barrel carburettor version with an 8.75:1 compression ratio that produced 155 bhp at 4,800 rpm with 210 lb/ft of torque. The four-barrel version, with a 10.75:1 compression ratio, mustered 195 bhp at 3,200 rpm and 235 lb/ft with a manual transmission (185 bhp and 230 lb/ft with an automatic transmission), which in a car with a kerb weight of around 1,222 kg (2,695 lb) gave the car lively performance.

The Buick/Oldsmobile 215 cu. in. aluminium V8 shared all the advantages of the Rover V8 but little of the success, at least in terms of numbers produced and years in production. In 1961, its first year of sales, the engine was produced in considerable quantity, the Oldsmobile F-85 selling 70,813, the Buick Special 90,000 and the more mechanically complex Pontiac Tempest 109,000. In its three short years of production, it went on to a total of around three-quarters of a million units.

But if the little 215 cu. in. engine lacked out and out power in production form, there were people who recognized its potential, and they were able to exploit it to the full. By mid 1961 Hot Rod Magazine had a Buick and an Oldsmobile engine on the Edelbrock dynamometers, and their methodical, step by step approach to performance improvements followed a familiar path. They went straight for more static compression by the simple method of fitting the flat top Oldsmobile pistons in the Buick engine, giving a healthy 12:1 compression ratio. They opened up the breathing first with more carburation and a pair of two-barrel Rochester's on an Edelbrock manifold, a prototype Isky E-2 camshaft, Hedman tubular headers and a dual point distributor. The result of their modest efforts was a best reading of 233 bhp, up from a standard 139 bhp at 4,500 rpm. Not bad for what was nothing more than an initial test and assessment session. They even had time to try an Isky roller camshaft.

Australia was the birthplace of a famous high-performance engine derived from the basic Buick/Oldsmobile aluminium engine design, although it was in many ways a fairly radical development. The Repco-Brabham Formula 1 engine of 1966 really only used the cylinder block of the Buick engine, with a steel flat plane crankshaft, of 2.37 in stroke and the standard 3.5 in bore giving a capacity of 2,994 cc. Special single overhead camshaft cylinder heads were designed for this engine, with unremarkable wedge-shaped combustion chambers and in-line valves inclined 10°. Power began at 285 bhp at 8,000 rpm (development saw that rise to 300 bhp) and peak torque of 230 lb/ft at 6,500 rpm.

The Rover aluminium V8 inherited the weight advantages from its Buick/Oldsmobile origins, weighing around 170 kg (375 lb). Being made of aluminium does not, of course, guarantee low weight. For instance the impressive Jaguar V12 aluminium unit of 5,443 cc produces in production form around 300 bhp at 5,500 rpm but it weighs a massive 309 kg (681 lb). As a point of interest, the most successful racing engine ever built (in aluminium alloys of course), the Cosworth DFV, weighs about 145 kg (320 lb).

That weight advantage is not the only factor that has made this engine so successful as a lightweight source of mass-produced abundant horsepower. It is not the lightest engine, nor the most powerful, nor has it been produced in greater numbers than any other engine, but as in a combination of weight, power cost and availability it has no equal. The glorious V8 sound is a bonus!

Australia was to see a second era of racing engine development using the Rover V8, when Rover designed, built and then sold on a big capacity version of the engine. The Leyland Australia version of this aluminium V8 had the standard bore of 88.9 mm (3.5 in) and an identical stroke, giving a capacity of 4.4 litres. With a modest twin-choke, down-draught, Stromberg carb it produced 192 bhp at 4,250 rpm and 285 lb/ft at 2,500 rpm.

The end of 1973 saw the unveiling in Australia of the Leyland Repco Formula 5000 racing engine based on the 4.4 litre version of the Rover engine used in the Leyland P76 saloon. Built as a collaboration effort between Leyland Australia and Repco, it had a 95.5 mm (3.7 in) bore and 89.9 mm (3.5 in) stroke for a capacity of 5 litres. The engine used the Leyland block, heads, water pump and timing cover and standard P76 crankshaft, considerably modified for racing with additional compensating weights. The standard block had steel back caps to the main bearings, each attached by four bolts. The cylinder heads were also P76, but fully prepared for racing with enlarged and polished ports and big valves, etc. However, the slightly longer than standard connecting rods and slipper-type pistons were Repco, as were all the bearings. Roller rockers were used with mushroom-type cam followers.

Induction was built around a magnesium butterfly-type manifold designed and manufactured by Repco, with individual port entry and injectors mounted on long curved trumpets. The fuel injection system itself was a Lucas high-pressure type with positive displacement metering unit and gear-driven, front-mounted pump. The ignition system was by a Repco Lorimer dual point distributor.

This remarkable engine weighed 158 kg (349 lb) (a F5000 Chevy weighed 231 kg/510 lb) and produced 425 bhp at 6,800 rpm with 375 lb/ft of torque at 5,000 rpm. The engine was raced both in Lola and Elfin Formula 5000 chassis.

The Leyland Repco engine was used by 1973 F5000 champion John McCormack, who in May 1975 unveiled a more radical development of the engine. The P76 cylinder heads had been extended upwards where the rocker cover normally bolts to the head and a new alloy rocker cover cast. This modification enabled the inlet port to be rewelded and angled upwards, making it much straighter, and allowing the inlet valve to be enlarged and re-angled to match the new fabricated inlet port. There was then room for larger Repco Holden valves. The heads were also changed to a six-bolt pattern (against the standard five), and a billet crank replaced the P76 item which was deemed too weak for the developed engine. Power was initially quoted as slightly more than 400 bhp.

Development continued and the modified P76 heads were eventually put aside in favour of specially designed castings. Appearing early in 1979 but now dubbed the IMC Leyland — the initials standing for Irving, McCormak and Comalco — it was part of the continuing evolution of the Leyland Repco project. This engine had completely new, specially designed alloy cylinder head castings, which were interchangeable to either side of the engine for ease of manufacture. The head incorporated all the earlier thinking on straight inlet port shape and bigger valves, which incidentally required two-piece pushrods, acting on a short slider retained in a bushed bore, acting in turn on Crane roller rockers. The block remained the basic P76. Irving designed Repco pistons set the compression ratio at 11.5:1

Much of the early competition development of the Rover V8 centred on parts and knowledge already acquired from tuning and racing the Oldsmobile/Buick V8, and with their American contacts John Wolfe Racing in Bedford were instrumental in sourcing and importing many specialist performance parts from such companies as Crane Camshafts, Edelbrock, Iskenderian, Hilborn, Crower Cams, Holley and Mallory, as well as building up a core of tuning knowledge which enabled many people interested in exploiting the Rover engine's potential to make a start.

Nothing accelerates automotive development like factory-backed competition efforts, and the Rover V8 was no exception. As an independent company, Rover had pursued their own modest racing and rallying programme, but not involving the Rover V8 engine. That all changed when the company became part of the British Leyland empire, and the BL Competition Department built a pair of Rover P6B racing saloons. These early racing engines did not benefit from any works engine development; they were in fact Traco/ Oldsmobile/Rover engines with little Rover content, built by Travers & Coons (Traco) in the USA. The exact specifications of these engines is now only of historic significance, but according to contemporary reports they used a 90.5 mm (3.563 in) bore and a 88.9 mm (3.5 in) stroke (the same as the Leyland P76 unit), retained hydraulic cam followers and wet sumps, but produced a reliable 360 bhp at 6,800 rpm on four down-draught Weber carburettors.

In late 1976, Leyland cars announced a motor sport programme that would involve the Triumph TR7 sports car which was very quickly evolved into the Triumph TR7 V8. Here the works did get enthusiastically involved in engine development, and the result was the first official competition version of the Rover V8 engine. The very first engines were modest affairs and even retained the hydraulic lifters. With a 10.5:1 compression ratio and a pair of 45 DCOE Webers mounted via an adaptor on to an Offenhauser inlet manifold, they produced 200 bhp and 225 lb/ft of torque at 5,000 rpm. By 1979 TR7 V8 rally engines were producing 285 bhp at 7,500 rpm (with a narrow power band) and 246 lb/ft of torque at 5,500 rpm. That was with 3.5 litres. Intensive development continued throughout the years of the programme, albeit on a limited budget, culminating in outputs of 300 bhp at 7,500 rpm and 268 lb/ft of torque at 5,500 rpm on four side-draught Webers, giving the TR7 V8 rally cars performance figures of 0–60 mph in 5.2 seconds and 0–100 mph in 12.8 seconds. Although the programme was cancelled at the end of 1980, hardware produced as a result of that exciting programme is still around today, and the pool of knowledge thus created for the Rover V8 engine expanded rapidly in the years that followed.

Even before the demise of the Triumph TR7 V8 rallying programme, BL Motorsport began exploring the racing and rallying potential of the Rover SD1 saloon. Factory-backed development of the engine for International

ROVER V8

Group A saloon car racing resulted in the production of the Rover Vitesse, and continued until 1986 with Tom Walkinshaw Racing while in private hands the Rover SD1 continued as a major contender of the British Touring Car Championship for another two years.

For saloon car racing the Rover 3500 (SD1) was initially built to Group 1 specifications. The Rover V8 engines produced a peaky and at first unreliable 260 bhp, but reached 280 bhp by the time Group A regulations were introduced. In October 1982 the Rover 3.5 litre V8 received fuel injection, and the Rover Vitesse became a more sophisticated racing machine. The power by now was 290 bhp with an overall broader power band and by the time the factory racing ceased in 1986 power was over 300 bhp (still with 3.5 litres). These Group A engines had to be built within a strict framework of regulations, regulations which no longer have any relevance in current competition, but again the hardware and knowledge built up from those days is still used by today's engine builders.

The engine has continued to play a major part in mainstream motor sport and development goes on, albeit in the hands of smaller, specialist companies. The Rover V8 engine still provides prodigious amounts of horsepower in the international arena by powering many competitors in the now famous Paris-Dakar Rally Raid and similar spin-off events.

The main performance road car application of the engine is now in the hands of TVR Power of Coventry (formerly NCK Racing) who build Rover V8 engines for use in the TVR sports car range, and continue research and development on behalf of the parent company. The TVR Tuscan Challenge, a one-make, identical engine series, has furthered the development process.

The availability of new products and components for the Rover V8 has been slowed by the economic downturn in recent years, which has reduced enthusiasts' spending ability for their road and weekend competition cars, and reduced the budgets of more ambitious motor sport programmes. The small Rover V8 specialist companies still thrive in the UK, and ideas for future products continue to receive their attention, but in order to commit themselves to the investment needed to finance manufacture they have to be satisfied that a market exists that will ensure sufficient demand for that product. This is especially true of more costly projects such as four-valve cylinder heads, which will undoubtedly be available in the future; but even smaller, higher volume items such as pistons or camshafts require investment that has to be recovered from retail sales.

THE PRODUCTION ENGINE

The production versions of the Rover V8 that have rolled off the Land-Rover production lines for the past 25 years have varied surprising little. But the engine has received constant and ongoing development at Solihull to ensure that it has always been capable of providing adequate, reliable power for the variety of applications that have been required of it.

Of course, for mass production there are a bewildering multitude of criteria which the engineers must meet. Rates of production, emissions, vehicle requirements, strict budgeting, warranty and servicing standards, consistency of product, manufacturing costs and feasibility to name a few all conspire to result in what many enthusiasts consider to be a very conservative product.

The engine remained in more or less one basic form throughout production of the Rover 3.5 litre (P5B), the Rover 3500 (P6B), the earlier Range-Rover and the MGB V8.

The Rover P5B and the P6B engine were one and the same in specification, having a 10.5:1 compression ratio and producing 160 bhp at 5,200 rpm with 210 lbf/ft of torque at 2,600 rpm, although in 1974 the Rover P6B engine had the compression ratio dropped to 9.25:1 with a change of piston.

The Rover V8 as used on the Range-Rover has evolved during the long production life of this marvellous vehicle, but basically it started out at 135 bhp at 4,750 rpm and 205 lb/ft of torque at 3,000 rpm (compression ratio 8.5:1) and in July 1981 went to 9.35:1 compression ratio and produced 125 bhp at 4,000 rpm with 185 lb/ft of torque at 2,500 rpm. Fuel injection was introduced in 1985 with a 165 bhp version.

The MGB V8 introduced in August 1973 was not given a particularly potent version of the engine. It was essentially the same as the versions fitted to the Rover P5B and P6B, but with a compression ratio of 8.25:1, its output being 137 bhp at 5,000 rpm and 193 lb/ft at 2,900 rpm.

Not until the "new" Rover 3500 of 1976, now universally referred to as the SD1, was the engine significantly altered in specification. The block remained the same with the exception of lip seals on the front and rear of the crankshaft which had been phased in a little earlier. The cylinder heads were new castings with larger valves, but the ports themselves were only slightly improved, and the cam followers were also altered to allow slightly higher revving. There were also improvements to the oil pump (higher volume), ignition and water pump, which were all of great benefit to the engine overall.

The factory Triumph TR8 had a fairly normal 3.5 litre Rover engine producing 152 bhp at 4,750 rpm and torque of 196 lb/ft at 2,750 rpm, except for the inlet manifold on the carburetted version which was unique, but only in as much as it allowed the twin Zenith/Stromberg carbs to clear the underside of the bonnet.

Fuel injection was the next major milestone in the engine's history, developed initially to meet tighter emission standards in North America. It was used to a limited extent on the Rover 3500 (P6B) and put into production on the later Rover 3500 (SD1) exported to both in North America and Australia as well as Californian-sold Triumph TR8s. The fuel injection system initially manufactured used different hardware to the system used on the Rover Vitesse, which although used extensively on production engines to the present was designed with racing in mind, and was further developed in conjunction with Lotus as the "twin plenum" system. The twin plenum injection system only found its way into a couple of hundred Vitesses. It is actually a slightly larger plenum chamber, with a pair of standard diameter Vitesse throttle bodies.

More recently we have seen the 3.9 litre Rover V8 engine introduced in North America for the Range-Rover and now available in the UK, using the injection system first seen on the Rover Vitesse and since adopted for all EFi Range-Rover models. The current Range Rover EFi with the larger 3.9 litre (actually 3,947 cc) fuel injected version of the engine is rated at 185.1 bhp at 4,750 rpm and 235 lb/ft of torque at 2,600 rpm.

The actual Land-Rover that we are all familiar with is known now in its current form as the Land-Rover Defender, and as well as the more mundane four-cylinder petrol and diesel engine options it is available with a carburetted 3.5 litre Rover V8, which produces 134 bhp at 5,000 rpm and 187 lb/ft of torque at 2,500 rpm.

The current 3.5 litre Rover V8 as offered in the Land-Rover Discovery EFi produces 163.3 bhp at 4,750 rpm and 219.9 lb/ft of torque at 2,600 rpm. It seems likely that the 3.5 litre version of the engine will cease production altogether at Land-Rover, to be superseded entirely by the 3.9 litre version. In September 1992 Land-Rover launched the new Range-Rover LSE powered by a 4.2 litre (4278 cc) version of the engine, the 94.04 mm (3.7 in) bore of the 3.9 litre version being combined with a new 77 mm (3.03 in) stroke crankshaft and a lowly 8.94:1 compression ratio. The engine, producing a disappointing 200 bhp at 4,850 rpm and only a slight increase in torque over the 3.9 litre version (250 lb/ft at 3,250 rpm), is said to have an improved torque curve, better suited to the needs of new long-wheelbase "super" Range-Rover LSE, with its adjustable height air suspension and much increased interior space.

After considerable low-key publicity and press speculation, the new MGB Roadster, the MG RV8, was unveiled late in 1992. When available in early 1993 it will be powered by a 3.9 litre Rover V8 producing 188 bhp and over 220 lb/ft of torque. Also revealed at the same time was news of a new vee engine under development at Rover based on the K-series, four-cylinder engine. Whether it will be a V6 or V8 (or both?) remains to be seen, but introduction is possible in 1994/1995. At the time of writing it is rumoured that a further development of the Rover V8 is to be unveiled in 1994 (?) which may be sufficiently different from the current design to be evolutionary. Certainly it seems that many parts, for example the cylinder block, will not be interchangeable with the present Rover V8, so we could be seeing the beginning of the end of the Rover V8 as we know it.

Chapter Two

The building bricks

One of the problems when building an engine is identifying the key components available in order to ascertain which have the greatest potential and those which should, if possible, be avoided. Many people may try to utilize second-hand components in order to reduce costs, and when examining engines or parts with a view to purchasing them, it is worth knowing which parts to look out for and which to avoid.

Many parts described in the following pages are not widely available. For instance the Australian P76 engines and parts were never used in any British vehicles, but quite a few of these engines have been imported at one time or another, and parts or complete engines do occasionally turn up in advertisements.

It might also be worth mentioning one or two facts about ex-racing parts that sometimes turn up for sale. During the years that the Rover 3500 (SD1) was enjoying success as a Group 1 and then Group A British and European Touring (Saloon) Car race car, there was a tremendous amount of research and development work done on the Rover V8 engine by many companies. The result of this was a substantial quantity of specialist racing parts/components, from cylinder blocks to valve gear and even complete engines, built to comply with strict construction regulations. As with any form of motor sport at this level, a great deal of time was devoted to exploiting these regulations, ie, pushing the letter of the regulations to the absolute limits in order to extract maximum advantage.

Such exploitation resulted in some very strange and indeed wonderful engine parts, many of which could just as easily have been replaced with less expensive and possibly even more efficient components had the regulations allowed. For example, for many years camshaft design in Group A was free with the single proviso that the valve lift must remain no greater than the standard camshaft. This led to Group A racing camshaft designs which made the best usable power within those lift limits. Camshafts were widely available from a number of sources which were better, but of course few could be used because of the valve lift limits imposed by the regulations.

In the area of valve gear alone there were many oddball parts specially made or more mundane components subjected to all sorts of machining in order to exploit the regulations, and in the hands of an inexperienced engine builder many of these parts could cause all sorts of unnecessary hassle when assembling an engine. Some racing cylinder blocks had no provision for supplying the cam followers with pressurized oil, so it would be possible quite unwittingly to fit hydraulic followers to one of these blocks and have one hell of a time trying to work out why there was a problem!

That is not to say that all such parts should be avoided. There are many Group A or works rallying parts widely available, such as con rods, which are acceptable (although expensive), and are an excellent choice for a competition engine.

Put simply, just because engines or parts (especially second-hand) are advertised or sold as "ex-works racing", do not automatically assume that they are going to be compatible with other Rover V8 parts you intend to use. If you have the opportunity to buy "complete ex-TWR short engine with a steel crank, Group A rods and forged pistons" for instance, by all means consider it a worthwhile purchase for a racing project, but take care. It may have all sorts of detailed alterations done either by machining or even during casting, which hopefully can be used to your advantage, but may cause assembly problems when mixed with less exotic parts.

CYLINDER BLOCKS

The Rover cylinder block closely follows the original GM design and is a one-piece aluminium casting, with cast iron cylinder liners. The block casting has cast iron "dry" cylinder liners – ie no cylinder block coolant comes into contact with the outer surface of the liner – which are dropped into the pre-heated block during manufacture. It is a rigid deep skirt design, ie, the block walls extend some way below the centre line of the crankshaft. A one-piece, die-cast aluminium front cover serves as a mount for the distributor and fuel pump, housing for the integral oil pump, retainer for crankshaft front oil seal, water pump scroll and dual water outlets. The main bearing caps are cast iron.

The prospective engine builder actually has several blocks to choose from, although from an availability point of view the production Rover item is the most practical. The Rover block has been revised four times during its production life, the revised casting always superseding its forebearer. In fact it is only now, with the 3.5 litre and 3.9 litre blocks being manufactured simultaneously, that more than one production block is currently available, and it is highly likely that the 3.5 litre block will disappear from production in the near future.

Early blocks These original blocks fall into two categories, engines built prior to 1973 with rope crankshaft seals in the rear of the block (and front cover), and those which have rubber lip seals for the crankshaft which were introduced on engines built from 1973 onwards. Rope crankshaft seals are found on the all original Rover V8 engines used in the Rover P5B and P6B saloons, MGB V8s and older Range-Rovers. The changeover from rope to rubber lip occurred during 1972–3. In material thickness and overall strength these early blocks are very similar to the Buick/Oldsmobile blocks from which the design is derived. They continued in this form through the introduction of the new Rover 3500 (SD1), but were revised during the SD1's production life. From 1984 onwards all production blocks were modified and are often referred to as the "Vitesse stiff block", although in truth they became the standard production block.

Later stiff block These revised blocks ("Vitesse stiff blocks") were introduced into production in 1984 (some were produced in 1983) and include slightly more material around the main bearing webs, thicker webs across the lifter gallery, between the cylinder banks, and more webs on the front of the block, behind the timing gear area. Introduced into production as a result of the Vitesse racing programme, post-1984 blocks are acknowledged as an excellent basis for a competition engine. There is a slight variation worth mentioning, known unofficially as the AE block, which can best be identified by having a fine lattice-type pattern cast into the exterior surface of the block sides. These AE blocks are not actually a production variation, but the particular foundry concerned uses a distinctive type of casting pattern, resulting in a very thick, robust block which is well worth seeking out as a basis for an engine build.

Leyland P76 block There are very few of

Early pre-SD1 Rover V8 cylinder block on the left and later post-'82/'83 stiff block on the right. Note the additional webbing on the front of the stiff block.

In this picture the early block is on the right and the later stiff block is on the left. Note the additional material above the main bearing area and either side of the main bearing cap location.

This view from the top of the block, again with early block on the right and the later stiff block on the left, shows the greater material in the valley area and thicker webs running across the valley.

On the left a Leyland P76 4.4 litre cylinder block with a standard 3.5 litre Rover early block on the right. The height difference between the two can clearly be seen.

these in the UK, although they are widely available in Australia where they were manufactured in considerable quantities from 1973 until the demise of Leyland Australia in 1975. They formed the basis of a 4.4 litre version of the Rover V8 and differ from a 3.5 litre production block in some respects. The cylinder bore is the same at 88.9 mm (3.5 in), because the extra capacity was due to a bigger stroke crankshaft. However, because of this longer stroke, the block is 17.463 mm (0.6875 in) taller overall, having longer cylinders. The "stroker" crank also had larger diameter main bearings, 63.5 mm (2.5 in) instead of the normal Rover's 57.2 mm (2.25 in) diameter, so the block has correspondingly larger main bearings. The cylinder head deck surfaces only have four bolt holes around each cylinder, as opposed to the Rover blocks which have five. The taller block also places the cylinder heads further apart, severely limiting inlet manifold choice, unless spacers are specially machined.

3.9/4.2 litre block In 1988, Land-Rover unveiled the Osprey engine for the North American market, which centred around a new 3.9 litre block with a 94.4 mm (3.7 in) cylinder bore. In all other respects this block is identical to the 3.5 litre block with the 88.9 mm (3.5 in) bore, but the new block does have more aluminium material around the cylinder liners than the smaller 88.9 mm (3.5 in) bore block. Because of their relatively recent introduction used blocks will be difficult to locate, although they can of course be bought new (for which read expensive) as service items. However, well-seasoned blocks are

A factory cross-bolt block. Note the difference in the side area of the main bearing cap compared with previous photographs of standard blocks.

always favoured for performance engine building, so converting a 3.5 litre block to 3.9 litre is a more sensible approach, although it must be said that theoretically a 3.5 litre block converted to 3.9 litres will not be as strong as a production 3.9 litre block. In practice this has never been a problem. This same block is used for the very latest 4.2 litre version of the engine, which adds a longer 77 mm (3 in) stroke crankshaft to the 94.04 mm (3.70 in) bore.

Cross-bolt block Also referred to as four-bolt mains or X-bolt blocks, these are the same as normal production 3.5 litre cylinder blocks, except that the main bearing caps are retained by four bolts instead of two. Because of the deep skirt design of the Rover block, the additional two bolts have to come through the side of the block into specially cast main bearing caps at right angles. This limits the length of the two extra bolts, but the design does tie the block/crank assembly together very well, and is widely regarded as the ultimate competition block.

Cross-bolt blocks come supplied from Land-Rover with hex bolts for the two extra bolts coming through the side of the block into the main caps. These have been found to be too weak and should be replaced with cap screws of the same size.

Cross-bolt blocks have never been used in any production vehicles. They were designed for use by BL Motorsport, later Austin Rover Motorsport, and borrowed by Land-Rover for the Iceberg diesel engine project which was eventually cancelled. Consequently these blocks are not widely available, but are produced in small batches periodically when the need arises, such as during Land-Rover's involvement in the Paris-Dakar Rally Raid. They can be obtained, but they are very expensive and are supplied unfinished, so there is additional cost involved in getting them ready for assembly. More than one company now produces a four-bolt conversion based on a two-bolt casting. For instance, Rovercraft of Maidstone do their own version of a cross-bolt block, machined from a standard two-bolt casting, and J. E. Developments can supply a four-bolt conversion based on a brand new 3.9 litre block with massive alloy main bearing caps. Either way, these blocks are an expensive option.

Buick block There is little to say about the original American-produced blocks that cannot be applied to the original Rover castings. The cylinder liners had heavily ribbed outer surfaces and were placed in the mould before the aluminium was poured so the block cast was around them, unlike the Rover liners which are dropped cold into a pre-heated block. They can be best identified by having the additional bosses cast in the lifter gallery, one to each cylinder, which on the Buick block are not drilled, but are drilled and tapped on the Oldsmobile version for the additional cylinder head retaining bolt. The main bearing diameter for the Buick and Oldsmobile crank was 58.4 mm (2.3 in).

Oldsmobile block General Motors used the 1961–3 aluminium engine in vehicles produced by their Buick, Oldsmobile and Pontiac divisions. Buick vehicles used the Buick engine, which is the design adopted by Rover, but Oldsmobile engineered their own variation of the engine. It is identical to the Buick version previously described, except for having six bolt holes around each cylinder, for the cylinder head retaining bolts.

TWR/competition blocks These are worth mentioning, for the simple reason that there are many about in circulation still being used in competition, and they may crop up in advertisements or be found in competition cars with a works competition history. There were two main phases of factory involvement. Firstly there was the Triumph TR7 V8 rallying programme which began in 1977 (officially 1978) and ended in 1980. Secondly there was the Tom Walkinshaw Racing assault on the British Touring Car Championship with the Rover 3500 (SD1)

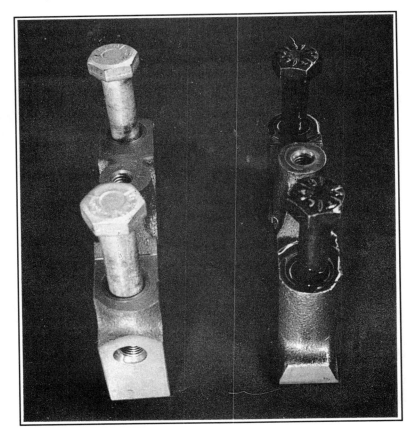

Bearing detail, with the cross-bolt block main cap on the left and a standard two-bolt cap on the right.

In this wider view of a cross-bolt block, the drilled bosses for the cross bolts can clearly be seen, but apart from that the basic casting offers no other advantages over the standard casting.

This is an original Buick block from 1961–3. It is identical to the Oldsmobile except that the bosses visible in the picture across the top edge of the block are drilled for a sixth cylinder head bolt (not used on the Buick).

which started in 1981 and was later expanded into the European Touring Car Championship which continued until 1986. In addition, there was a limited works rallying programme with the same car and a number of substantial private teams who campaigned

Triumph TR7 V8s and Rover 3500s (SD1s), as well as several campaigners of the Rover 3500 (SD1) in British Touring Car Racing. There were many blocks taken as bare castings during this era that were subjected to all sorts of special machining in the name of

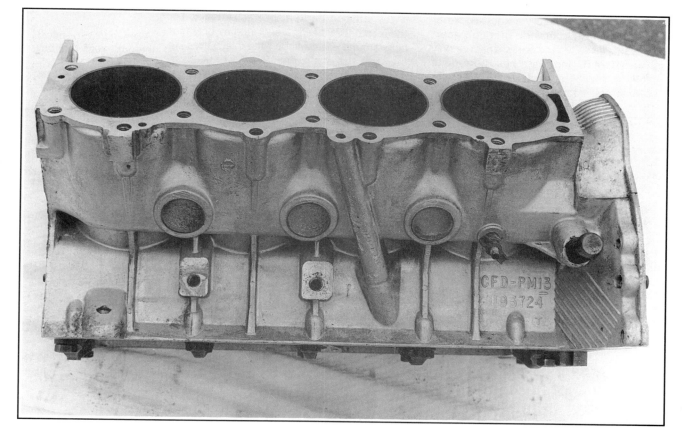

ROVER V8

development. For instance, oil feed drillings were altered or omitted altogether, adaptions were made for dry-sump systems, and details modifications were often made in the course of development to optimize a particular block for a particular racing or rallying application.

The rarest block of all must be the limited number of Oldsmobile turbocharged engine cylinder blocks which had taller, meatier (but still two-bolt) main bearings caps retained with special twelve-point fasteners.

CYLINDER HEADS

The Rover V8 production cylinder heads have been designed for good emissions and low-end torque, so as a consequence possess combustion chambers with excellent mixture swirl effect. The Rover V8 cylinder head design is sound, although the basic design has its shortcomings for performance, but then so have most engine pieces designed for mass production. Land-Rover have produced two distinct castings, but the choice of available heads for the engine builder is actually six.

Rover P5B/P6B These are the original heads produced from the time the Rover V8 was first introduced until the launch of the Rover 3500 (SD1), so can be found on all other Rover V8 engines used in the MGB V8, Range-Rover and Freight-Rover V8 vans until 1976. This head is generally acknowledged as inferior to the SD1 version, although apart from its smaller valves the port shapes are only slightly different, and these heads are quite capable of flowing enough air for 230 bhp. The 36 cc cast combustion chamber has 38

mm (1.5 in) inlet valves and 33 mm (1.3 in) exhaust valves, with three angle valve seats, and uses 12.7 mm (0.5 in) reach spark-plugs with five bolts around each cylinder (as do all Land-Rover-produced cylinder heads).

Rover SD1/Vitesse/Current All cylinder heads are basically the same since they received some revisions to port shape and valve size for introduction in the Rover 3500 (SD1) saloon in 1976. The combustion chamber volume remained the same at 36 cc, but the inlet valves, again with three angle seats, were increased in size to 40 mm (1.6 in) and the exhaust to 34 mm (1.3 in) with 19 mm (0.7 in) reach spark-plugs. The object of these changes was to extend the useable rpm range of the engine in its new application.

The Rover Vitesse heads are superior to the SD1 type but are the same casting. Their superiority comes from the valves used. The valve diameter is the same, but the valves have waisted stems and are machined immediately behind the valve head (the underhead area) to increase flow, which they do successfully. The valve throat has been machined to increase the diameter some 40 thou, but more interestingly the valves have been recessed approximately 120 thou into the combustion chamber, restricting low valve lift inlet flow but assisting overall exhaust valve flow.

Leyland P76 These heads differ considerably from the Rover version, but the differences offer no performance advantages. For the record, P76 heads are located by only four bolts around each cylinder, the inlet valves are the same size as the pre-1976 Rover heads at 38 mm (1.5 in), as are the exhaust valves at 33.3 mm (1.3 in). These heads have no rocker

A Leyland P76 cylinder head uses only four bolts around each cylinder. Valve sizes are the same as early Rover heads.

Rocker arm detail on the Leyland P76 cylinder head. It is unique to this engine, with rocker gear oiling via hollow push-rods.

shaft, but instead the stamped steel rockers are stud-mounted in pairs (like the small-block Chevrolet engine) and top-end oiling is via hollow pushrods.

Buick 300 (1964) For 1964 only the Buick 300 cast iron engine had aluminium cylinder heads which, because of the design ancestry of the Buick 300 engine, fit the Rover V8 engine. These heads only have four bolts around each cylinder head and have a large 54 cc combustion chamber.

With these heads it is the inlet valve diameter that is really interesting, being 41.2 mm (1.6 in), while the exhaust valve remains a disappointing 33.3 mm (1.3 in). These heads will take Manley 38 mm (1.5 in) VW inlet valves and TRW 43.7 mm (1.7 in) Volvo exhaust valves, although the VW inlet valve will have to be ground to the same length as the Volvo exhaust valve. The ports – particularly the inlet – are reputed to be superior to the Rover heads, although in reality the interest in these heads stems from their superiority over the original Buick/Oldsmobile heads which the Rover redesign – that is post-1976 engines – went a long way towards addressing.

Buick heads Basically the same as the original (pre-1976) Rover heads, with five bolts around each cylinder but with an oblong hemispherical chamber of 37 cc machined into the head. The Buick version is considered to have an inferior exhaust port design (which the Rover inherited) to the Oldsmobile head, being fairly restricted behind the valve and flaring out towards the port.

The 38.1 mm inlet (1.48 in) and 33.3 mm (1.3 in) exhaust are located towards the upper side of the cylinder bores with the spark-plugs located almost in the centre of the cylinder bore. Aluminium rockers are located on a conventional rocker shaft like the Rover heads.

Oldsmobile The heads have a wedge-

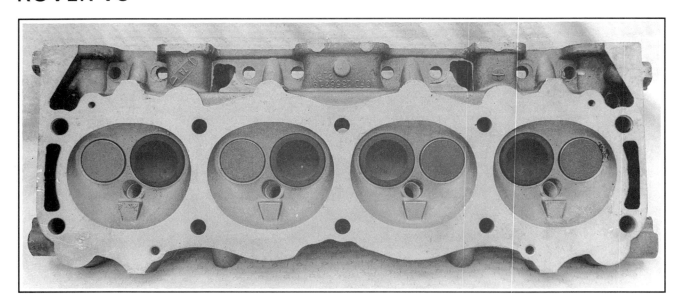

Buick 300 aluminium cylinder head, again with only four bolts around each cylinder. These heads do have performance potential when used with the Rover V8, but are not so easy to obtain.

shaped combustion chamber machined into the head with the valves lying in line almost across the centre line of the bore and the spark-plugs offset towards the lower side of the bore. There were two distinct heads produced by Oldsmobile: those for use with a single two-barrel Rochester carb had 51 cc combustion chambers, and those using a single four-barrel Rochester had 38 cc chambers giving a higher compression ratio. All Oldsmobile heads had six bolts around each combustion chamber. The inlet valves were 38.6 mm (1.5 in) diameter and exhaust valves 34.3 mm (1.3 in). The Oldsmobile engine had steel rockers with the rocker shaft pillar bolts going right through the head into the block.

CRANKSHAFTS

A view of the Buick 300 aluminium cylinder head, looking at the exhaust ports.

For the majority of enthusiasts the crankshaft choice for a 3.5 litre or 3.9 litre engine is limited to the stock 71 mm (2.8 in) stroke, cast spheroidal graphite iron, five-bearing item. It has 58.4 mm (2.3 in) diameter main bearings and 50.8 mm (2 in) diameter big end bearing. It is certainly not a bad choice since it has proved itself in racing and rallying competition, and in thousands of high mileage production engines.

The Rover V8 crankshaft weighs 36 kg (79 lb). This is not particularly heavy for this type of engine and is certainly not a handicap in the overall weight of the Rover V8, and it lacks nothing in strength, given the material from which it is made.

There are steel crankshafts available in virtually any stroke (more on this subject later).

However, steel crankshafts have never been used in production engines and are only available – at a price – from specialists. They are not legal in some racing classes.

Another view of the Buick 300 aluminium cylinder head, looking at the inlet ports.

There are other crankshafts, with production origins which can be used when building Rover V8 engines of various capacities. Their application is discussed in more detail in Chapter 5.

The crankshaft from the later 1964–7 cast iron version of the Buick/Oldsmobile engine design, known as the Buick 300, has a crankshaft that can be made to fit in the Rover block. The Buick 300 crank has 63.5 mm (2.5 in) main bearing diameter (so will not drop straight into a Rover block) and is externally balanced, unlike the Rover which is *internally* balanced. However, the biggest problem with the Buick crankshaft is the fact that it is longer, ie the flywheel flange is 14.2875 mm (0.5625 in) further back, which will cause problems if used with an automatic transmission. Perhaps more difficult to overcome are the differences in the rear main oil seal arrangement which requires machining and the design of a "labyrinth" oil seal. However, the Buick 300 crank does offer a stroke of 86.3 mm (3.4 in) which is an increase of 15.2 mm (0.6 in) over the standard Rover crank. The Buick 300 does have less overlap between bearing journals so is inherently weaker, although this has never manifested itself in this application.

The Leyland P76 crankshaft, with its 88.9 mm (3.5 in) stroke is the largest stroke crankshaft ever used in production in the Rover V8 engine. The 4.4 litre P76 saloon car engine in which this crankshaft was used was also found in the Leyland Terrier light truck, but these truck engines have crankshafts with larger (and heavier) counterweights. The P76 crank has 63.5 mm (2.5 in) main bearing journals so will not bolt straight into a Rover V8 block.

Billet cranks There are a number of companies who can machine crankshafts to any required design from solid steel billet, hence billet cranks. A number of 5.2 litre Rover V8 engines have been built using a combination of 96.5 mm (3.8 in) bore and 88.9 mm (3.5 in) stroke billet cranks, and in fact a 5.5 litre Rover V8 engine has been built using such a crankshaft which would require a stroke of 98.0 mm (3.8 in). They are of course very expensive and require work to block for clearance of the counterweights inside the crank case.

In September 1992 Land-Rover unveiled the new Range-Rover LSE with a 4,278 cc engine. The factory-manufactured long stroke cast iron crankshafts has a 77 mm (3.03 in) stroke but remains identical to its 71 mm (2.8 in) stroke counterpart in design. These cranks will fit any Rover V8 block although the longer stroke will require compatible pistons (see *Chapter 5*).

PISTONS

When considering piston choice for the Rover V8 there are some general points about piston design that should be considered. The piston should not burden the engine with excessive operating friction; it has to transfer the maximum amount of combustion heat into the cylinder walls; it should be of low overall weight; and provide adequate gudgeon/wrist pin support.

The total piston area of standard Rover V8 with an 88.9 mm (3.5 in) bore is 496.5 sq cm (777 sq in). On a standard factory-built engine the particular piston used is the deciding factor in establishing specific mechanical compression ratios. However, when discussing

23

Crankshafts. Left to right: Buick 300 (86 mm stroke), Billet Steel (71.1 mm stroke), Leyland P76 (88.9 mm stroke), J. E. Engineering cast (80 mm stroke), Standard Rover (71.1 mm stroke).

pistons for use in individual engines other factors may have to be taken into account, such as the combustion chamber volume of the particular cylinder heads used, the volume of the cylinder/piston crown when at TDC (top dead centre), and the cylinder head gasket thickness.

Current Rover V8 production pistons are either 88.9 mm (3.5 in) or 94.04 mm (3.70 in) diameter because of the different bore sizes between the 3.5 and 3.9 litre. Throughout the long production period of the Rover V8, the numerous applications of the 3.5 litre engine has given rise to a range of different compression ratios/pistons, from 10.5:1 of the early Rover saloons to the 8.13:1 of the Land-Rover Defender. The factory piston choice and thus compression ratio variants for the 3.9 litre versions of the engine are far more limited because the engine is fairly new. Likewise the 4.2 litre version released in September 1992 has a compression ratio of 8.9:1, and although it still has a 94.04 mm bore, it uses a dimensionally different piston with a different (lower) compression height than the 3.9 litre engine, even though it shares the same bore diameter.

Some early (pre-SD1) Rover V8 pistons gave a compression ratio of 10.5:1 (slightly lower when used with SD1 heads), and it has long been considered a hot tip to fit these pistons in later engines to boost the compression ratio.

The Leyland P76 engine pistons are dimensionally identical to the Rover 3.5 litre items in terms of diameter, ring package and

Factory pistons. From left to right: Rover P6B with a compression ratio of 10.5:1, Rover SD1 with 9.35:1 and a Range Rover piston with a deeply dished crown giving a 8.13:1 ratio.

wrist pin placement. Although the compression height is about 0.07 in more, the compression ratio is only 9:1 because the piston has a deep dish cast into the crown.

Like the Rover V8, the Buick engine's two production compression ratios (for two or four-barrel carbs) of 8.8:1 or 10.25:1 depended on the piston used. The Oldsmobile version was the odd one out, because it used a single type of flat-top piston and altered the compression ratio for the two and four-barrel engines (the two-barrel was 8.75:1) by having cylinder heads with slightly differing chamber volumes. (See *Cylinder heads* above.)

All factory piston rings up to the start of the 3.5 litre EFi engines have 2 mm (0.078 in) wide compression rings, after this point the compression rings changed to 1.5 mm (0.0585 in). This is because older type rings could not maintain sufficient radial tension in narrower sizes, but modern materials have made it possible to reduce the width without compromising ring life. Some racing pistons do use 1 mm (0.039 in) wide compression rings because they are less prone to ring flutter at high rpm.

CONNECTING RODS

The Rover V8 engine builder now has an excellent choice of connecting rods from aftermarket sources, but the range of production con rods is severely limited.

The standard Rover V8 connecting rod is an alloy steel forging with a press-fit gudgeon (or wrist) pin. The big end has a diameter of 50.8 mm (2.0 in) and the small end is 22.1 mm (0.87 in) in diameter. There are three distinct versions of the production rod, each with a unique rod bolt (see photo). The early rod, used in the Rover P5B, Rover P6B, MGB V8 and early Range-Rovers has no machined pad on the rod sides near the big end, and the rod bolt is marked with a small circle.

With the arrival in 1976 of the new Rover 3500 (SD1), its version of the engine and all subsequent production engines had a new, although not drastically altered, version of the con rod, with a smaller machined pad near the big end and the rod bolts marked with a slot on the bolt head.

With the Vitesse fuel injected engine came a slightly different rod, with machined pads near the big end and the rod bolt marked with a dot. This rod superseded the SD1 rod and became the standard production rod for all versions of the Rover V8 engine, including the 3.9 litre engine. The latest rods are the best production rod available, although there is really little to choose between them. The rod bolts used on these current rods are reputed to be the best of any available and if new rod bolts are being selected for use with production rods these are the ones to use.

Possibly worth including here, since they are production-rod based, are the Group A rods which are identical in appearance, forged from the same pattern, but in stronger EN24 material. They are considerably stronger and also heavier, weighing 540–546 g (1.19–1.20 lb) as opposed to the standard production rods 501–509 g (1.10–1.12 lb).

The Leyland P76 4.4 litre engine had con rods 158.8 mm (6.25 in) long and superficially they are exactly the same design as the Rover rods (apart from being longer, obviously), so they share the same design weaknesses.

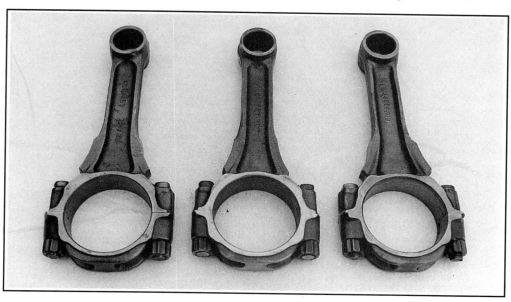

Production connecting rods. On the left the early rod, superseded in 1973 by the Rover SD1 rod, and then replaced again in 1983 by the Vitesse rod.

Connecting rod identification. From left to right: Rover P5B, P6B and early Range-Rover, the latest type as fitted to the Vitesse and all production engines that followed, and finally the Rover SD1 con rod. The key is in the different markings on the bolt heads, which should be checked to see if they match the other rod details in the picture.

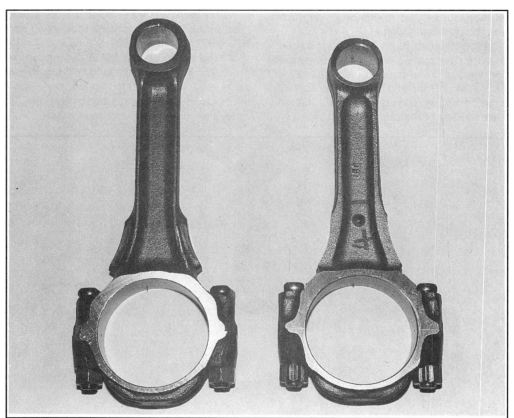

Leyland P76 4.4 litre connecting rod on the left and the standard Rover connecting rod on the right. The design is almost identical. Only the length differs.

CAMSHAFTS

Land-Rover have used a limited number of camshaft specifications in the Rover V8 in the many years of engine production but none has any performance potential, although some good strong road engines have been built retaining the standard production camshaft. There have been half a dozen different camshafts fitted in these engines, starting with the original which the factory refer to as the '66 four-barrel camshaft (referring to the Rochester carburettor used on the original Buick version of the engine), and the difference between them is of no consequence to anyone contemplating performance tuning. The standard Rover saloon camshaft specification stated in most manuals, however, bears no resemblance to the spec of the original Buick/Oldsmobile camshaft, which was 22/58/60/20 (duration 260°) with a 0.384 in lift.

The normally quoted specification for a Rover V8 camshaft is 30/75/68/37, this camshaft being quoted for P6Bs, SD1s being used in the Triumph TR8 and retained in the vast majority of Rover Vitesses.

In 1980 came the two-barrel camshaft which increased torque slightly and coincidentally (or otherwise) was introduced to the production line about the same time as the fuel-injected engines.

The "Eagle" engine, which was the code name for the emissions-legal version of the engine developed for the North American export version of the Range-Rover, had a new camshaft strictly for emission purposes, and the later 3.9 litre version of the engine had the same camshaft advanced 2° by changing the keyway position.

The introduction of the 4.2 litre factory engine in September 1992 added a further camshaft variation which by all accounts has potential, being a mild road performance camshaft.

Most controversial was the WL-9 camshaft which most definitely was used in a considerable proportion of what are known as the twin plenum injection Rover SD1 saloons. At least 200 were built for homologation purposes, and most were sold through normal Rover dealers. The WL-9 camshaft is still available from many specialists.

INDUCTION SYSTEMS

The potential of the factory inlet manifolds/induction systems for performance applications will be discussed later. The majority of Rover V8 engines, and all carburetted

The MGB V8 had a particularly useful variation on the twin SU carburettor theme, although the manifold design was essentially unaltered except for an additional casting mounting the carbs.

versions, have been manufactured with the well-known pent roof inlet manifold. It mounts either a pair of SU or Zenith-Stromberg carburettors low down in the vee of the engine for good under-bonnet clearance. There were some variations on this basic manifold design; for instance the Triumph TR8 manifold mounted the Zenith-Stromberg carbs especially low (but in the conventional position), and the MGB V8 was essentially the standard Rover manifold except that the carbs faced towards the rear of the engine on a specially cast adapter, again to facilitate under-bonnet clearance.

More recently fuel injection has taken precedence in Rover V8 production engines, and these are also supplied to Morgan, TVR, and other specialist car manufacturers. There was an early type of fuel injection system, using a two-piece inlet manifold, but this was never used on vehicles produced for the UK market. This early system was available mainly in North America and Australia where it was designed to meet emission criteria rather than performance. Current EFi versions of the Rover V8 owe their fuel injection system with its redesigned three-piece inlet manifold to the performance/racing requirements of the Rover Vitesse which was introduced in 1982 as a high-performance version of the Rover 3500 (SD1) saloon. This Vitesse fuel injection system later became the EFi version of the engine, but essentially changed little from the system designed for the Vitesse.

EXHAUST MANIFOLDS

As you would expect, no factory-installed Rover V8 was fitted with anything other than cast iron exhaust manifolds, but the number of different production applications has left the engine builder with an equal number of castings.

There are several designs of factory castings available. In fact, every production application of the Rover V8 required a unique exhaust manifold design, although the majority were designed around the need to fit into a limited space and the need to keep production costs down.

Not surprisingly it was the Rover 3500 (SD1) which received the first exhaust manifolds which could be said to have given a positive contribution to the engine's performance. Indeed they are better than some so-called performance tubular/extractor designs.

Cast manifolds are considerably cheaper than tubular types, of which there are a large number available. They generally last a lot longer since they are weakened less by corro-

sion, suffer less from vibration fatigue, and they result in a good deal less cabin noise. J.E. Engineering manufacture an excellent design of cast exhaust manifold, originally for their Dakar Range-Rover conversion. The manifold was necessary to limit cabin noise, essential in a refined application such as this, but does not restrict engine performance which the standard items most certainly do. The result is a large-bore, free-flowing, cast exhaust manifold, which is also more durable than a steel-fabricated manifold.

There are a large number of tubular exhaust manifold designs that could be considered "productionized", such as those used by Morgan on the Morgan Plus 8, the TVR sports cars using the Rover V8, of which there are more than one type, the Marcos Mantula/Mantala/Spyder, and more recently some of the mid-engined specialist car applications also have tubular manifolds designed especially for them. In addition there are tubular exhaust manifolds available from specialists in steel or stainless steel which are specifically designed to fit Rover V8 engines in particular production applications, such as the MGB V8, Rover 3500 (SD1), Range-Rover and Triumph TR8. More recently we have the MG RV8, which has used a new design of tubular exhaust manifold specifically designed to overcome the severe limitations imposed by previous Rover V8 installations in the MGB bodyshell.

OIL SYSTEM

Considering the number of production applications to which the Rover V8 had to be adapted, there are few variations in oil system and sump design.

The sump itself has few design variations and the range consists of an early design common to the Rover P5B, Rover P6B, and early Range-Rover, which can best be described as having the main oil pick-up area central to the sump. The sump designed for the Rover 3500 (SD1) had a shallow front and carried the oil at the rear of the oil pan with a separate windage tray inside to help control the oil and separate it from the whirling crankshaft. The current Range-Rover sump is very similar to the SD1 type, but has a shorter shallow area at the front and has a welded in horizontal baffle.

Oil is pumped around the internals of the engine by a conventional gear pump which feeds oil under pressure to the crankshaft and camshaft bearings, hydraulic tappets, the rocker arm bearings via the hollow rocker shafts, and the skew gear (distributor drive) on the

The MGB V8 manifold can be particularly useful for providing an exceptionally low profile induction system for specialist applications, such as in this kit car.

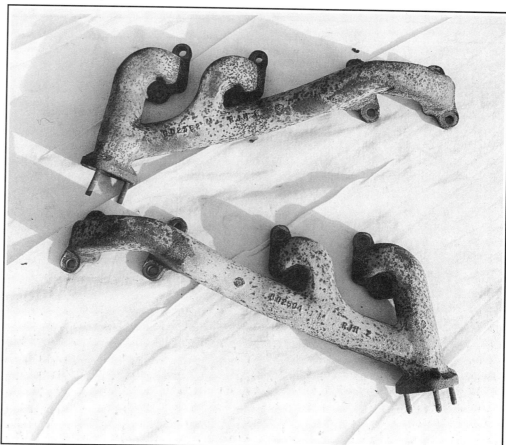

Rover P5B saloon exhaust manifolds.

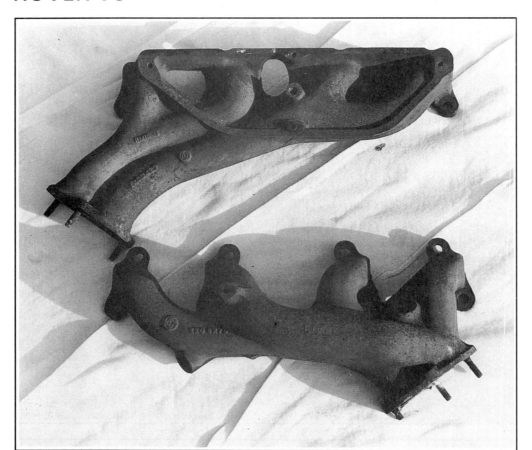

Rover SD1 saloon exhaust manifolds.

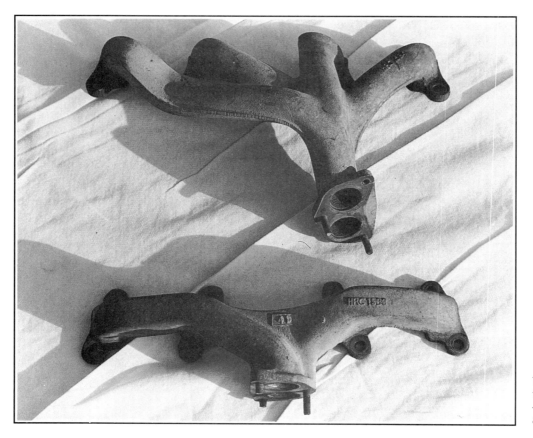

The latest Range-Rover twin outlet cast manifolds – Part No. HRC1584 (LH) and HRC 1583 (RH).

The J. E. Engineering cast iron bog bore exhaust manifolds specifically designed for large capacity Rover V8s.

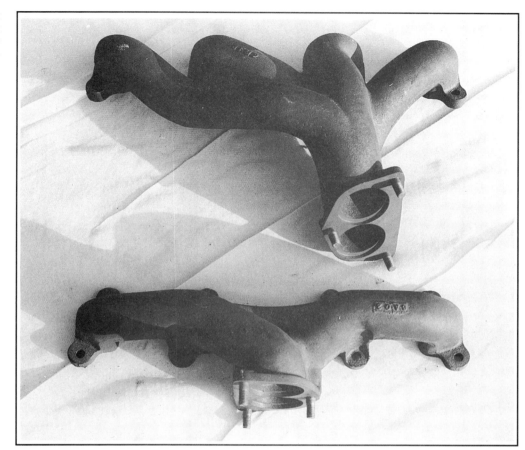

These are a fairly restrictive tubular design for the MGB V8, which is the best that can be done to fit the space available. The new MG RV8 has a far less restrictive design because it exits through the inner wheel arch.

31

ROVER V8

Rover P5B saloon oil pump cover/filter mount.

32

Rover SD1 saloon oil pump cover/filter mount.

Front covers. On the left is the pre-SD1 type with rope front oil seal, in the middle is the post-SD1 type with lip seal, and on the right is the Range-Rover type with lip seal and retaining plate.

Rover SD1 saloon sump pan on the left. The plate on the front of the sump has two bolt holes which attach it to the bellhousing. On the right is a Range-Rover sump pan.

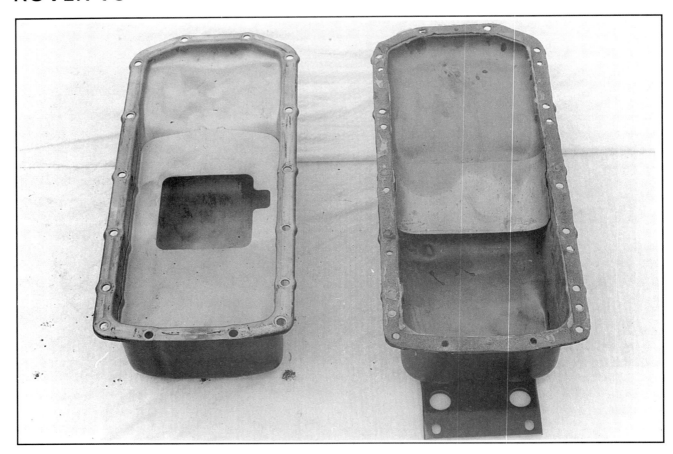

camshaft nose. The gudgeon pins, timing chain and cylinder walls are all splash fed. The standard oil pressure is 35 lb/sq. in nominal at 2,400 rpm. Substituting the oil pressure relief spring from an MGB V8 will increase the pressure to 55 lb/in^2, a "tweak" favoured by many, but in essence the Rover V8 system depends on volume, not pressure

The system was improved for the SD1 engine by altering the skew gear drive to the oil pump and more rigidly supporting the pump shaft to avoid binding. The oil pump was increased in size to increase the volume of oil pumped through the engine. There have only been two basic oil pumps in production form, the pre-SD1 and the post-SD1. Uprating kits are available, but they essentially upgrade a pre-SD1 oil pump to post-SD1 specification.

IGNITION SYSTEMS

Prior to 1976, all Rover V8 engines used the Lucas 35D series distributor with single contact breaker (points). These early distributors are not interchangeable with later, post-1976 engines, and likewise the later electronic distributors cannot be fitted to the early pre-1976 engines, because the distributor drive will not mate with end of the oil pump drive shaft. If you wish to fit a later electronic distributor to a pre-1976 (ie P5B or P6B) engine you will have to change the entire front cover assembly (which of course incorporates the oil pump) for that of a post-1976 (SD1) type, or the cheaper alternative would be to have a set of post-1976 oil pump gears machined down to fit into the earlier housing.

With the introduction of the Rover 3500 (SD1) in 1976, the Rover V8 engine got its first electronic distributor, the 35DE series Opus (Oscillating Pick-Up System). The 35DE Lucas Opus system was one of the first electronic distributors, having been proved in Formula 1, no less, and used first in production on the Jaguar V12 engine.

In 1982 a new Lucas Constant Energy System was introduced, coded 35 DM, which up until 1986 had a separate ignition module, but after 1986 the module was incorporated into the distributor body.

Internal view of the Rover SD1 saloon (right) and Range Rover (left) sump showing the difference in internal baffling. The SD1 engine also has a windage tray beneath the crankshaft (not shown).

Chapter Three

The road car engine

This chapter will look at the techniques and options involved in building a strong road car engine within a realistic budget. The parameters which differ between road engines and competition engines are not easily defined, but the object here is to offer guidance for enthusiasts of limited engine-building knowledge who are perhaps tackling their first Rover V8 engine build, or considering how to go about putting together a strong powerful engine for a road-driven vehicle as opposed to a vehicle built for some form of competition. It may be that some readers will consider that some of the modifications and components examined in the next chapter on competition engines should be included here, but the object is to look at basic techniques and "budget" components. In addition we will look at some of the theoretical aspects of engine tuning to give beginners a broader knowledge of how and why an engine's characteristics may change as that engine is modified to produce greater power.

Rebuilding a Rover V8 engine for use in a high performance road car has many advantages over using a smaller capacity engine, which may need to be in an even higher state of tune to provide the level of performance required. The Rover V8 offers a horsepower and torque advantage over the majority of four- and six-cylinder engines even in its standard form, and its size and weight make it ideal for transplanting into cars originally built for the smaller engines.

Peak brake horsepower (bhp) and maximum torque figures are often quoted to impress, but a major part of the practicality and enjoyment of a powerful road car comes from good low- to mid-range power and torque, which are needed to get a relatively heavy road vehicle moving quickly. Of course torque alone does not provide vehicle performance; the engine has to also produce some useful horsepower to maintain the momentum, which means it needs to be capable of revving freely, smoothly and without fear of breaking internal components.

It might be appropriate at this point to discuss torque and horsepower (and the relationship between the two) in more detail. Torque is the measure of an engine's ability to develop effort as a turning motion and is usually expressed in lb/ft. Imagine a bar 3 ft long attached to one end of the crankshaft and the other end of the bar attached to some weighing scales. If the scales registered 100 lb of force then the torque would be 100 x 3, or 300 lb/ft. Of course you could not actually attach a bar and scales to a running engine, but this is in principle how a dynamometer measures torque.

Horsepower (or bhp) is the amount of work (torque) of which an engine is capable relative to time, and is calculated from the torque figure reading given by the dynamometer and the rpm of the engine at which the reading was taken. For instance, if an engine produces 245 lb/ft of torque at 4,000 rpm, then the calculation goes thus: (245 x 4,000) divided by 5,252 =186.6 bhp (at 4,000 rpm). It is important to understand the relationship between horsepower and time, the time aspect being the key word in the term rpm – revolutions per minute. As crankshaft revolutions per minute increase, the actual amount of time the combustion process has to act upon the crown of each piston (and thus produce power) goes down. But the number of instances of these combustion processes acting on pistons goes up in the same period of

ROVER V8

time, so more horsepower is produced. This is the key to why for a given engine capacity an increase in power generally involves an increase in the engine's operating rpm. However, if the useable rpm level of the engine is increased, the engine must have an induction and exhaust system capable of flowing more fuel/air through the cylinders if more horsepower is going to be produced. You also have to ensure that the engine is capable of operating at higher rpm without sacrificing reliability. So before getting carried away with the idea that more power automatically involves high rpm, it should be reemphasized that peak power at high rpm is not a desirable characteristic for a road car. It needs good low- to mid-range power, and once the relationship between bhp and torque is understood, the desirability of a good torque curve, ie generous torque produced over a wide rpm range without peaking or falling off sharply, can be appreciated.

Engine power, ie torque/bhp, can either be measured on a dynamometer (at the flywheel) or on a rolling road (at the wheels). Dynamometer readings will always be higher because the engine power is not dissipated by frictional losses through the transmission, and drive line and the actual exhaust system used on the vehicle may alter the reading slightly.

SELECTING YOUR CORE

Basically sound used Rover V8 engines are available for about £200 in automotive breakers all over the country, and anyone contemplating rebuilding a Rover V8 that is already in their road car would be well advised to buy a second used engine and rebuild that. The pressure of having your vehicle off the road is lessened by being able to build the additional engine at a leisurely pace and the swap from worn out to freshly rebuilt engine can be done in a weekend. If you are concerned with matching chassis and engine numbers, do the swap first, running your car on the spare engine in its original form and rebuild the car's original engine, then swap them back. You will be guaranteed to do the second swap in less than half the time!

If you are going to tackle a task such as building an engine from the block up, do it properly. Having your road car/daily transport laid up while the engine is being rebuilt can put pressure on the rebuild and possibly result in a rushed job. Building an engine properly is something that should not be hurried. You can do a lot of work on an engine, such as a camshaft swap, over a weekend without removing the engine from the car, but you will

see little benefit if the engine is tired, well worn and in need of a thorough rebuild.

Rebuilding an engine to original factory specifications is strictly speaking not what this book is about, and most good workshop manuals cover this subject admirably, while it is hoped that anyone reading this book be more interested in engine building. But a lot of basic engine work for road cars is concerned with ensuring the engine is healthy, assembled to factory tolerances, and capable of giving its absolute best. There is not much point in spending money on a new camshaft and fitting it to a high mileage engine. Much of the disappointment experienced by enthusiasts installing performance parts for the first time is down to fitting the parts to a worn, tired engine, as well as poor assembly, and not spending sufficient time on the final setting up.

Building a good road engine is also about setting realistic budgets and goals. If there is money to spend, then spend it wisely on components and machine work that will be of the most benefit to the engine in its intended application. Anodized roller rockers might look superb when the valve covers are removed, but it is highly unlikely that they have any place in a road car engine, and the money spent on these finely crafted precision components may be entirely wasted if the engine they are installed in has not been built to compliment their use.

There is no real justification in using an early type Rover V8 engine as a basis for building a good performance engine. Of course, some highly impressive, successful power units have been built using these early engines as a base, but with so many post-SD1 units about using these older engines makes little sense unless you are restoring a car and wish to retain the original "matching" engine. The MGB V8 is a perfect example, having the pre-SD1 engine, but even in this case many enthusiasts who rebuild the original engine choose to take advantage of later engine developments, such as doing away with the rope oil seals, and perhaps incorporate performance-improving components. Incidentally, the cost of the machining involved in converting the older blocks and their front covers to lip type rubber oil seals is very reasonable. The block has to be machined and you can buy a later type front cover, but they are expensive so it's more sensible to have the original machined too.

There are now a considerable number of fuel-injected engines available from breakers or through parts advertisements which make an excellent upgrade once they are rebuilt, but apart from the valves and the entire induction

Rover SD1 saloon front pulley.

system they are still basically a post-SD1 engine. Improving these engines' performance is still relatively straightforward, but the fuel injection system is more complex and ultimately expensive to alter and tune if it is to go beyond a certain level. The fuel injection system will be examined in detail in *Chapter 7*, but at this stage it's fair to say that if you can afford to go with one of these engines then do.

Using an engine with a known history as a basis for a rebuild – for example the engine in your own car – has obvious advantages over choosing an engine from a breaker's yard or advertisement, but if an engine is being rebuilt any problems should become apparent during the examination phase and can be corrected. However, careful visual checking is essential when buying second-hand engines, preferably removing the cylinder heads and sump for a good look at the engine internals. The compression ratio of the engine is stamped on the block by the factory. On early engines the stamp can be found on the rear of the block above the bellhousing flange. On later (post SD1) engines it is on a small extension to the left-hand deck surface, visible between the middle two cylinders when looking down through the exhaust manifold on that side. Remember though that the compression ratio

does not depend on block or heads but on the pistons used. If the boss has no compression ratio stamped on, or has some other markings such as "EXP-2" or a compression ratio higher than, rather than compatible with its origins, then the engine has probably already been subjected to a specialist build since it left the factory, and will need very careful examination to determine its component parts.

Having decided on the engine to be used for the basis of the build, it is necessary to strip it down completely in order to examine all the components and establish what is to be retained, what will need machining, and what is to be scrapped and replaced. Because V8 engines tend to go on forever without complaint, always starting easily and running smoothly, they are often neglected, and many second-hand engines will have some signs of infrequent oil changes and resultant excessive wear in certain areas, usually obscured by a heavy build-up of thick black sludge inside the engine. Before dismantling, the engine should be examined externally for oil or coolant leaks, and as the oil is drained it should be strained to reveal any possible gritty or metallic particles. If the oil has been already drained, remove the sump and check the residue inside for displaced bits. Make a note to investigate anything suspicious as the engine is disassem-

37

Sherpa V8 front pulley.

Rover P5B, P6B and MGB
V8 front pulley.

38

Range-Rover front pulley.

Group A racing poly V
belt pulley with Zytek
engine management
trigger/cutter.

This is probably the largest front pulley, a Land-Rover with a number of take-offs for power steering, air-conditioning etc.

bled. Once the coolant has been drained remove the water pump and check for signs of excessive corrosion in the water passages. Aluminium engines need the correct anti-freeze in the cooling system at all times as a corrosion inhibitor, and some engines are not as well cared for as others. Remove the inlet manifold and the metal gasket beneath to reveal the lifter gallery. A relatively clean gallery will indicate an engine that has had regular oil changes, which should mean that even a high-mileage engine should still be in good condition.

The Rover V8 needs no specialist tools to dismantle, although the crankshaft front pulley may need a puller. All the moving parts should be carefully checked for wear, particularly the camshaft and valve gears, bearings and valve guides. Refer closely to a good workshop manual. Learn to understand and use some basic engineer's measuring instruments, and at the very least obtain a good quality pair of dial callipers, a 1 in micrometer and a dial gauge with a magnetic base. If the engine is being completely stripped, it is most important that all the oil ways, particularly in the cylinder block and the crankshaft, should be thoroughly cleaned and if possible blown out with compressed air. The camshaft will need to be removed with extreme care to avoid damaging the lobes or bearing.

After stripping and cleaning the block it must be thoroughly and minutely inspected for cracks and a note made of any stripped threads which will also need to be helicoiled while the block is at the machine shop. Cleaning the bare block and head castings is best done properly in a "hot tank" which consists of a strong alkaline solution capable of restoring the aluminium to an as new condition.

From this point the plan of action has to depend on the budget available and the extent to which the engine is to be modified. Some of the engine rebuilding techniques in the following pages may be considered by some to be overkill, too expensive or not necessary, and it must be left to the choice of the individual as to what is considered optional or essential.

BLOCK PREPARATION

The main bearing caps can be torqued into place and the block align honed to bring them up to perfect diameter (or bore size) and in exact alignment with one another. One point to watch here is that the crankshaft centre line is not moved upwards in relation to the camshaft. This can produce too much slack in the timing chain. A certain amount of slack is essential to prevent excessive wear, but too much slack gives poor camshaft timing and can lead to failure.

Whether the main bearing caps should be

A very smartly presented Rover V8, in an equally smart MGB.

Rover V8 in muscle guise, sitting in the engine bay of a Cobra replica and looking the part.

fastened to the block using the standard bolts or whether studs should be substituted is a matter of personal choice, but it is worth giving some thought to this at this stage. A big end bearing stud kit such as the one available from Real Steel is not expensive, but a new set of 10 standard bolts is about a quarter of the cost. Studs do offer superior clamping ability, with less distortion, and with the studs themselves going into the aluminium block at less torque than bolts they are less likely to pull threads from the block. However, you should really use studs with waisted shafts, because the aluminium will react with the steel and the resultant corrosion can make disassembly at a later date difficult. This is especially true of cylinder head studs, where getting the heads to separate from the block can be very difficult if they have been left for some time.

If required new camshaft bearings can also be installed while the engine is at the machine shop. Surprisingly new camshaft bearings are not available from Land-Rover as a service part, but can be obtained from many Rover V8 specialists such as Real Steel and John Wolfe Racing. Installing them is not a DIY operation, unless you have a fully equipped engine assembly shop in your garage!

Assuming the engine selected has done

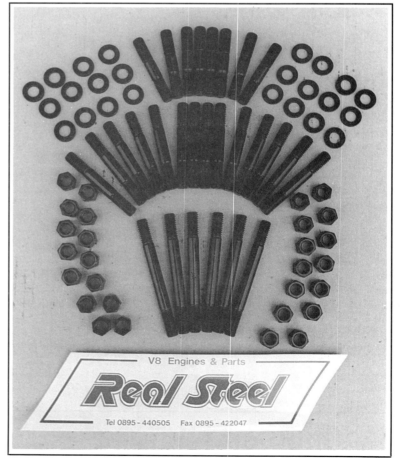

Main bearing stud kit from Real Steel.

relatively low mileage then the bores may be in perfect condition, and assuming you are not changing the pistons they may require only a cross-hatch pattern hone to deglaze the cylinder walls, and a new set of piston rings. However, this will involve retaining the OE (original equipment) cast pistons which are of open-type design, having expansion slots below the oil ring line. These gaps separate the so-called "ring belt" from the piston's skirt. It helps reduce piston skirt distortion and control piston/bore clearance as well as keeping the oil ring free from distortion caused by piston skirt loading. This helps oil control and the maintenance of cylinder pressure over the high mileages expected of a production engine, but the end result is a piston not particularly strong for performance applications, having less material holding the skirt to the crown and allowing them in extreme circumstances to separate! Factory pistons can be used quite safely for many applications, but an engine rebuild does present an opportunity to change the pistons for a change of compression ratio. If you are rebuilding a low compression version of the Rover V8 from perhaps an MGB GTV8, Land-Rover or Triumph TR8, the obvious and cost-effective tuning ploy is to raise the compression to at least 9.75:1 or even 10.5:1 by using OE factory pistons from a higher compression version of the engine. Those used in the Rover P5B and P6B give a compression ratio of 10.5:1 (very slightly lower if used in an SD1 engine), and Rover Vitesse fuel injected engine pistons give a compression ratio of 9.75:1, but this is still a cast piston and is of the same potentially weak design as other OE pistons. On a budget road engine they will give a healthy performance boost and should be reliable at reasonable rpm limits.

Cast pistons are inferior to forged pistons and of course cheaper, but they are perfectly adequate for a road car engine. Budget permitting, it is wise to choose one of the stronger closed slotless designs or "performance" cast pistons, which have no separation slot between the ring belt (or piston head) and the skirt. They provide good resistance to cylinder pressure, excellent transfer of heat and good piston ring support. Omega cast pistons available from J.E. Engineering are a flat-top piston with valve cut-outs (for use with high-lift camshafts), and have a nominal compression ratio of 10.5:1, although this varies with application. Forged pistons will be discussed in *Chapter 4*.

If the choice is new pistons, most aftermarket replacement pistons are available in +.020 in or +.040 in oversizes which will require reboring of the cylinders followed by plateau honing (more expensive than cross-

hatch honing) to finish the bores. You will probably find that when installing the piston rings the specified end gap for each ring will be larger than required in the engine specification. This is because most piston ring manufacturers recognize that the majority of road car engine builders do not take the time and trouble to file and fit (ie blueprint) each ring. Consequently the end gaps fit the bores straight out of the packet, and have an end gap bigger than they should be for a performance engine. If you have the dedication to file each piston ring so that the end gap is as specified, you will need to obtain oversize rings from the bore size you are fitting and file the ends carefully, pushing them down into the bore with an inverted piston and measuring the end gap with a feeler gauge.

The other major option at this stage is to go for an increase in engine capacity such as the popular 3.9 litre conversion, which involves not only a set of new pistons but also re-sleeving the cylinder bore with new liners. Increasing the capacity is examined in detail in *Chapter 5*.

CRANKSHAFT

The standard Rover cast spheroidal graphite iron, five-bearing crankshaft is tough enough for any road engine use, and has stood up to a considerable range of competition applications too. Before any work is done on the crankshaft it is as well to check the crankshaft end-play. Place the crank in the block with a new set of main bearings torqued in position. With a dial gauge placed on the nose of the crankshaft, lever it with a large screwdriver towards the rear of the block, set the dial gauge to zero and lever the crank toward the front of the block. The amount indicated on the gauge will be the crankshaft end-play. If the end-play is excessive, then the crankshaft is scrap. Obviously it's worth checking this before the crank is subjected to any expensive machining.

It is a very good idea to have the crankshaft crack tested, although again it is not essential for a road car engine, and checked for straightness. This should be done by inserting the crank in the block with only the front and rear main bearing inserts in place, and the bearing caps in place and torqued down. Place a dial indicator on the centre main bearing surface of the crank and rotate the crank. Ideally the dial indicator should show zero runout but is it is no more than 0.002 in then it is acceptable. If it is greater, either the crank will have to be straightened or, if the problem is bearing ovality, the bearing will have to be

Cylinder head stud kit from Real Steel.

43

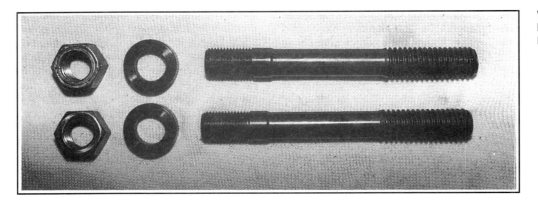

Waisted stem main bearing studs from J. E. Developments.

Camshaft bearing kit from Real Steel. Camshaft bearings are not available as Land-Rover spares.

Cast OE-type pistons 88.9 mm bore size and 9.75:1 compression ratio.

Performance-type solid cast pistons, both for a 94.04 mm bore size, but high compression on the left and low compression on the right.

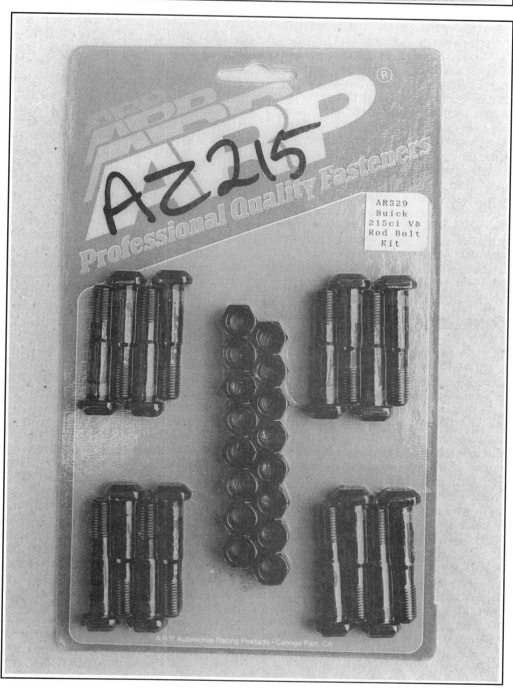

An ARP rod bolt kit for the Rover V8/Buick 215 V8.

reground and oversized bearings used. Bearing ovality or taper across the surface will make it difficult to obtain acceptable bearing to crank clearance, essential for good oil pressure. It might be worth mentioning here that when a healthy engine is running, the crankshaft never actually touches the bearing surface (likewise the big end bearings). While the pressures of combustion acting on the pistons are trying to force the crank against the bearings, the two are held apart by a layer of oil, forced between them under pressure. If the two ever do touch it is time to get out the chequebook! The standard Vandervell bearings are excellent quality and adequate for most performance applications.

Assuming everything checks out then the crankshaft can be "indexed" or "restroked"; that is the big end journals are machined 0.01 in undersize (if necessary) to equalize the strokes and ensure that each piston reaches top dead centre (TDC) exactly 90° of crankshaft rotation after the previous piston. At the same time any damaged or oval journals, including the mains will be reground (if necessary further undersize ground to -0.02 in) to remove any signs of bearing surface damage and the oil holes chamfered to improve oil flow to the bearings. Regrinding bearing journals does reduce the strength of the crankshaft, but this should not be critical in a road car engine. The crank should then be tuftrided, and the journals repolished.

CONNECTING RODS

Buying connecting rods is an expensive exercise. Even brand new OE rods are not cheap, so for a road engine the sensible choice is to retain the rods already in the engine you are building. Given the rpm limits imposed by the use of a hydraulic camshaft the standard rods are adequate for the task, but there is much that can and should be done to them if the engine is being upgraded. Rod reconditioning and preparation can only be done by a competent machine shop, so the cost can mount up to something in the region of 50 per cent of the cost of new rods. However, they will be reconditioned to a standard higher than production rods, and peace of mind is worth every penny.

The first thing is to have used rods Magnafluxed to check for cracks and then checked for alignment and ovality. This ensures that the rod is not twisted or otherwise out of end to end alignment, and also that the big and small ends are not distorted in any way. They should then be beam polished longitudinally to remove casting flash

and surface imperfections which may be a source of potential weakness, and the rods should be shot-peened to induce surface hardness. The original rod bolts should not be reused except for trial building purposes, and brand new rod bolts should be used for final assembly. Some engine builders consider that the bolts used in the current 3.9 litre engines are the best available, while others consider ARP (Automotive Racing Products) bolts forged from 8740 chrome moly (molybdenum) steel and tested to 190,000 psi to be a worthwhile upgrade.

CAMSHAFT SELECTION FOR THE ROAD

Most engine builders will agree that the single most important component in the four-cycle internal combustion engine is the camshaft. Probably the most important consideration in camshaft selection is where in an engine's rpm range are optimum volumetric efficiencies going to be required. Camshafts designed for low to mid rpm use are decidedly different from those intended for high rpm use.

With one camshaft an engine can have an effective power range from 1,500 rpm to 4,000 rpm, and the same engine with only a change of camshaft can then have a power range of 4,500–7,000 rpm. A camshaft can be made to give a low-compression engine the characteristics of a high-compression engine, going some way towards making up for deficiencies in cylinder heads, induction systems etc. We now have camshaft companies that have been in business for over 50 years, and in that period a great deal of information has been amassed about what camshaft specifications work and do not work.

In more recent years, thanks to computer technology and competitive racing, even great advances have been made and the enthusiast has the pick of catalogues of camshafts and the technical back-up to go with them. Unfortunately there is very little visual difference between one camshaft and another, so in order to select the one for your engine it is important to understand what the various specification figures mean.

It is the camshaft's job to provide the correct amount of valve timing (and lift) to ensure optimum cylinder filling in a specific range of engine rpm. In controlling this valve motion the camshaft must not open an intake valve too early, lest cylinder pressure is lost by reversion into the intake tract, or too late for full and effective cylinder filling. Likewise if the exhaust valve is opened too early, again cylinder pressure will be lost, and if it closes too late exhaust gas might be drawn back into the cylinder, diluting the fresh incoming fuel/air charge.

Since this combustion process takes place at high cylinder pressures, it is important that the inlet and exhaust valves seal effectively to contain this pressure and thus provide useable power. However, these same valves must open to admit a mixture of air and atomized fuel into the cylinder of an engine and to allow the burnt gases to leave it. When these valves open and close is called the timing and how long they remain open is the duration. These two factors govern how a particular camshaft affects power output.

The camshaft lobe raises the lifter (or cam follower), which in turn raises the pushrod, which tips the rocker arm to push the valve open. How far off its seat the valve is raised is the lift, and this can be seen in two ways. Net lift is the amount of lift seen at the valve and theoretically consists of the cam lobe lift multiplied by the rocker arm ratio, minus any clearances. If the lift at the valve is 0.45 in and the rocker arm ratio is 1.5:1, then the actual lift at the cam lobe is 0.3 in. That is the theory, but with a typical V8 camshaft mounted in the vee of the cylinder block with its pushrod and rocker arm, a number of valve lift variables can result in a net valve lift somewhat less than intended. Lift is one aspect of camshaft choice that the enthusiast should consider very carefully, because it also has a bearing on two very

important aspects of engine building. The standard Rover V8 camshaft has a valve lift of 9.906 mm (0.39 in), and it should be possible to fit camshafts with valve lifts of up to 11.43 mm (0.45 in) without problems. Above that and it becomes necessary to consider other internal clearances very carefully. Increase the valve lift and there may be problems with the valve collet striking the top of the valve guide, increase the lift or hold the valve open longer and you change the relationship between the valve and the piston, requiring piston to valve clearance checks. Valve spring coil binding should never be a problem if attention is paid to valve spring installed height. Unless you are prepared to address these problems, either by seeking professional assistance or by virtue of having sufficient experience in engine building to have whatever machining may be required done to your calculations, it would be best not to be over ambitious with camshaft selection.

Duration is the time a valve is off its seat, and is expressed in degrees of crankshaft rotation. The camshaft is driven via a chain drive and rotates at half the speed of the crankshaft (the crankshaft rotates twice for every rotation of the camshaft). Duration can vary from the camshaft specification due to the mechanical arrangement of the valve gear, more so at higher crankshaft speeds as the cam follower or tappet tries to track the camshaft lobe.

Before we move on to another important aspect of camshaft selection, let's look briefly

Kent Cams camshaft kits. Four kits are available for the Rover V8 with the H180, H200, H214 and H224 camshafts. They include cam, valve springs, retainers, cam lube and timing disc. Additional machining may be necessary on the H214 and H224 cams.

ROVER V8

at the theoretical four-stroke cycle. The intake valve should open as the piston reaches top dead centre (TDC), so that the entire downward stroke of the piston will be available to inhale the fuel/air mixture. Then when the piston reaches bottom dead centre (BDC), it should close so that the entire upward stroke of the piston compresses this mixture. Then ignition occurs at or near TDC, with the resultant rapid rise in pressure driving the piston downwards on its power stroke. At BDC the exhaust valve opens, and the upward stroke of the piston drives out the spent gases via the exhaust system. We are all familiar with the theory, but as a result of camshaft design (and to a certain extent ignition system development) the actual timing during the four-stroke cycle at which these events occur varies. It was quickly established that for optimum engine performance the intake and exhaust valves should not be opened and/or closed precisely at TDC or BDC because of the low gas flow inertia at low rpm and high inertia at high rpm. Thus we have valve overlap.

Overlap therefore is the period of time during which both inlet and exhaust valves in the same combustion chamber are off their seats simultaneously. To be exact, this is a time when the exhaust valve is closing (ending the exhaust cycle) and the inlet valve is opening (beginning the inlet cycle). As this overlap period is increased, the effective cylinder pressure at lower rpm decreases, thus camshafts with long overlap require higher rpm operation to provide good cylinder pressure (or horsepower) and enable higher static compression ratios to be used on high rpm engines, such as race engines. Remember also that good cylinder pressure means good torque, so if you have a camshaft with a relatively short overlap period, you get better cylinder pressure at lower rpm and thus more low rpm torque, but there is then a trade-off when the engine rpm rises and the shorter overlap begins to restrict engine breathing and thus engine power.

To calculate overlap look at the intake valve opening period, say, 36° opening before TDC and an exhaust period of 40° after TDC. The overlap period is the total of the two, ie 76°. Lobe separation angle has largely replaced overlap in camshaft terminology and is the angle between the centre line of the intake lobe and the centre line of the exhaust lobe for one cylinder in the camshaft. Narrowing the lobe separation angle increases overlap – the time that both intake and exhaust valves on one cylinder are simultaneously open – but it also increases the time that both these valves are closed. Camshafts with long duration need wider lobe centres, 110–114°, to maintain idle quality and mani-

fold vacuum at low rpm, but if idle quality is not a problem then a camshaft with narrower lobe centres, 108–110°, will give good torque in the mid range, where it is needed on a road engine.

While on the subject of camshaft lobes there are one or two other terms to clarify. The base circle of the camshaft lobe is the surface on which the cam follower rides during the time the valve is fully closed. As the lobe rotates, the cam follower then rides up the opening flank of the lobe, thus opening the valve. Then the point on the camshaft lobe at which maximum lift is achieved is the nose, after which the follower descends down the closing flank. It is interesting to note that when the cam follower is on the nose of the lobe, not only is maximum lift achieved but also the valve opening acceleration and velocity are zero.

Some camshafts have identical intake and exhaust lobes, while other designs may have one lobe pattern for intake and one for exhaust. These dual pattern camshafts take into account the differing cylinder head flow capabilities between intake and exhaust valves/ports, perhaps giving slightly longer intake timing duration. Dual pattern camshafts should not be "degreed in" during installation in the same way as a conventional camshaft. Asymmetrical lobe designs, such as the Piper Blueprint, have a faster valve opening rate coupled to a slower closing rate.

Ultimately the valve opening rate is limited on a flat tappet (or lifter) camshaft, as opposed to a roller camshaft, by the diameter of the lifter and also the valve spring pressure. A small diameter lifter will dig into the flank of a steeply profiled cam lobe (the steeper the flank the faster the rate of valve opening). So the larger the lifter diameter, the steeper the lobe it can remain in contact with, hence the "mushroom tip" lifter design used on some engines, but large diameter lifters can be difficult physically to fit into the confines of a V8 engine's lifter gallery. More on this in *Chapter 4*.

Radical camshaft profiles also require greater valve spring pressures to keep the lifter in constant contact with the camshaft lobe at higher rpm, as failure to do so produces valve float as a side effect. Such strong valve spring pressures cause rapid camshaft wear, drag, friction and stress on valve gear components. You should never use valve springs stronger than required for the camshaft selected for this very reason, not to mention the waste of money involved!

Because the Rover V8 has such superb flexibility in standard form and will pull quite happily from around 500 rpm, the final drive gearing on cars fitted with the engine (such as

48

the Rover 3500 SD1) is quite high. If the engine is then tuned and loses some of this low rpm pull, it will become necessary to use higher rpm and more clutch slip to get the car moving from stationary or low speeds. The heavier the vehicle, the worse this problem will become. The answer would be to fit a lower final drive ratio but this then loses the cars long-leggedness for motorway cruising and does nothing for fuel economy.

So, you should first establish your realistic operating speed/engine rpm. For example, the vehicle may spend a considerable amount of time on the motorway cruising at high speed. What engine rpm is being used at 112 km/h (70 mph) in fifth gear? Unless the car has a low final drive ratio, the rpm will be fairly modest, maybe 3,000–3,500 rpm (which is good for economy), so you do not want a camshaft that produces peak power at 5,500 rpm. Likewise, if you examine carefully the rpm at which your engine is operating when being driven in urban areas, even when taking part in the odd traffic light Grand Prix, you will find that rpm rarely rises above 5,000. So once again we arrive at the conclusion that a camshaft producing good low to mid range power is the sensible choice.

The next factor to consider is the engine's compression ratio. A low compression ratio with a long duration camshaft will produce poor combustion pressure at lower rpm, because pressure will be lost with the intake valve remaining open as the piston rises up the cylinder. Having said that, you can of course run a high compression ratio (eg 12:1) with a long duration camshaft, but by definition a long duration camshaft is designed to produce high rpm power and is not suitable for road use. But since a relatively high compression ratio, eg 9.75:1, is good for performance, the opportunity is there to extend the camshaft duration over that of the standard camshaft and still maintain good cylinder pressures.

The vehicle weight is also an important factor. Heavy vehicles (or when towing) require more low rpm power to produce good acceleration, whereas lighter vehicles can still be acceptable with higher rpm camshafts because they need less torque to get them moving from rest. Relatively heavy vehicles, such as Range-Rovers benefit especially from larger capacity Rover V8 engines, as the factory have demonstrated so the extent to which the 3.5 litre engine can be tuned, without resorting to forced induction perhaps, is limited as heavier vehicles are not ideally suited to tuned engines.

Automatic transmissions absorb more power than a manual gearbox and clutch, so need low rpm power just to maintain an acceptable idle. More radical camshafts will need a smaller, high-stalling speed torque converter to reduce the bhp absorbed at idle and raise the engine rpm during acceleration from rest.

In addition to all these factors, we also have to consider very carefully the efficiency of the modified engine itself, which will determine just how quickly the cylinders can be filled with fresh fuel/air mixture and emptied of spent exhaust gases. Longer intake duration will help an engine with restricted intake breathing to pack more fuel/air mixture into the cylinders, while longer exhaust duration can help a restrictive exhaust system. The problem is that long duration camshaft require higher rpm to produce these benefits, and this can often be beyond the flow (breathing) capabilities of standard or slightly modified engine.

Do not underestimate the standard camshaft. Many people build excellent 3.5 litre engines for road cars without changing the camshaft from standard, because even a modest Crane 216 will reduce low rpm power for a modest increase in peak power at slightly higher rpm. On the other hand, some people rather like an engine to respond sharply with a strong increase in power at a higher rpm as the engine "comes on the cam", and provided the driver does not tire of this novelty and find himself longing for that lost low rpm flexibility, it can be acceptable on a road car. If you do want to upgrade your camshaft, the sensible choice is a "road" or "mild road" camshaft: for instance, the Kent 200 is highly recommended. If you insist on something slightly more peaky, go for a "fast road", such as the Piper Blueprint 270. This is available as a kit with hydraulic followers and a set of compatible valve springs. A recent addition and well worth considering is the Hurricane camshaft from Real Steel, which if used on a 3.5 litre engine with raised compression (9.75:1) gives excellent results, with only a marginal loss of low rpm torque. You can build an engine around a Kent or Crane 238 which has acceptable road manners – in fact you can go as far as a 256 and still consider it perfectly driveable – but these cams should really only be used on a competition car which for various reasons has to be driven on public roads to and from a meeting. Hot camshafts have great novelty value when first tried out on a road car, but they soon become tiresome when the car is driven every day in all weather and road conditions.

Rhoads lifters are very similar in appearance to other hydraulic lifters, but they have a unique bleed-down feature below 3,500 rpm improving low- and mid-range performance.

CAM FOLLOWERS (LIFTERS)

With a road car engine, the choice of camshaft will be limited somewhat by the decision as to whether you intend to continue with hydraulic lifters (cam followers) or whether you wish to go for solid lifters. The Rover V8 engine uses hydraulic lifters because they are quiet, require little or no maintenance because they automatically regulate rocker arm to valve clearance, and their action effectively limits maximum rpm (to about 6,500 rpm on post SD1 engine, 5,500 rpm prior to that), because they eventually "pump-up" and hold the valves slightly open. This, of course, is a useful engine-preserving feature when the engine has not been built to withstand high rpm. Solid lifters cannot simply be substituted because you will be unable to set valve to rocker arm (tappet) clearance unless you also fit either adjustable push-rods (expensive and awkward) or adjustable rockers, which in the Rover V8's case means roller tipped rockers (even more expensive). Solid lifters are discussed in more detail in *Chapter 4*, so for a road car engine we will limit ourselves to

hydraulic lifters. If you change the camshaft, be it a performance item or just a new standard cam, you will have to replace the cam followers for a new set. You can choose simply to buy a new set of OE lifters if you are intending a fairly modest rebuild, and if you are rebuilding an early engine the post-SD1 lifters are a useful upgrade. Beyond that you can fit a set of "hi-rev" lifters which resist the pumping up action until higher rpm are reached, eg 7,000 rpm, allowing the use of a "hotter" camshaft.

The other choice of hydraulic lifter is the Rhoads lifter, which is not only hi-rev but also "bleeds down" below 3,500 rpm, thus reducing valve lift and overlap, improving flexibility and fuel consumption at lower rpm when using hotter camshafts. Over 3,500 rpm, these Rhoads lifters act exactly the same as a normal hi-rev lifter. Again one must consider the practicalities of using even moderately radical camshafts in a road car, not to mention the limited choice of hydraulic camshafts designed to produce power up to these rpm limits, and by all accounts this type of lifter is noisy in operation.

LIFTER PRELOAD

One very important aspect of performance engine assembly frequently neglected by less experienced engine builders is checking the lifter preload. Incidentally, when installing new hydraulic lifters they have to be filled with oil, which can be done either by submerging them in engine oil for several hours or, a far more practical method, by pushing the nozzle of a pump action oil can against the small oil hole in the side of the lifter and literally pumping the lifter full of oil. It is quick and easy.

When replacing hydraulic lifters during an engine build, it is easy to assume that after opening a box of brand new lifters, be they standard or of the hi-rev type, they can just be filled with oil and dropped into the lifter bores. Well, of course they *can*, but this would neglect a simple check that would ensure that the camshaft and valve train worked with maximum efficiency.

When using non-adjustable rocker arms or push-rods, the lifter preload should be between 0.508 mm (0.02 in) and 1.524 mm (0.06 in) (ideally 1.016 mm/0.04 in). When the short engine is assembled and the heads in place with the valves, valve springs, rocker gear and push-rods installed, the preload can be checked. Many experienced engine builders can visually assess whether the preload is within acceptable limits, but it can be done more methodically.

The crankshaft should be rotated until the lifter is on the heel or base circle of the cam lobe, and the distance between the lifter snap ring and the push-rod seat checked. It can be measured with a wire feeler gauge or visually examined to see whether the push-rod seat is level with the chamfer immediately below the snap ring. If the push-rod seat is below the chamfer, a shim will have to be inserted under each rocker shaft pillar to increase the distance between the lifter and the rocker arm. If the snap ring is above the chamfer, the rocker pillar will have to be machined to bring the rocker arms closer to the lifter. It may vary from one side of the engine to the other; ie, adjustment may be required on the rocker pillars of one cylinder head but not the other, or one side may need shimming up and the other side machining down.

The lifter preload should always be checked when installing a new set of hydraulic lifters, but there are many types of engine work or component replacement that may significantly alter the critical dimensions of the engine, thus affecting the lifter preload. For instance, thicker head gaskets will place the cylinder heads higher on the block, increasing the distance between the lifter and the rocker shaft, increasing or decreasing the length of the pushrods will alter the preload, as will milling the surfaces of the block or heads.

You can adjust the lifter preload by using adjustable rocker arms or adjustable length push-rods, but this is a needless expense. Once you understand the principles of what you are doing it is very straightforward, and the cost of a shim kit is nothing compared to the cost of a set of adjustable push-rods!

However, you may already have adjustable rockers fitted to the engine for another reason; for instance, you may wish to fit roller tipped rocker arms, which invariably have adjusters but for some reason are still using a hydraulic lifter cam. Lifter preload is still as important and must be adjusted. This is done by rotating the crankshaft until the exhaust lifter just starts to move up the lifter bore, then adjusting the tappet clearance (or valve lash) of the intake valve on the same cylinder to zero then adding half to one turn. Rotate the crankshaft again in the same direction until the intake lifter is almost at its lowest point in the lifter bore, and set the exhaust in the same way. Repeat this for all 16 valves and the preload will be correct.

FINAL SHORT ENGINE MACHINING

If each piston does not reach exactly the same point up the cylinder bore at TDC, then it follows that the cylinder volumes above the piston at TDC may also vary and hence the compression ratios too. Not recommended! We must therefore equalize the deck heights. To do this the crankshaft, con rods and pistons are assembled in the block and the piston-to-block height is measured on each piston (at TDC). The block face on each bank should then be machined using the lowest piston on each bank as the reference point, and the remaining pistons machined to match.

It is possible to forgo this operation and still achieve something like equal piston heights by putting the longest piston and con rod assemblies on the shortest crank throws and vice versa to end up with approximate equality on all eight cylinders. It can take a little time, but it is possible to do a reasonable job that will suffice on a road car engine. At this stage, assuming all the pistons are identical in dimensions, it is recommended that the crankshaft, rods and pistons are balanced.

BALANCING

There is one aspect of Rover V8 tuning on which every professional agrees, and that is **51**

ROVER V8

A Rover V8 cast crankshaft undergoing balancing. Note the counterweights attached to the rod bearing journals.

Tungsten inserts used for balancing when additional weight is needed in the web area of the crank. Tungsten is approximately 22 per cent heavier than the equivalent amount of crank material.

the importance of having the whole recipro-cating assembly balanced. It is not essential if the engine is being built with a hydraulic camshaft for a maximum of 6,000 rpm with the occasional burst to 6,500 rpm, but very highly recommended for any engine being built with performance in mind.

The Rover V8, in common with the major-ity of production V8 engines, has a paired throw crankshaft. It does not have mirror sym-metry and is balanced by having suitable coun-terweights cast as part of the crank structure, the main ones forming part of the front and rear crankshaft webs. Concentrating the bulk at the front and rear webs in this way enables the other webs to be made thinner and thus the crankshaft shorter.

Twice the rotating weight (which is the big end of the con-rods plus the bearings) and once the reciprocating weight (which is the little end on the con rod plus the pistons/rings, plus the gudgeon (wrist) pin) are taken as fac-tors in calculating the weight of four bob weights. In principle, were these bob weights clamped to a straight metal shaft of suitable diameter they would balance themselves, ie the shaft could be rotated at high speed with-out vibration.

On to these bob weights can be mounted a set of big end bearings of the correct size and weight, and the bob weights are clamped around the big end journals of the crankshaft, without flywheel or front pulley. The crank is then balanced by removing metal from the crank counterweights or, in the case of bigger capacity engines, by adding metal by drilling a hole in the counterweight and inserting a plug of tungsten which is 30 per cent heavier.

Once the crank has been balanced the fly-wheel, clutch cover and front pulley are added and balanced. Substitution of any of these items will not then affect previous crankshaft balance, provided they are balanced in their own right. The con rods then have to be bal-anced end to end, so the all big ends are the same weight (including the weight of the bearings) and all little ends are the same weight. Likewise all eight pistons are weighed, and equalized to the weight of the lightest. The whole balancing operation requires a skilled operative and can take between one and three hours.

Drilling two small holes in the front of the lifter gallery will aid oil drainback and timing chain lubrication.

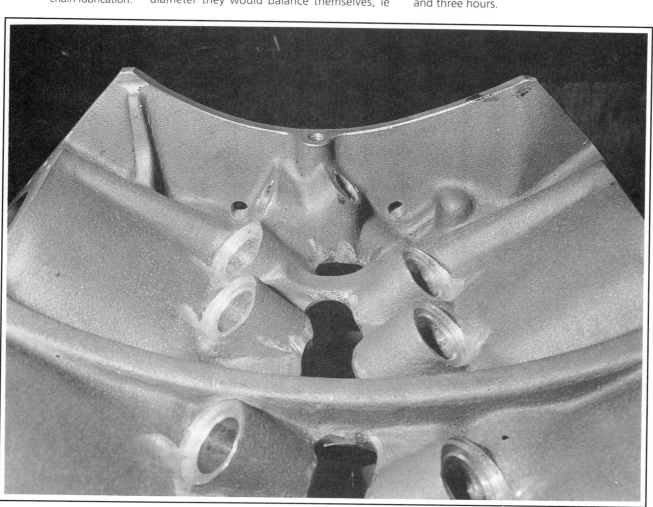

ROVER V8

It is possible to influence the harmonics of the engine by external balancing, but this is race engine tuning to the *nth* degree. On many American V8 engines the flywheel and front pulley are used to influence the balance of the crankshaft itself, but because of its alloy block the Rover V8 is internally balanced.

FINAL PREPARATION

When a bare cylinder block has been returned from the machine shop it can now be prepared for assembly, and this preparation should be done as thoroughly as time allows. Be careful to deburr the top and bottom of the bores very carefully, then with a small grinding tool remove all casting flash from the block, both externally and internally, keeping well clear of the cylinder bores and the camshaft bearings. This polishing will prevent flash from breaking off inside the engine and getting in the oil system with obvious results. It helps prevent the formation of stress risers that could lead to cracks forming, and if the lifter gallery is well cleaned and opened out it will help oil drain back in the sump from around the valve gear. Another trick is to radius the angle where two oil passages meet, in particular those visible in the front of the block when the timing cover is removed. Also, drilling a couple of holes through from the front lifter gallery bridge into the timing gear area not only helps to return oil drainback but also adds lubrication to the timing gear itself.

When this operation is complete, wash the whole cylinder block thoroughly in warm soapy water, using pipe cleaners to scour every nook and cranny. This will ensure no machining swarf or other harmful debris remains in the engine and contaminates the oil, with obvious damaging effects to new bearing surfaces. It is a good idea, if you have the block on an engine stand, to take it outside and hose it down, using the water liberally. After rinsing with plenty of cold water, dry the bore surfaces immediately and coat with WD40 or some similar water-repellent light oil. If engine assembly is to be delayed, the bores should be coated with clean engine oil.

CYLINDER HEAD PREPARATION

The most straightforward way to prepare a pair of heads for use on a street engine is to buy professional assistance, either in the form of a pair of exchange modified heads or by having your existing cylinder heads modified. It is true that a good pair of heads are the key to good engine performance, but it is easy to go overboard and spend too much time and money in this area for disproportionate returns. Use your own judgement when choosing a pair of cylinder heads and look closely at the quality of the workmanship. If possible talk to the person responsible for preparing the heads, and find out his views on airflow and port shape. Ask to see flow charts and the flow bench. If they don't possess a flowbench, they are not doing or have not done a great deal of research. If the heads they sell are prepared by a third party they should at least be able to show you a flow chart. Different flowbenches will produce different figures and other values have to be taken into account during tests, such as ambient temperature and the pressure drop used on the flow bench to draw the air through the port, eg "28 in of water" because flow figures will vary with the pressure drop used during the tests.

Look first at that flowbench's figures for a standard Rover V8 head, and then look for improvements over as wide a valve lift as possible. Remember that when an intake valve opens it only dwells at maximum lift once, while it moves through the lower lifts as it opens and again as it closes. It is during the opening and closing motion that the port/valve needs to flow well, and good flow at lower lifts will mean the gases start moving in faster earlier in the valve opening cycle and keep flowing longer as the valve closes. Buy heads from companies that have a good reputation, that are prepared to discuss your particular requirements, and will recommend the best specification.

The minimum requirements of road heads are valve seats cut to three angles ("three-angle seat job") and the port opened out to exactly match the internal diameter of the valve seat. It is also of paramount importance that all the valves when closed sit at exactly the same depth in the cylinder head, and therefore get the same lift when opened by the camshaft. Beyond that you need polished ports to increase the speed of the gas flow, and if the engine is being increased in capacity you need to look for ports that have been increased in volume.

When buying/preparing cylinder heads it is also necessary to know the camshaft you are going to install in the finished engine, because the valve lift and the valve spring installed height information, as well as whether you intend using single, double or triple valve springs, are all vital to the machine shop.

Pre-SD1 Rover V8 engines used dual valve springs, and after the SD1 all production engines use single valve springs. Dual valve springs are considered safer on a performance

Sectioned exhaust port from a post-SD1 cylinder head.

Sectioned inlet port from a post-SD1 cylinder head. Note the position of the waterways.

engine, as well as being considered more suitable for performance camshafts, because in the event of a spring breaking there is less likelihood of dropping a valve. However, dual (or even triple) valve springs cannot be fitted to post-SD1 heads without some machining to the valve spring seats. Some camshaft manufacturers specify single springs for some of their camshafts because they do not want their customers to have the additional expense and trouble of having the machining done. It is possible to buy "performance" single springs (eg, Real Steel – part no DW060; or Piper – part no V8SC) and these are a good choice for mild road camshafts, but if the seats can be machined then a set of heavy duty dual springs (eg, Kent VS14) should be seriously considered. Triple springs are an option for serious competition work. Try to use the valve springs recommended by the camshaft manufacturer.

There are two key aspects of cylinder head preparation that are often taken for granted or ignored by enthusiasts doing their own engine assembly. One is valve spring installed height, and the other is valve guide height.

It is essential when installing a performance camshaft that close attention is paid to the valve spring specified height, which is the height of the spring as it sits between its seat on the cylinder head casting and the underside of the valve retainer. The correct height enables the spring to exert the specified spring pressure and ensure that when the valve is at full lift the coils of the spring will not come into contact with each other, making the spring solid and breaking either the spring or damaging some other valve train component.

Actually measuring the installed height of the spring is probably the most daunting aspect of this vital task. If you look at a valve spring in position around the valve, you will see that the cylinder head casting in the vicinity of the valve spring seat makes taking that measurement rather tricky. The secret is to make a 25.4 mm (1 in) cylindrical spacer, with the outside diameter equal to that of the valve spring and the internal diameter sufficient to allow it to slip over the valve guide. With the spacer positioned in place of the valve spring and the valve cap with collets held in position by finger pressure or any weak wire spring, the distance can be accurately measured between the top of the spacer and the underside of the collet with a good pair of dial callipers. Add 25.4 mm (1 in) for the spacer and you have the dimension which represents the valve spring installed height. It is then a simple matter to have the seat machined accurately if the distance needs to be increased, or to install a shim under the spring if the distance is too great. Don't be tempted to just install the valve springs and hope for the best. *Do it right!*

The valve guide height is similarly crucial. When using performance camshafts that give a higher than standard valve lift, it is possible for the valve retainer to come into contact with the top of the valve guide with obvious results. The solution is to have some material machined from the top of the valve guide, the amount depending on the maximum lift of the valve, but 0.1524 mm (0.006 in) clearance

Simple but very important, rocker pillar shims for accurately setting lifter preload, amongst other things.

To calculate combustion chamber volume accurately, the cylinder also has to be "cc'ed" at TDC.

between retainer and valve guide should be enough for any lift of camshaft.

With those two factors in mind, what other modifications can be made to street cylinder heads at reasonable cost? There are big valves available that will fit into Rover heads with a small amount of machine work to the standard valve seats, but for a quarter of the cost the OE valves from the fuel injected (Vitesse/EFi) version of the Rover V8 can be a straight swap (assuming the heads you are working on do not already have these valves). The latest 3.9 litre EFi exhaust valves also have a slight lip machined in the back side of the valve head to help resist exhaust gas reversion. With a 3.5 or 3.9 litre engine bigger valves should not be necessary for road use, and good heads should not need them.

If the valve guides are worn, avoid using valves with oversize stems, if you can. The thicker stems make them heavier and valves should be kept as light as possible. If the guides

are worn have them replaced with shortened, "bulleted" guides which protrude less into the port and cause less restriction to gas flow.

The combustion chamber volumes should be equalized (or balanced) by the cylinder head supplier, but it does no harm to check it if you can. This is done by measuring the amount of fluid displaced from a chemical burette into the combustion chamber, with the valves installed. The smallest chambers are then enlarged to equal the volume of the largest and equal combustion chamber volumes are vital for equal static compression ratios on all eight cylinders.

As with the block, time should be taken to grind away all casting flash, paying close attention to the push-rod holes. Then the heads, like the block, should be thoroughly cleaned with plenty of warm soapy water, rinsed and dried, preferably with an air line. A light coating of clean oil should then be applied to valve guide bores and valve seats.

ROVER V8

TRIAL ASSEMBLY

With the block, crankshaft and con rods checked and machined, it is time to think about trial assembly. When assembling, always keep the work area scrupulously clean and ensure that all fasteners have clean threads and are tightened to the correct torque, lubricating them with a 50–50 oil/paraffin mix. Carefully inspect all new parts to ensure that they have no imperfections and that they are correct to specification. Do not assume that because they are straight from the box and brand new they are perfect or even correct. Check them, and if necessary compare them with the part they are replacing.

Many enthusiasts building engines on a tight budget save money by doing much of the assembly work themselves, and although the new components may have cost a lot of money it should never be expected that everything will just bolt together. Engine building is about care and thorough checking. The main reason that professional engine building is so expensive is because an enormous amount of time and skill goes into building any engine, especially one that is being put together from a collection of parts from a variety of different sources. A built engine, either supplied ready to fit, or installed in a car which has been taken to the engine specialist, has probably been slowly and carefully assembled to fine tolerances, the rotating and reciprocating parts checked at every stage and when everything had been trial built, with grinding, polishing and relieving were necessary, the whole engine is dismantled, re-checked and then finally re-assembled. It is possible to build a good engine at home in the garage or workshop, but only with the careful choice of parts, specialist help in machining and balancing, a sensible, methodical approach, care and patience. *Never assume anything* – check and recheck.

Assuming new pistons are part of the programme they must first be examined carefully for imperfections, paying particular attention to the machined surfaces such as the ring grooves and the wrist pin bore. Then, if all is well, polish off any rough edges around the piston skirt. With the block cleaned and dried it is time to install the camshaft, lightly coating the bearing surfaces with oil. Next is the installation of the crankshaft, but the main bearing clearance must first be checked. This can be done satisfactorily using Plastigauge, but professional engine builders torque the caps into position with the bearings in place but without the crankshaft. Then using a micrometer they measure each main bearing journal, and use a hole gauge to measure the internal diameter of each bearing. Subtracting one from the other gives the bearing clearance which should be 0.02286 mm–0.0635 mm (0.0009 in–0.0025 in). Insert each piston/con rod assembly into the bore without rings and check each big end bearing for clearance in the same way as the mains bearings, with Plastigauge or micrometers, and then check the rod side clearance 0.1524 mm–0.3556 mm (0.006 in–0.014 in) with a feeler gauge. If it is too little excessive heat can build up, so the rods will need to be machined to achieve a correct clearance. Too much clearance will mean excessive oil being thrown on to the cylinder walls.

With the block assembly complete the cylinder heads can be bolted on, with the fasteners torqued in stages of 30, 45 and 68 lb/ft.

With the engine "buttoned up", perhaps it would be appropriate to consider some of the other engine components which can be retained or replaced in a road engine. The first and most obvious at this stage is the cam drive gear, which on the standard Rover V8 consists of an iron crankshaft gear and a nylon toothed, alloy camshaft gear connected by a simplex chain, with no tensioner. The cheapest upgrade option is to replace the OE camshaft gear with an iron version, which will reduce the chances of failure but still leaves the problem of accurately degreeing in the camshaft. Those who understand the principles of degreeing in the camshaft will know that it can be done simply by using a three-keyway crankshaft gear, and for the Rover V8, Cloyes make an excellent steel timing gear set with a duplex chain. However, for those wishing to degree in the camshaft using a vernier camshaft gear there are two options. The OE camshaft gear can simply be replaced with an all-steel vernier gear retaining the standard simplex timing chain, or better still a vernier gear that comes as a complete duplex chain drive, which is stronger and much less prone to stretch in performance applications.

When cylinder heads were discussed earlier, it was more in the context of port modifications, airflow and valve size, but when the time comes for final engine assembly there are other components connected with the heads that need careful consideration.

The standard alloy rocker shaft pillars should be perfectly adequate for a road engine (steel ones are available), as are the standard rocker shaft, although a tuft-rided version can be obtained (or indeed a new pair could be tuft-rided) at slightly more cost. The Rover V8 rocker arms are one-piece alloy with steel inserts for the push-rod and valve tip contact points, but heavy-duty steel versions can be obtained from many Rover V8 specialists, such as Real Steel and John Wolf Racing.

Standard alloy timing gear with nylon gear teeth.

A steel camshaft gear to accept the standard timing chain (American manufactured).

Left A vernier timing gear for use with a standard timing chain.

Right High volume oil pump uprating kit for use on pre-SD1 Rover V8 engines only. A selection of oil pressure springs is included.

The standard push-rods are also perfectly adequate with hydraulic camshafts but they must be straight. Even brand new ones should be checked before installation, either by spinning them in a drill chuck or rolling them on a sheet of glass.

THE OIL SYSTEM

Fortunately the Rover V8 engine has an efficient and effective lubrication system. It is, of course, a wet sump system, with oil pumped around the internals of the engine by a gear pump which feeds oil under pressure to the crankshaft and camshaft bearings, hydraulic tappets, the rocker shaft bearings and the skew gear (distributor drive) on the camshaft nose. The gudgeon (wrist) pins, cylinder walls and timing chain are all splash fed. The system was improved for the SD1 engine by improving the skew gear drive and supporting the pump shaft more rigidly to avoid binding. Also sump baffling was improved in anticipation of higher cornering speeds, and overall oil capacity was increased. The first rule is to ensure that the engine has regular oil and filter changes. The standard oil pressure is 35 psi, nominal at 2,400 rpm and is perfectly adequate for road-going applications, although

Left to right: Rover P5B/P6B oil pump gear, the current EFi type gears, and a set of high volume gears requiring an oil pump spacer plate.

pre-SD1 oil pumps will benefit from an uprating kit. The MGB V8 oil pump used a different relief spring which increases the oil pressure to 55 psi and many people like to fit this spring to tuned road engines, but the system depends on high volume, not high pressure. Do not forget that the oil pump has to be primed when an engine is rebuilt before start-up, either by using a priming tool or the tried and true method of packing the oil pump with Vaseline during assembly.

If oil temperature becomes a problem on a hard-driven road car, fitting an oil cooler may be the answer, but it should also have a thermostat to ensure that the oil is routed through the cooler only when high temperatures are reached. Further modifications will be discussed in *Chapter 4*.

THE INDUCTION SYSTEM

For all practical purposes the Rover V8 engine builder has the following choice of induction systems:

1. Twin SU carburettors 44.45 mm (1.75 in) or even 50.8 mm (2.0 in) on standard Rover pent-roof inlet manifold.

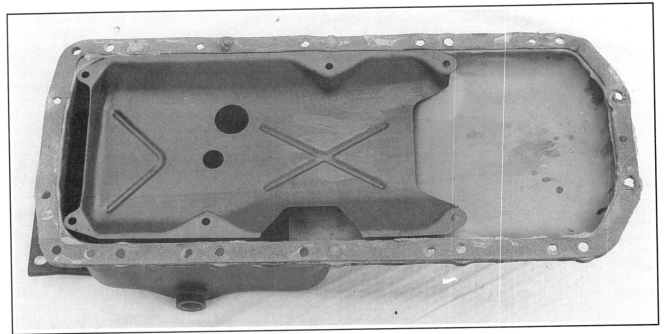

2. Holley four-barrel on appropriate manifold, of which there are a limited choice.
3. Dual sidedraught Webers via adapter to four-barrel type manifold (as above).
4. Quadruple sidedraught Webers on pair of "swan neck" manifolds.
5. Quadruple downdraught Webers or Dellorto carburettors on pair of cast manifolds.
6. Fuel injection based on the OE Rover Vitesse or EFi models.
7. Supercharger.
8. Single or twin turbocharging.

Quite a choice, but once again cost is a significant factor. Fuel injection is an excellent option for a road engine and is examined in detail in *Chapter 7*. Supercharging and turbocharging (as well as nitrous oxide injection) also have a separate chapter devoted to them. There has been no mention so far of the standard manifold mounting a pair of Zenith-Stromberg carbs which have been used on many production Rover V8s. They can be used on a mildly tuned road car engine, but the limited range of needles when compared with the SUs make them less versatile.

Quadruple downdraught or sidedraught Webers or Dellorto will be discussed in *Chapter 4*, but it is worth mentioning at this point that for road use a water-heated manifold manufactured by Mangoletsi is available to mount quadruple Weber or Dellorto carburettors. It is a rare sight on Rover V8s, because the paired cast non-water-heated manifolds

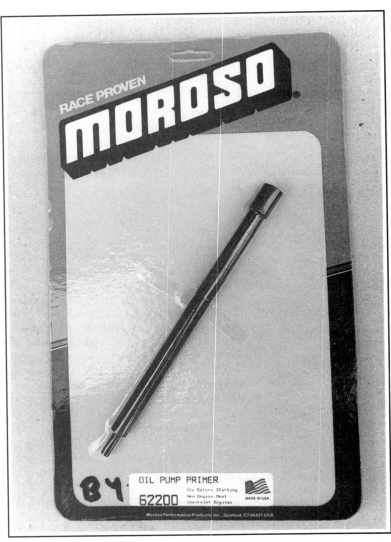

Left The standard Rover SD1 sump is quite capable of handling performance applications. The windage tray in the sump was fitted with higher cornering forces in mind.

Below left An oil pump priming tool (pre-SD1 engines only) allows the oil pressure to be raised using an electric drill before the engine is started.

Oil cooler kit for Rover V8 engine with 13-row cooler.

are far more popular with engine builders and enthusiasts.

SU CARBURETTORS

To the average British motor enthusiast the SU carburettor is common enough, so common in fact that it is usually treated with only passing interest on a performance engine. The SU is a very simple carburettor, but that does not undermine its ability to perform its function, nor its potential as part of a high performance Rover V8.

The SU was patented in 1905 by George Skinner, who in 1910 set up the Skinner Union (SU) in London, with his brothers Carl and John.

The Rover V8 in its many guises used three main models of SU carburettor. The first Rover P5Bs had the HS6 type, the Rover P6B started out with the HS6 but changed to the HIF6, which was also used on the MGB V8,

and this model continued with the Rover 3500 (SD1).

In all 10 different needles were used in Rover V8 productions engines fitted with SU carbs, the main one being listed below.

Rover P5B 1967–9 KL needles
Rover P6B 1968 KO needles
Rover P6B 1969–70 BAC needles
Rover P6B 1971–2 BAK needles
Rover P6B 1972–3 BBG needles
Rover P6B 1973 onwards BBV needles
Rover SD1 1976 onwards BAK needles

Any modification that increases airflow through the carburettor, such as the removal of the air cleaner, fitting of a ram pipe, or any engine modifications that increase volumetric efficiency, will require a richening (from standard) of the mixture to compensate; ie, the carb is passing more air, therefore more fuel will have to be introduced to that air to main-

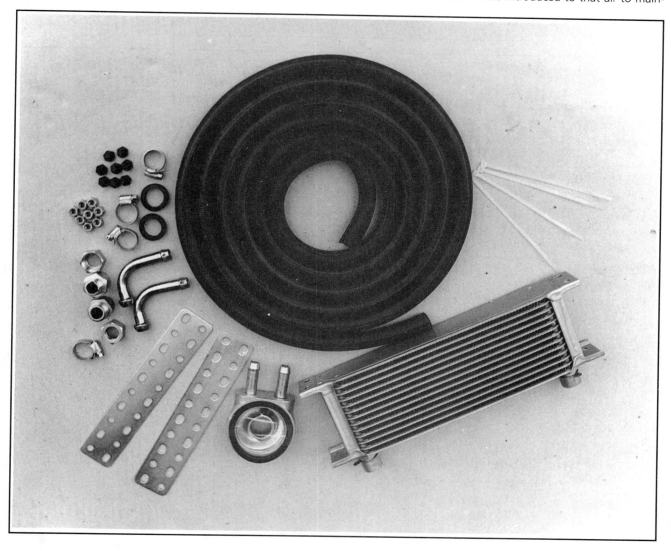

ROVER V8

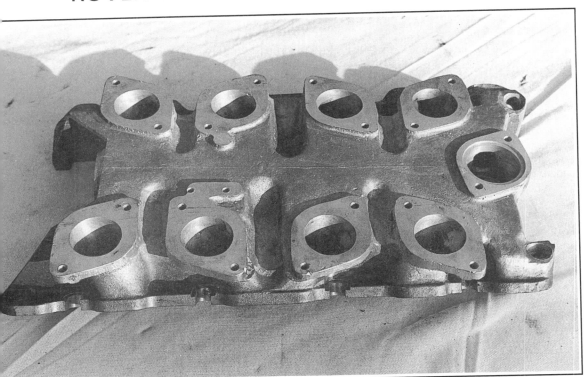

Mangoletsi water-heated manifold to mount four downdraught Weber or Dellorto carburettors.

The familiar twin SU carburettors on the standard Rover inlet manifold do have performance potential on a road car, and can be made to look good, too.

Modified standard SU inlet manifold adapted to mount Holley 350 cfm carburettor.

Modified standard SU inlet manifold adapted to mount a single sidedraught Weber.

tain correct mixture ratio. The thinner the needle, the richer the mixture.

One of the more well known modifications to the SU carb when tuning the Rover V8 is the fitting of BAF (with H214 camshaft) or BBW (with K & N air filters) needles. But this apparently simple information does need elaboration if the engine is to give its best with these carburettors. There is no simple progression of needle sizes to work through when tuning the engine, since the huge range of needles, each with their own taper, can provide enrichment at quite specific rpm points. To achieve perfection would require a dynamometer and an extensive range of needles, not to mention considerable expertise. There is an excellent book *SU Carburettors Owner's Workshop Manual* by Haynes Publishing which is recommended

reading for anyone intending to work with these carbs.

Strictly speaking the 3.5 litre Rover V8 required two 50.8 mm (2 in) SU carbs to meet its requirements, but HS6 or HIF6 44.45 mm (1.75 in) SUs were used in production for greater mid-range response and economy. On a tuned engine they are capable of flowing enough fuel/air for a 3.5 litre engine up to about 230 bhp, but beyond that they begin to restrict breathing. The production type air cleaner is restrictive, so replacement with a good pair of free-flow filters such as those made by K & N with slightly richer needles are an immediate improvement. It is a relatively simple matter to fit a pair of HS8 50.8 mm (2 in) SUs from a Jaguar or Rover 2000TC to the standard Rover V8 inlet manifold, with possibly AAB needles, but although they bolt right

Modified standard SU inlet manifold adapted to mount a Weber DGAS carburettor.

on the manifold flanges they are taller, and can have under-bonnet interference problems. The carburettor linkages will also need to be reworked, but the adaption is not difficult.

The standard "pent roof" Rover V8 manifold, on which are mounted the usual SU or Zenith-Stromberg carburettors, is of particularly good design and does have further potential if the enthusiast has access to some machine tools or modest fabrication facilities. Adapting it to mount a Holley four-barrel carburettor will be discussed later, but with a little work it can be adapted to mount other carburation. In all cases the pent roof area of the manifold, which mounts the twin SUs will have to be machined off flat, and once that has been done it remains to weld or fasten (without air leaks) a number of flanges to match a number of carburation options. A Holley flange can be used to mount a Holley two-barrel 350 cfm (cubic feet per minute) carb, which is no where near as popular as the bigger four-barrel, but which is a perfectly acceptable option for a road-driven 3.5 litre Rover V8. The Holley flange will also take a cast adaptor which mounts a pair of sidedraught Webers, which was one of the original works rallying set-ups, although it was not that successful due to poor fuel distribution and consumption. If as an enthusiast you have experience with Weber carburettors, but perhaps do not wish to go to the expense of a dual or quadruple set-up, it is possible to mount a single Weber 40 DCOE sidedraught via a 90° adaptor or even a single IDA downdraught, as was done during the early racing days of the Group 1 SD1 saloon. Yet another Weber option is a 28/37 DCD type such as the DGAS used on the Ford V6.

The Rover V8 in Buick/Oldsmobile guise was originally designed to operate with a Rochester four-barrel carburettor (as an option). The Rochester is no longer available and neither is the Carter 9410 400 cfm four-barrel which at one time looked so promising. Carter have resumed production of some of their carbs but unfortunately the 9410 400 cfm is not one of them.

For road use we will consider only one Holley carburettor which is very popular with many enthusiasts – the Holley 390 cfm four-barrel with vacuum secondaries and mechanical choke, which comes with side pivot fuel bowls. Side pivot bowls are all right for road cars, but for competition use the centre pivot bowls are superior, also having greater internal volume and individual fuel inlet systems. Real Steel have been able to optimize this carb for use with the Rover V8, and when bought from them its comes with a 51 primary jet, and a secondary plate equivalent to a 53 jet.

It is possible to use a bigger 465 cfm Holley on a road car, especially if the car has a manual transmission, but the Holley 390 cfm with vacuum secondaries really is the optimum for a road car or a four-wheel drive vehicle, and works well with standard torque converter equipped automatic transmissions. The vacuum secondaries work by sensing engine demand, metering air in quantities which maintain velocity in the induction system.

Installing the Holley 390 cfm on a road car begins with an adequate fuel supply, which should be via a good filter, and pump at a pressure of 4.5 psi. High rpm misfiring may be due to fuel pressure dropping off, so make sure the delivery stays at 4 psi, (nitrous oxide users will need 7 psi). Investment in a proper fuel pressure regulator and even a fuel pressure gauge is worthwhile.

With the fuel supply sorted, the carburet-

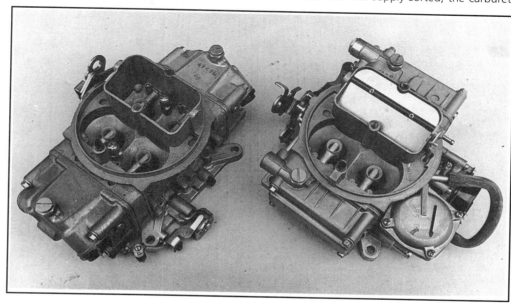

Right A Holley 390 CFM four-barrel "double pumper" with centre pivot fuel bowls and no choke for competition applications, although it could be used on the street. On the right is a normal Holley 390 CFM four-barrel with vacuum secondaries, electric choke and single inlet fuel bowls, a more suitable road car version.

tor itself needs to be mounted without vacuum leaks, so check that the mounting flange of the inlet manifold is absolutely flat, with a straight edge, then plug or cap all unused vacuum tubes. When the engine is up to operating temperature and the choke fully open, the float level should be set with the external adjusting screw, with the sight plug in the side of the float chamber removed. You can buy clear plastic sight plugs which prevent the possibility of fuel spillage during this simple, but vital operation. However, adjusting the fuel level this way can be difficult because of the vibration present when the engine is running. Getting the adjustment spot on is vital because it effects the fuel metering to both the main and idle circuits within the carb. Once done, the tick-over can be set using the external stop. Next the idle mixture must be set, using the two screws on the sides of the metering blocks (primary and secondary) which are sandwiched between the body of the carb and the float chamber. They need to be adjusted, more or less equally to obtain the highest possible tick-over engine speed (or manifold vacuum reading), after which the tick-over should again be set via the external stop.

If when turned the idle mixture screws seem to have little effect on the engine rpm, there is either a vacuum leak or the primary throttle plates are having to be set too far open to get any tick-over. If this is the case it will be necessary to remove the carb from the manifold and adjust the secondary throttle plates from underneath so that they allow slightly more airflow. Try to adjust them so that the fuel transfer slots, cut into the body of the carb, are just visible.

Eliminating any "bogs" or hesitation during hard acceleration is the next step. This is caused by a delay in the secondary throttle plates, which are opened by inlet manifold vacuum, not opening quickly enough to feed the engine's sudden increase in demand for air and fuel. This delay has to be tuned out by trying progressively heavier diaphragm springs (they are colour-coded) and increasing the size of the accelerator pump squirters. These pump squirters are numbered according to the size of their nozzles (eg, No 26 is a 0.026 in diameter nozzle) and they should be increased one step at a time until the hesitation clears up, while trying to stick to the smallest possible.

If the car just seems sluggish in response to full throttle acceleration, but not actually bogging, then a lighter diaphragm spring should be tried, but if there is no improvement then more fundamental causes need to be investigated.

The other areas of the carb for tuning are the main circuits and the power circuits, but these rarely need adjustment. The main circuits – which on the Holley 4160 390 cfm four-barrel are regulated by a metering plate – are best left alone. Other Holleys may have a metering block. The metering plate must be changed to change the jet, while the metering block has removable jets that are simpler and cheaper to change than the plate. The power circuits are controlled by power valves, which augment the fuel supply to maintain correct metering under hard acceleration. They can be changed to improve off-idle acceleration, but again, in general they should be left alone.

When fitting a Holley it is possible to end up with an erratic idle, depending on the type

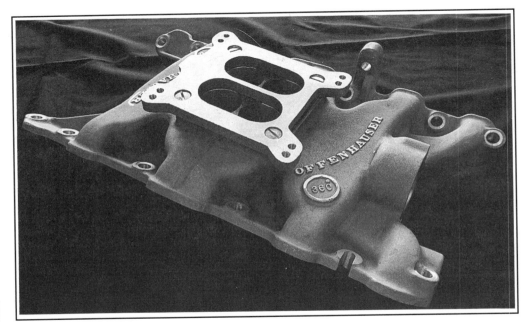

The very popular Offenhauser 360 inlet manifold, which is a dual plane design, and again mounts a single four-barrel carburettor.

On the left is the standard Rover alloy thermostat housing and on the right is the cast iron housing for use with the Offenhauser 360° manifold.

Accelerator cable kit for use with the Holley carburettor and Offenhauser manifold has cast bracket and either ball or barrel-type pedal connector.

69

ROVER V8

Kick-down linkage for the SD1 Borg Warner automatic, for use with the Holley carb and Offenhauser inlet manifold.

The John Wolfe Racing dual port inlet manifold for mounting a single four-barrel carb. It is a very good street manifold because it is a bolt-on replacement for the standard Rover item.

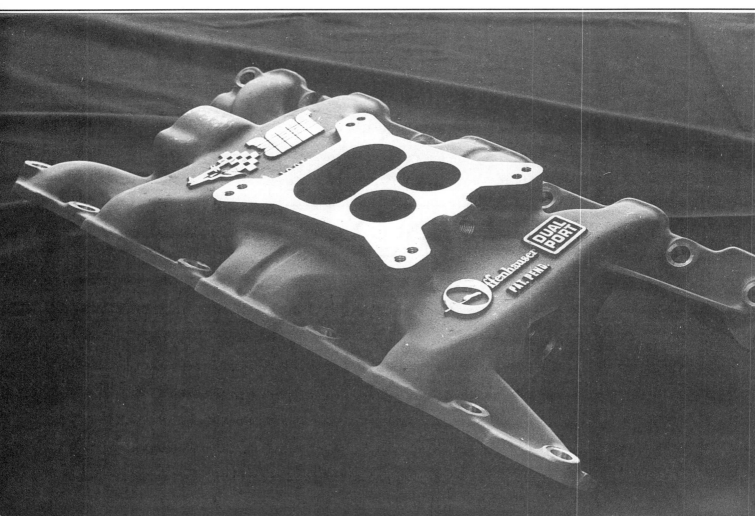

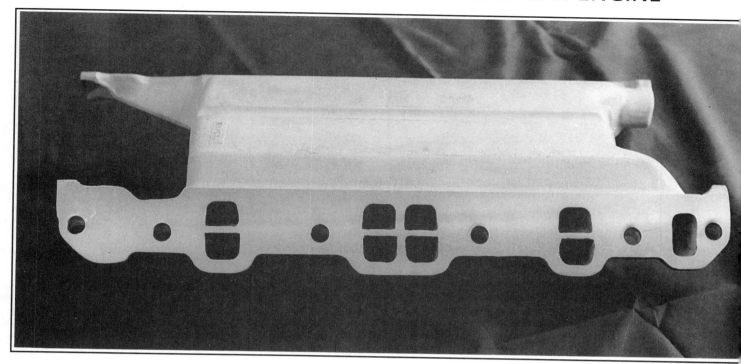

The underside of the John Wolfe Racing dual port inlet manifold, showing the unique split-level manifold runners.

of air cleaner fitted. This is caused by insufficient clearance between the bowl vent tube and the air cleaner lid. Put you finger over the tube: if the symptoms are repeated the problem lies there.

Inlet manifolds for mounting the Holley four-barrel are fairly limited, but the range is adequate. For road use the simplest and cheapest way to mount a four-barrel carburettor (eg, Holley, Edelbrock) is on the standard Rover SU/Zenith-Stromberg manifold. It will have to have the twin carb pent roof mounting machined off and a Holley mounting flange welded on. The result is not only very cheap, but also extremely effective when compared with the Offenhauser 360 dual plane manifold, which is probably the most popular manifold used with the Holley carb. Dual plane manifolds are divided internally so that one side of the four-barrel carburettor supplies the fuel/air mixture to one side (or cylinder bank) of the engine, and the two sides are in no way interconnected, which is supposed to increase low and mid-range throttle response. They are also water-heated, although slight work is needed to fit them to the Rover V8 because they are derived from a Buick design.

Dual plane manifolds are not the same as dual port. Specifically designed for road use is the Offenhauser/JWR Dual Port manifold, developed in the UK by John Wolfe Racing from an Offenhauser design. It is effectively two manifolds in one casting, with the inside of the manifold runners divided horizontally to correspond with the primary and secondary fuel/air flows of the Holley carburettor. The

primary mixture is fed into the bottom portion of the manifold runners, giving high mixture velocity at low rpm. For full power, the secondary mixture from the carb is fed into the top half of the manifold runners, giving maximum flow. In theory the manifold provides the right mixture flow/velocity for the engine's needs at all throttle openings. It is also a direct bolt-on replacement for the Rover V8 engine, not an adapted Buick/Oldsmobile casting, so has the correct water temperature sender outlet, heater hose clearance channel underneath, correctly positioned vacuum take-off point and has ample under-bonnet clearance.

Newest on the scene is the Edelbrock "Performer" 2198 dual plane manifold for all 1968 and later 3.5 litre Rover V8s and 1961–3 Buick/Oldsmobile 215 aluminium V8s. This manifold is really a road car piece, more so than the evergreen Offenhauser 360 manifold which is popular for mounting a four-barrel. The Performer's dual plane design gives good low rpm fuel distribution and mid range torque, providing enhanced performance off-idle up to 5,500 rpm, increasing bhp across a wide rpm range. The angle of the equal length manifold runners exactly matches the angle of the inlet ports. The Edelbrock is slightly taller than the Offenhauser design, but not to the extent of causing severe clearance problems, and it is a good halfway house towards the single plane Huffaker manifold which will be discussed in *Chapter 7*. Edelbrock recommend either the Holley 390 cfm four-barrel (8007) or the Edelbrock Performer 500 cfm (1404) on the Rover V8.

71

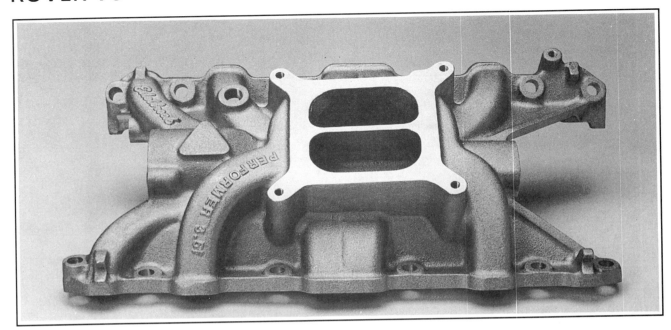

The Edelbrock Performer carburettor range, of which the 500 cfm is the smallest, is manufactured by Weber USA but it is a traditional American four-barrel design. The Edelbrock features metering rods for part throttle tuning. This is a tapered steel rod which seats in the main jet, and the rod's depth into the jet changes according to engine vacuum, thus altering fuel flow, rather like the SU tapered needle and seat system. There are a range of these metering rods available, making tuning easier than with the Holley.

More induction system options are discussed in other chapters.

EXHAUST SYSTEMS

Just about every production application of the Rover V8 has involved a unique cast iron exhaust manifold, and several specialist applications such as the Morgan and TVR models have used tubular manifolds of varying designs. In addition, other specialist companies have made tubular exhaust manifold replacements for most production applications, so the choice, is very large indeed, without having to resort to building one-off systems.

The only OE cast exhaust manifolds that have any performance potential are those used on the Rover SD1 saloon, which were used on all Group A racing SD1 saloons, albeit fully "ported" inside to maximize their flow ability. If the budget is especially tight these manifolds will do a good job on a road car engine, and can be squeezed on to engines used in other applications too, such as the TR7 V8 conversion.

A good pair of tubular exhaust manifolds are worth about 15 bhp on a Rover V8 engine. These tubular manifolds are sometimes referred to as extractor manifolds for good reason, and it might be worth delving into this aspect of an engine's breathing a little more deeply.

When the exhaust valve opens, the rising piston has to force the spent cylinder gases into the primary pipe of the exhaust header, which is already full of air at atmospheric pressure. The gases flow at high speed into the primary pipe until the piston stops rising and the exhaust valve closes, after which the pulse of hot gas continues to travel down the primary pipe, but now with the exhaust valve closed it leaves in its wake a low pressure area in the primary pipe. As the pulse of exhaust gas enters the larger diameter collector, its speed and pressure decrease, but it still has sufficient energy to cause a slight pressure drop in the other three primary pipes also. So when the next cylinder's exhaust valve opens the exhaust gases will get an extra boost out of the cylinder, because the pressure in the primary pipe will have been lowered by the passage of the previous cylinders exhaust gases pulsing through the exhaust system. Furthermore, it will get that extra boost when it is most needed because the piston has only just begun rising up the cylinder and gas pressure is therefore relatively low. So, with eight cylinders sending a rapid sequence of hot exhaust gas pulses through the exhaust system, there is an opportunity to create low pressure conditions in the primaries to suck the spent cylinder gases through the exhaust port when the valve initially opens. After that the rapidly rising cylinder will do the rest.

The superb new Edelbrock Performer manifold for the Rover V8. This company have produced inlet manifolds for the Buick/Oldsmobile version in the past, and this new piece looks a real winner.

Small bore tubular headers like this are available from many speed parts emporiums. They do not do any harm, but they are little better than cast manifolds.

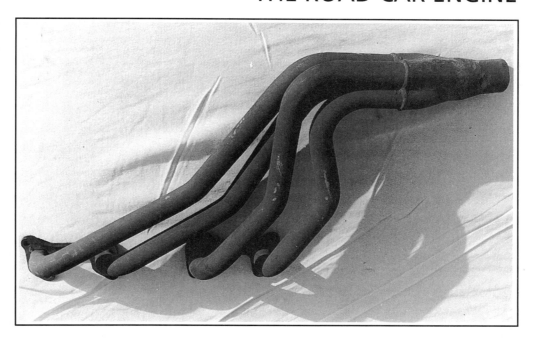

The more effective the exhaust system the less exhaust gas reversion can occur, when early on in the opening of the intake valve the incoming fresh fuel/air charge is diluted by left over exhaust gas. During the end of the exhaust cycle the rising piston is still pushing the exhaust gases out of the cylinder but the gas velocity is decreasing, so improving the velocity of the remaining gases greatly assists cylinder scavenging. The amount of time available for scavenging decreases as rpm increas-

These are more like it. A pair of big bore 4-2-1 manifolds for an SD1 installation, ideal for a 3.9 or 4.2 litre engine.

es. Exhaust gas velocity is related to the id (internal diameter) of the tubes constituting the exhaust system. Increase the id and decrease the velocity. As with intake runners, peak velocity is related to peak volumetric efficiency as the higher the operating rpm, the bigger the diameter of pipes needed. When you have one id of primary pipe flowing into a collector of bigger id (as they all do), the peak velocity occurs at different rpm. It is a fact that longer collectors produce more low end

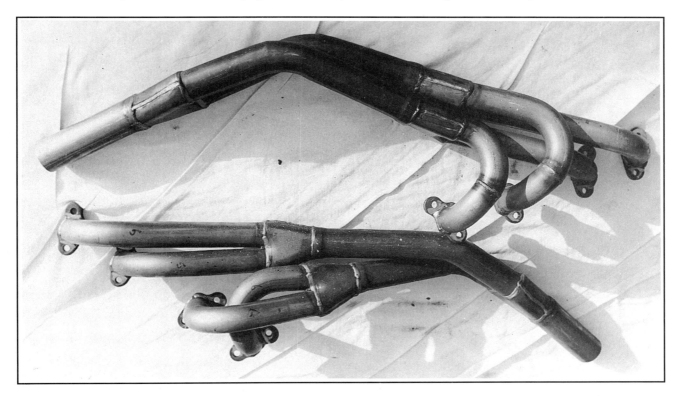

Opposite (both pictures)
This Range-Rover
chassis affords a good
opportunity to see the
design and fit of a good
pair of big bore 4-2-1
exhaust manifolds.
Tubular manifolds like this
can produce some
additional cabin noise in
such a refined vehicle.

torque and that shorter primaries produce more top end horsepower. The collectors therefore contribute to the torque output until the rpm is reached at which peak torque is produced, but beyond that point it is the primary pipe id and length that influence torque. So there are many factors that enable an exhaust system to be finely tuned to a particular engine's needs.

Most road car tubular exhaust manifolds are constructed from 34.925 mm (1.375 in) id tubing, but most Rover V8 tuners now consider 38.1 mm (1.5 in) more effective, although it is not unusual to see 41.275 mm (1.625 in) on big capacity road cars, although these and the mammoth 44.45 mm (1.75 in) primary pipe headers are more usually reserved for racing. The mismatch of header (primary) pipe and exhaust port size is not a problem with the larger diameter pipes. Obviously there is the aforementioned gas velocity issue to consider, and velocity will drop as the gases enter the large diameter pipe, but exhaust gas pulses back into the port tend to be blocked, reducing reversion and thus intake charge contamination.

Some exhaust system specialists favour using a balance pipe on the Rover V8, ie, a short pipe joining the two collectors. A balance pipe can improve low rpm torque, but its effectiveness decreases as back pressure increases, as in the case of a fully silenced road car. If fitted, it needs to be located just past the point where the primaries enter the collector and be 60–70 per cent of the collector's diameter.

The remainder of the exhaust system is really a matter of fitting sufficient silencing in the space available, although here again there are special single or twin performance systems available for some applications, and there seems little difference in power output between single and twin except of course that a single pipe system in 63.5 mm (2.5 in) tube is usually cheaper.

IGNITION SYSTEMS

Whilst is it true to say that the Rover V8 engine is very tolerant of ignition inadequacies and even timing inaccuracies, that is no reason to neglect this important aspect of performance.

The ignition system is very important. Many problems of poor starting, power loss and rough running can be attributed to ignition maladies, so from the plugs to the distributor/coil the whole system needs to be *good*.

The pre-SD1 engine was fitted with a Lucas single contact breaker system (their first for an eight-cylinder engine), but when the engine's peak rpm was raised to 6,000 rpm with the introduction of the SD1 it was deemed unable to cope, and the solution of using a twin contact breaker system was rejected because of possible service problems.

The Rover SD1 saloon used a Lucas DE8 with Opus electronic ignition. The oscillator, timing rotor, pick-up amplifier and power transistor are all housed in the distributor body. This compact system, if in good working order, is an excellent choice for performance road cars, right down to the plug leads, but it can be prone to misfiring and deterioration of the system because of heat from the engine in tuned applications. The system used on the Rover Vitesse is probably the best OE system, having an ignition amplifier underneath the coil. The latest specification Range-Rover EFi engine systems have the ignition amplifier on the side of the distributor where once again engine heat can affect it.

The early pre-SD1 systems suffer from above-average spindle wear, points bounce and poor dwell angles. It can be improved by fitting a good electronic ignition kit, such as the Lumenition.

UNLEADED FUEL

The Rover V8 engine can be modified to run on unleaded fuel. Any post-1970 standard engine has valve seat material compatible with unleaded fuel. Those engines with a 9.35:1 compression ratio will have to have the ignition timing retarded by 3°, but those with a lower compression ratio can run on unleaded without any problem. However, the official line is that the above information applies only to Land-Rover installed-engines, ie, engines in Land-Rover vehicles (including Freight-Rover). Rover (formerly Austin Rover etc) do not approve of unleaded fuel being used in any Rover V8 engine installed in their vehicles, yet the MGB V8 was set up for 94 octane fuel!

KEEPING UP APPEARANCES

This visual aspect of a newly rebuilt Rover V8 should never be neglected, and can be the icing on the cake after all that hard work and expense. There are many excellent products on the market now for dressing up the engine, and most have practical advantages to offer as well as giving the engine a professional look.

Let's begin by looking at rocker covers. Land-Rover have produced two factory types, both in cast aluminium, the pre-SD1 shape

being rounded with the Rover legend and the SD1 saw the introduction of the current, more angular style. The MGB V8 had a version derived from the earlier design but they were finished in black and bore the "MG" legend.

It was in mid-1976 that the rocker covers were changed to the current, more angular finned type which are powder coated grey at the factory but can be custom finished in black, red, blue or simply left as bare alloy and polished. This exact pattern of rocker cover has also been duplicated in stamped steel with a bright chrome finish. Available through Roverpart in Norwich they are light, reasonably priced and very attractive.

Real Steel manufacture an adaptor kit which enables any small block Ford rocker cover to fit the Rover flange. This provides exceptional rocker gear clearance, sometimes a problem with different types of rocker gear and also allows the use of an impressive choice of stamped steel rocker covers in chrome or various anodised colours by such manufacturers as Moroso or Edlebrock and cast alloy rocker covers, even those bearing the "Cobra"

Above and below (a) Early type Rover V8 rocker cover used on all Rover P5B, P6B, and early Range Rover engines. (b) Current type of rocker cover used on all production Rover V8 engines introduced with the Rover SD1 in 1976.

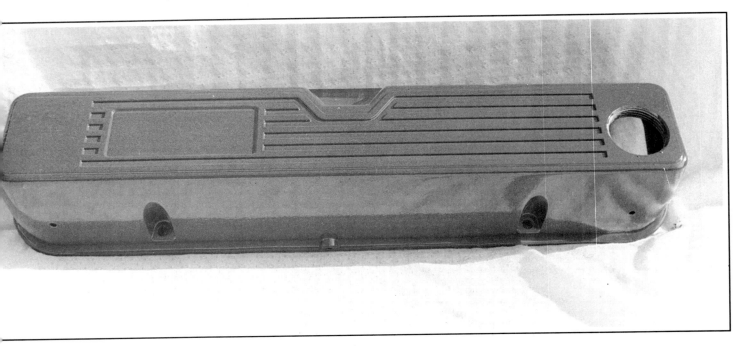

Right Real Steel rocker cover adaptors allow the mounting of any small-block Ford rocker cover on the Rover flange, giving improved rocker gear clearance and superb looks.

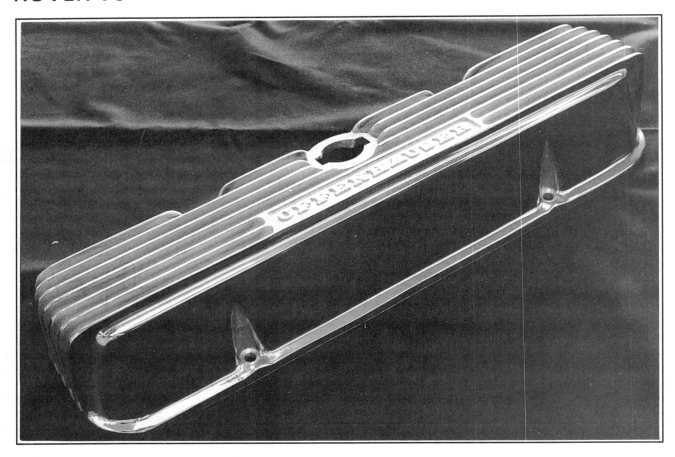

The cast polished alloy Offenhauser rocker covers have an excellent period look and are superb quality.

legend which are ideal for any Rover powered Cobra or even Ford GT40 replica.

Air cleaners are another obvious choice for the custom touch, and the range available becomes bewildering when taking into account the fact that the air cleaner depends on the type of induction system being used on the engine. The Holley carburettor flange will accept any number of American-manufactured air cleaners in chrome or anodized finish, and even machined alloys by such esteemed names as Moroso, Holley and Mr Gasket.

CONCLUSIONS

For an enthusiast now contemplating the building of his first Rover V8 engine, perhaps for installation in a Triumph TR7 roadster, the information so far given has simply laid out a multitude of bewildering choices and said little about the costs involved. Let's just put power outputs into proportion before we consider possible options. The Rover Vitesse engine when launched in 1982 produced 190 bhp at the flywheel, and a good used Vitesse will be making over 100 bhp at about 3,500 rpm and peaking at about 125 bhp around 4,500 rpm at the wheels. A standard SD1 engine pro-

duces 155 bhp and a carburetted Range-Rover 125 bhp at the flywheel.

So what would constitute the main ingredients of a good road engine without breaking the bank? Assuming the engine is based on a 3.5 litre version, which will probably be the engine available to most enthusiasts, the first decision to be made is whether to remain with that capacity or go to 3.9 litres. It is extremely difficult to be specific about what an individual should do to their particular engine, without knowing how much they have to spend and what they want from their vehicle. The cost aspect is further complicated by which engine is being used as a basis for the build, for instance a late EFi or early Rover P5B unit, the condition of the engine, and how much reconditioning of the engine is needed or whether any second-hand tuning parts are available for incorporation into the engine which might help keep the costs down (as well as dictate, in part the route taken).

If 3.5 litres is to be retained, the power output can be realistically boosted to 215–220 bhp while retaining acceptable road driving characteristics, although there will be a slight sacrifice of low rpm torque for greater peak bhp. A good route would be a pair of Stage 1 cylinder heads with standard sized Vitesse

ARP stainless steel inlet
manifold bolt kit.

ROVER V8

valves, Vitesse pistons with 9.75:1 compression ratio, Kent 200 or 214 camshaft, a Holley 390 cfm carb (vacuum secondaries) on an Edelbrock Performer inlet manifold, and pair of 44.45 mm (1.75 in) tubular exhaust manifolds. This specification should produce an engine with good road characteristics but the 214 camshaft will still give the engine a definite peaky feel to anyone used to the standard engine.

The ideal, given a reasonable budget but still using good value as a criterion, is putting the bulk of the budget into two main areas – increasing the capacity to 3.9 litres (staying with a 9.75:1 compression ratio) on a second-hand Vitesse or EFi unit and investing in a good pair of cylinder heads. This route does not even need a change of camshaft from standard (although it can be part of the plot), and with a pair of tubular exhaust manifolds will be good for at least 200 bhp at the wheels. A mild road camshaft will boost this even further. The value of a good pair of cylinder heads cannot be overstressed on this engine, and they are the pivot point of building a good Rover V8. More work and investment can be put into an engine as more money becomes available, but the heads should be considered a prime requirement for serious power.

Higher outputs are always possible, especially if the capacity is taken beyond 3.9 litres, but this would significantly increase the cost. For a big vehicle like the Range-Rover it would be difficult to beat the benefits of 4.4+ litres without using forced induction, but sports cars could certainly make good use of a tuned 3.5 litre Rover V8 provided the engine remains tractable and untemperamental. Push for too high power outputs, and road manners and tractability become increasingly compromised as we move into the realms of the road-driven competition car or the out and out racing unit.

Chapter Four

The competition engine

Assembling a competition engine using any production-based V8 with parallel inclined valves operated via push-rods might for many engine builders be a contradiction in terms. Using push-rods to actuate the valves involves more valve gear complexity, the weight of which can seriously restrict the engine's ability to achieve high rpm. Such complex valve gear means loss of rigidity and a number of clearances, both of which reduce the precision with which the camshaft profile is transferred to the valves. Furthermore, the weight of this valve gear imparts an inertia which has to be overcome, even before the additional load of actually opening the valve is encountered. In order to reduce the effect this complexity has on overall gas flow, it is considered vital to reduce the weight of the valves, rockers and push-rods. Ways of lowering loads by reducing friction are also employed, such as roller tipped rockers, which reduce the sliding motion of the rocker across the valve tip as it opens and closes. Many other aspects of the engine may also prove unacceptable to a competition engine builder, and a major part of the art of making it work is surmounting those shortcomings.

So, it would seem that in the very principles of its design, the production-based V8 competition engine has its drawbacks, just as one could say that one of the major drawbacks of using a Cosworth DFV is actually finding the money to buy it! What we are talking about here are compromises, pipe-dreams versus realistic goals, and production design limitations versus racing technology. You need to have a very healthy bank balance to run a pukka racing engine, but a properly built Rover V8 can produce an enormous amount of wonderful-sounding power, quite capable of powering anything from weekend rally car or clubman circuit racer, to a modern single-seater for national hillclimbing or sprint competition, all in a package light enough to maintain a vehicle's poise and balance on the racetrack.

Building a Rover V8 for use as a motor sport power unit involves fewer compromises than for use in a road car. Of course there will always be a crossover of components and building techniques, as enthusiasts' definitions of what constitutes a road car and what constitutes a competition car differ. Many road cars are used for limited weekend competition, while some drivers are prepared to be more tolerant of a competition engine's "manners" when driven on the road, and many enthusiasts either cannot afford to own a second car for motor sport or are forced for various reasons to drive their car to the sporting venue. As the road car may be required to fulfil a dual role, or the road car engine builder may wish to employ greater sophistication in seeking higher power outputs, so the division between a road engine and a competition engine cannot be so easily defined.

That the Rover V8 has, and indeed is having, a very successful competition career cannot be disputed. Probably the most well-known racing series currently using the engine is the popular and very exciting TVR Tuscan Challenge. These specially built racing machines are powered by 4,441 cc (94 mm bore x 80 mm stroke) Rover V8 engines with 12:1 compression ratios and quadruple 48 DRLE Webers. They produce 348 bhp at 6,750 rpm and 297 lb/ft of torque at 5,500 rpm, which is sufficient to give these lightweight racers a 0–60 mph time of 3.7 seconds and a top speed of 246 km/h (153 mph).

This mighty 4.4 litre TVR Tuscan Challenge power unit produces over 350 bhp and over 300 lbs/ft of torque. Note the forward-facing exhaust manifolds.

Few enthusiasts can afford to build an engine regardless of cost, but it is possible to build a perfectly acceptable Rover V8 for racing or rallying on a limited budget. Compromises are involved when building any engine to a set budget (few are ever built with "money no object"), but it is important to consider very carefully how available money should best be spent. A basic specification needs to be decided on for the intended engine build given the budget involved, and one should not be over-ambitious with what can realistically be achieved.

As part of that compromising process, it is essential to consider the intended application of the engine, and take into account factors such as total vehicle weight, final drive ratio, overall gearing, and the type of competition the vehicle is involved in. For instance, if the vehicle is an off-road 4 X 4 trials type, then lots of low and mid-range torque is needed to haul it over the tough terrain, but if the engine is being installed in a lightweight circuit racer, torque becomes less important but horse power is needed. Of course, things are never that simple, and any competition vehicle needs torque for pulling away from slow corners, and then as the straights open out and the rpm builds up it is its horsepower that is going to build up the speed rapidly and sustain it. Too much torque applied to a racing car that has class-imposed tyre width restrictions can lead to excessive wheel-spin off the start line, and when accelerating out of slow corners so to a certain extent torque can be traded in favour of peak horsepower.

The weight advantage of the aluminium Rover V8 over iron block engines has frequently been emphasized. It has also been said that there are many cheaper ways to remove weight from a competition vehicle than indulging in the luxury of aluminium block and heads, but of course once the vehicle has been lightened as far as possible by other means, this is the next logical route to take. With the Rover V8 this rather exotic material comes as standard, not as an additional cost, so with a competition vehicle using a Rover V8 engine there is an opportunity to make maximum use of the weight advantage already afforded by having an aluminium powerplant.

CYLINDER BLOCK

Make no mistake about it: the cylinder block is the solid foundation of any engine project, and never more so than in a competition engine where power and reliability are the key to success. The money spent on preparing and machining the block can be considerable, and the result is not visually apparent when the engine sits in the engine bay. It may be money well spent, but you will have little to show for it!

If the engine is being built from scratch, blocks manufactured from 1984 onwards should be considered the minimum requirement for a competition engine. Of course this is not a hard and fast rule, but if the choice is there these later blocks are superior.

Selection of a suitable block requires a little more care than one would perhaps take for a road engine. A well-seasoned block that has become dimensionally stable is the best starting point, the engine having gone through repeated heating and cooling cycles and settled the internal stresses created during casting and machining. Of course, used blocks such as this will require very careful checking to ensure nothing is amiss before subjecting

them to expensive machining. Some builders may prefer and be able to afford using a brand new block as the basis for their project, but it will still need to be thoroughly checked and subjected to certain machining before it is considered race-ready.

If you intend to build an engine with the standard 88.9 mm (3.5 in) bore with perhaps just 0.508 mm (0.02 in) overbore to restore the bores, it is worth checking that the engine has not already been overbored. In theory every overbore will reduce the strength of the block, but in practice this is hardly a problem. The standard 88.9 mm (3.5 in) liners will only take a 0.762 mm (0.03 in) overbore before becoming unacceptably thin, so if this has already been done the only solution would be to have new cylinder liners inserted in the block. Assuming this stage has been reached, the option of going for a 3.9 litre conversion is well worth considering. There is obviously plenty of aluminium block material around the cylinders, bearing in mind the popularity and reliability of larger capacity conversions with their 94 mm (3.8 in) bores, so one hardly need worry about block strength with this larger bore.

The standard two-bolt main bearing caps are capable of handling high power outputs, but they begin to show signs of weakness as rpm limits rise. Sustained high rpm produces extraordinary stresses in seemingly solid materials and structures. These stresses will lead to failures if the engine is not capable of withstanding them. The main bearing caps, in particular the bolts fastening them to the block, will loosen at high rpm, allowing the steel bearing caps to move or "fret" against the block: obviously an undesirable phenomena.

A full race competition hill climb/sprint Lola 87/50 single-seater using 4.2 litre Rover V8 power.

ROVER V8

This 1972 vintage F5000 Rover V8 block has a simple alloy plate and thick steel straps across main bearing caps.

A close-up of the F5000 block showing how the main bearing caps are locked into the straps and girdle, and the special steel spacers on the caps.

This is one of the reasons the four-bolt or cross-bolted block was developed. The most that can be done with the standard two-bolt main bearing caps is to fasten them down using studs, rather than the standard bolts.

If the cost of a cross-bolted block is outside the budget – and many engines have to be built without the benefit of this luxury – some form of block stiffening plate or girdle has to be fitted if rpm limits are to be raised beyond 7,000 rpm. Such girdles used to consist of a fairly thick steel plate cut to the same shape as the sump flange, with strips running across the line of the main bearing so that extended bolts could go through the stiffening plate, through the main bearing caps themselves, and into the block. The plate would also be sandwiched between the sump and the sump flange of the block, thus adding to the strength of the block in a critical area. Large areas of the plate were cut out, of course, to allow for crankshaft rotation and oil drainback.

These steel plate girdles were crude and of dubious benefit, but they were relatively inexpensive and certainly did no harm. In the late 1970s Janspeed designed and cast a dry sump for their twin turbocharged Rover V8 Le Mans racing project, which dispensed with the standard main bearing caps and incorporated sump and bearing caps in a one-piece alloy structure. This in effect became an integral part of the block and tied together the bottom end in a far more positive way. Nowadays substantial girdles, following on from the Janspeed design, but for wet sumps are cast and then machined from aluminium alloy. The crankshaft is placed in the block on the main bearings, and then the girdle, with its integral main bearing caps, is bolted down using longer main bearing cap bolts, cap screws or studs. The sump is then attached using longer bolts which have to go through the girdle (around the sump flange) and then into the block. The oil pick-up pipe has to be extended by the thickness of the girdle.

A more recent development, which in theory is almost bullet-proof (no, make that bomb-proof), is the cast alloy girdle in conjunction with a cross-bolted block. The cross-bolted block has not proved to be the ultimate answer to block/main bearing integrity in some extreme cases, so a girdle, very similar to that designed for the normal two-bolt main's block, has been designed for the cross-bolted block, with the added advantage of being further tied into the block structure with the additional two bolts for each of the three centre main bearing caps which come through the block just above the sump flange.

There are two distinct types of four-bolt main's blocks. The "factory" blocks were originally made for BL Motorsport for the Triumph TR7 V8 rallying programme, adopted by Land-Rover for the Iceberg diesel engine project, and subsequently resurrected during their involvement in the Paris-Dakar Rally Raid. Since then they have been made available in very limited numbers and are much prized, but their cost and rarity have always been a major drawback. In practice, their special cast caps have not proved the ultimate answer, which is why some specialists resorted to using them in conjunction with a girdle. The scarcity and cost of the factory four-bolt blocks has led to more than one company machining normal two-bolt blocks to accept billet four-bolt caps.

Mention should be made at this stage about the part played by the inlet manifold in overall block strength. It has long been the opinion of Land-Rover production engineers that the Rover V8 block structure benefits greatly by having the two cylinder heads tied together by the inlet manifold, which of course forms a solid bridge across the top of the engine. When fitting paired inlet manifolds, such as those used with quadruple downdraught carburettors, this strengthening is lost. Most competition engine builders do not consider this to be a problem, while others see it as a potential source of block failure, usually along the main bearing webs.

CYLINDER BORE PREPARATION

On a competition engine you will have to spend a lot more money trying to regain the power your engine will be losing because the cylinder bores have not been properly prepared and are therefore not capable of giving the best possible seal between bore surface and piston rings.

The only acceptable preparation for the cylinder bores is for them to be properly honed on an automatic power honing machine to produce perfectly round, straight properly textured cylinder walls. Ask the machine shop if they can hone to a plus or minus 0.0254 mm (0.001 in) of the required bore size throughout the length of the bore, and if they express doubts take your block elsewhere. If you do not have the necessary bore gauge to check the machining yourself, ask the machine shop to show you using their gauge, and don't accept the block until you are satisfied. When the bores are finished, chamfer the inside edge of the bore slightly to ease the installation of the new piston rings during assembly.

Block preparation does not stop there. The block should be thoroughly deburred,

An upper view of the F5000 block showing the welded bar on each cylinder bank. There are holes not only for the push-rods, but also for U bolts which went around the inlet port castings to provide additional cylinder head clamping! Note also the oil baffle and the sleeved cam follower holes to allow the fitting of Ford mushroom lifters.

Standard two-bolt mains block fitted with an alloy block girdle, incorporating main bearing caps.

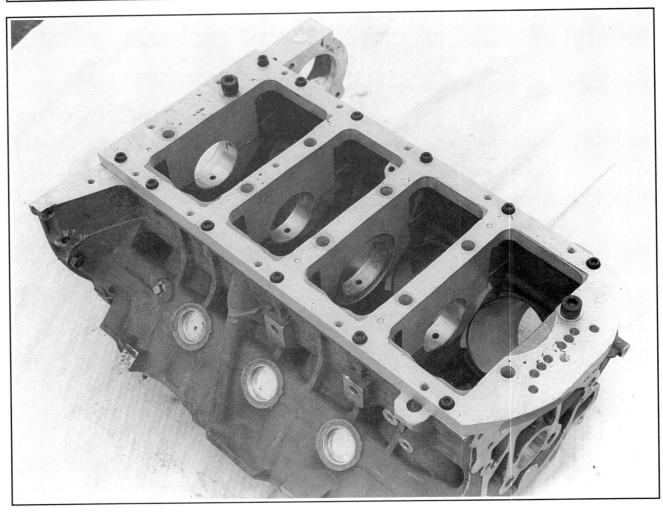

Factory cross-bolt block with alloy block girdle incorporating main bearing caps. (This example still has to be line bored.)

Finishing the bores on an automatic power honing machine. The cylinder on the left has yet to be done, but the two cylinders on the right have clearly been honed. This is the way to have bores finished.

ROVER V8

Proper bore finish also depends on accurate bore dimensions. Insist on bores honed to plus or minus one thou over the entire bore depth.

Polishing the lifter gallery like this is done on many competition engines to aid oil drainback to the sump. It is a time-consuming but inexpensive tweak for enthusiasts building their own engines.

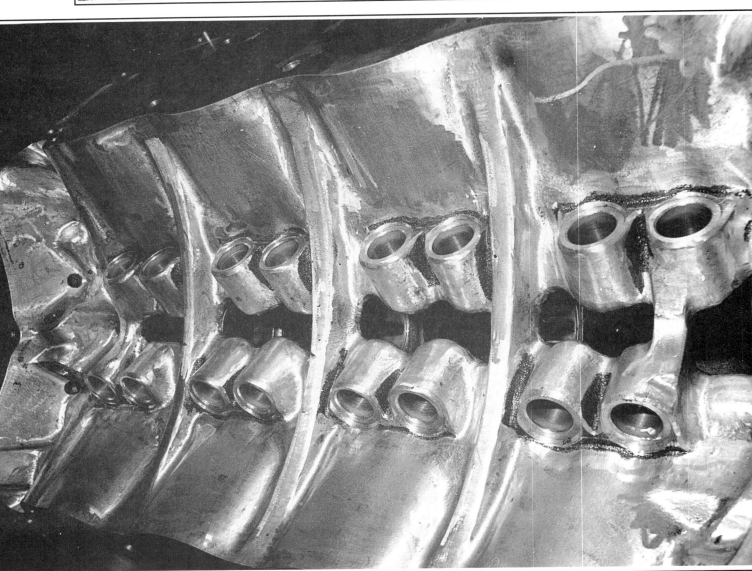

grinding off all sharp edges which might give cracks a starting point, and removing any casting flash which may break off inside the engine at a later date and cause damage. This is also the time to open out the oil drain back areas in the lifter gallery between the two cylinder banks, and if you are dedicated it is worthwhile polishing all the cast aluminium surfaces in this area to speed up oil flow as it returns by gravity to the sump. This polishing of the lifter gallery surface has long been a popular "tweak", mainly because of the Rover V8's tendency to retain large quantities of oil in the upper part of the engine during high rpm operation, and it is felt by many that anything that speeds up the drainback of the oil to the sump is obviously of benefit. However, it might be worth mentioning the other school of thought which maintains that the cast texture of the gallery provides a greater surface area of alloy to transfer engine heat into the oil as it returns to the sump, and of course one of the primary functions of the oil is engine cooling.

The main bearing bores should be align-honed to correct any distortion in the main bearing bulkheads, but more importantly sizing the main bearing bores and leaving a smooth finish on the bore surface which will accurately crush the bearings when they are inserted in the bores and give a precise bearing to crank journal clearance across the width of the bearing. An equally important machining operation on the block is equalizing the block (to cylinder head) decks so that they are the same distance from the crankshaft centre line both at the front and rear of the block. Dimensional accuracy of the cylinder block is vital in any racing engine and is best left to expert machinists.

One major advantage of having an aluminium cylinder block is that it can be repaired much easier than cast iron. Aluminium can be welded relatively easily and often major damage can be repaired at the fraction of the cost of buying and preparing another block. Many companies involved in racing engine preparation can undertake aluminium block repairs.

CRANKSHAFT

The standard spheroidal, cast graphite iron, five-bearing crankshaft has proved extremely durable in a number of demanding competition applications. It is generally considered that the standard cast crankshaft, when properly prepared, is capable of withstanding 7,500 rpm, and indeed BL Motorsport claimed 8,000 rpm was produced by their engines using these cranks. We do know that these crankshafts,

certainly in the TWR racing Rover SD1s, were fillet-rolled on all the journals, ionized and cross-drilled for maximum lubrication, and crankshaft failure has never been a weakness of these engines

If the standard cast crank is going to be used it really should be crack (Magnaflux) tested first, and checked to see that it is straight. It will need to be deburred for the same reason that the block is deburred – it removes stress risers which are potential sources of cracks – and shot-peened, ie, bombarded with tiny steel balls to compress the metal on the surface of the crank casting and make it more difficult for cracks to get started.

The bearing journals need to be checked for size and if necessary reground, but beware of using a crank that has had any bearing journals reground by removing more than 0.254 mm (0.01 in). During the regrinding the big end journals can also be indexed to put the crankshaft throws exactly 90° apart, and ensure that the crankshaft puts the pistons at the same height up the bores at TDC. Variations in rod and piston dimensions will be addressed later.

For maximum strength a crankshaft should have the maximum radius joining the bearing's journals to the crankshaft "cheeks". If the crankshaft is being reground, a good machine shop can grind in these generous radii, or alternatively a crank can be prepared from a raw casting, keeping the maximum journal diameter and generous radii. But beware that when installed the bearings have to have an equally generous chamfer on their outside edge to avoid interference.

Cross-drilling the crankshaft and chamfering the oil holes is another important procedure when preparing the crankshaft for performance use. In cross-drilling the existing oil holes to the main bearing journals are drilled through completely, resulting in a second oil feed hole located 180° opposite the original. This is preferably to using fully grooved bearings because it does not involve reducing the loading capacity of the bearing. All oil feed drilling should also be chamfered around the edges but not excessively flared (before the journals are ground!). It is also worthwhile making sure that when the upper main bearing half is inserted in the block the oil hole in the bearing exactly matches the oil supply hole behind it in the block.

Forged steel cranks have never been made for the Rover V8, so any that are available have been machined from billet. Many people involved in circuit racing are using steel crankshafts, but they are only available to special order from one of the specialist crankshaft manufacturers, such as Laystall Engineering.

ROVER V8

Never buy a second-hand steel crankshaft without first having it Magnafluxed. Despite being an excellent choice for an out-and-out racing engine they are prone to radial cracking, and it is possible that the crank is being offered for sale for that very reason. Such cracks are difficult to detect, and if you buy a cracked crank, install it in your engine and it breaks, the resultant destruction may make it very difficult to prove that the crank was at fault. Steel cranks are unquestionably stronger than cast cranks, but they are more likely to develop stress cracks in the event of engine blow-ups. Cast cranks seem less likely to crack, but their ultimate strength is lower.

Before moving on, a word about flat-plane crankshafts. One of the reasons a pukka racing engine such as a Cosworth V8 does not have that familiar uneven V8 sound is that is uses a flat-plane crankshaft, that is, the crank throws are all on the same plane, not phased at 90° to each other like a conventional V8. Some flat-plane cranks have been manufactured for the Rover V8, engines have been built with these cranks and some racers have dabbled with using them. The flat-plane crank has a different firing order to the conventional cranks – 1 4 5 2 7 6 3 8 as opposed to 1 8 4 3 6 5 7 2 – which means that a special camshaft also has to be used to match this altered firing order, and of course the firing order of the distributor has to be altered, too. For someone determined to pursue this option as part of an engine project the parts do exist. In fact, flat-plane cranks have been made in both cast iron and billet steel, but they are not widely available (probably about a dozen exist) and would need to be sought via specialists.

PISTONS

Apart from the OE cast pistons available from Land-Rover, only Omega (available through J.E. Engineering Ltd) manufacture pistons specifically for the Rover V8. But that does not mean that there are limited options when choosing pistons for this engine; on the contrary, the choices are many and varied.

Rover V8 engines have been built using pistons from not only Land-Rover and Omega, but also Cosworth, Mahle, Venolia and a few others besides. A piston is a piston, and what matters is its critical dimensions, ie, diameter (bore size), compression height (the distance from the piston pin to piston crown), overall height (or length), weight, wrist pin diameter, and whether it is press fit or floating wrist (gudgeon) pin.

There are then further refinements to the specification, such as whether they are taper and ovality (barrel) ground. OE pistons are taper-ground, but some specialist pistons are also ovality-ground which means they need less bore clearance. Piston crown thickness is important if the engine is being supercharged, turbocharged or using nitrous oxide injection. Valve clearance pockets may also be already cast or machined into the piston crown, important with high-lift camshafts or larger valves, and the piston ring package should be suitable for the intended application.

The Rover V8 engine OE cast pistons are available in a variety of compression ratios, and this is accomplished by having bowls in the piston crown of varying depth. The deeper the bowl, the greater the volume of the bowl and therefore the lower the compression ratio. So for a performance engine the bowl is shallower, reducing its volume and raising the compression ratio. Thus with a bowled piston, the volume of the bowl must be added to the overall combustion chamber volume when calculating the compression ratio. Reducing the bowl volume can only be taken so far until a flat top piston is the result. To raise the compression further involves adding more material to the top of the piston, ie, raising its compression height, but this has its limitations. Eventually the stage will be reached when the piston is almost coming in contact with the cylinder head at TDC, and the only option then to raise the compression ratio further is to mill the cylinder head or use domed pistons. Milling the cylinder head is not desirable for a number of reasons, not least of which is the fact that it moves the valves closer to the edge of the bore, aggravating the valve shrouding problem already encountered with the standard 88.9 mm (3.5 in) bore, reduces the thickness of the cylinder head deck thus threatening cylinder head gasket sealing, and this can affect inlet manifold alignment. The Rover V8's squench-type combustion chamber works best with a flat top or dished piston. Achieving an even higher compression ratio will require using domed pistons, not an option for the faint-hearted – that is assuming you can find a set of domed pistons to fit. They were made by Mahle and used in the Group A racing 3.5 litre Rover saloons 88.9 mm (3.5 in bore) where compression ratios went to around 14:1, but are no longer widely available, and finding a set suitable for the bigger 94.04 mm (3.7 in) bore would be even more difficult. The more readily available flat-top pistons, obtainable in both common bore sizes, give a nominal 11:1 or 12:1, and depending on the usual variables they should suffice for most applications.

Cast or forged? Forged pistons have a much denser molecular structure than cast pistons, and although there are good die cast pistons

Flat plane crankshaft. This is a bare unmachined casting and one of only a handful in existence.

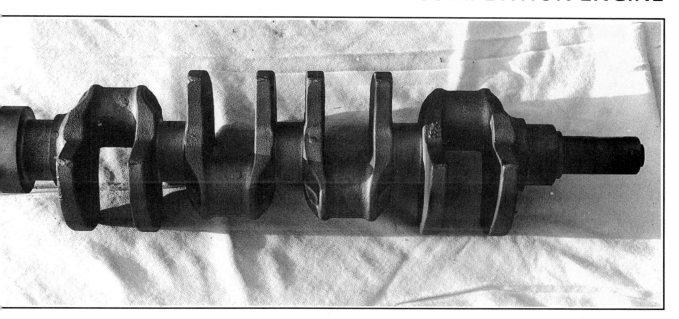

Pistons. Left to right: Cosworth Group A high-compression raised crown (forged), Bemak semi slipper type (forged), and Mahle Group A (forged).

that are eminently suitable for budget competition engines, the serious engine builder will want a good set of forged pistons.

A good piston design will take into account the expansion characteristics of the piston as different areas are subjected to differing rates of heating and cooling. The design will also take into account the need to keep the piston as light as possible, without compromising strength and durability, because piston weight is an important factor in the stress loading on the piston pin, connecting rod and the rod bolts. However, providing that the piston is not especially heavy, its weight has no effect on overall engine performance, so there is little point in trying to machine the piston underside in order to par off a few grams when there is potential for weakening or altering the expansion characteristics of the forging.

If a 3.5 litre engine is being built with an 88.9 mm (3.5 in) bore, Real Steel can supply an excellent Ross-forged piston, available in +0.020 in size for reboring, with race quality 4340 steel pin and weighing 605 g (21.3 oz) (less rings). Omega pistons (from J.E. Engineering) are available in a considerable range, both cast and forged range for the larger 94.04 mm (3.7 in) bore size. There are flat-top with compression heights of 43.2 mm (1.7 in) and 48.3 mm (1.9 in), and a lower compression type with a bowl in the piston crown. There are then a number of die-cast pistons in the range, which are excellent budget competition designs with a number of compression heights, etc.

The standard Rover V8 wrist (gudgeon) pin is an interference fit into the connecting rod small end, with the piston itself floating on

91

ROVER V8

Forged flat-top piston in 88.9 mm bore size (+0.2.0 in) from Real Steel.

Speedpro plasma moly-chilled iron piston rings. File fit 6.35 mm with 1.59 mm compression ring and 4.76 mm oil ring for 88.9 mm bore size.

the pin. The pin therefore has to be pushed into the connecting rod small end with the aid of a press capable of exerting a pressure of at least 8,128 kg (8 tons). This is hardly practical for a racing application, where a piston may need to be changed at the race track, so most forged pistons are fully floating, ie, the pin is a push fit into the con rod small end and the piston, being held in place by circlips (or Tru-Arcs) located into grooves in the piston at either end of the wrist pin bore. The failure of one of these circlips for whatever reason will result in the wrist pin moving and coming into contact with the cylinder wall. Not a pretty sight! Never re-use circlips in this application; always replace them with new ones at every rebuild and install them with the smoother, rounded edge facing the piston pin.

It is also very important that the wrist pin diameter is taken into account when deciding on a particular piston/connecting rod combination, because if the small end internal diameter is sized for interference fit but the piston chosen is fully floating, then the small end will need to be reamed out to a slightly larger diameter, as it would be if a piston using a larger diameter pin, either press or floating, was being used.

Using pistons with a larger wrist pin diameter is yet another consideration worth dwelling on for a moment. Some engine builders choose to use pistons in a Rover V8 which have a larger wrist pin diameter than standard which, if the standard rods (or Group A pattern) are being used, will mean reaming out the connecting rod small end to a diameter that might unacceptably weaken this part of the rod. If steel or aluminium rods are being used this is not so much of a problem, but the principle of sizing the small end to fit the wrist pin for either press fit of floating remains the same. Note, too, that a connecting rod converted to take a floating pin will need a small hole drilled in the top to lubricate the pin.

The whole question of increasing the capacity of the Rover V8 is dealt with in a later chapter, but it should be made clear at this stage that longer stroke crankshafts need a dimensionally different piston. If a longer stroke crankshaft is fitted, a piston with the gudgeon pin located higher up the piston has to be used. Therefore as the stroke is increased the compression height of the piston has to be reduced by 50 per cent of that increase (50 per cent because the piston will move further down the bore as well as further up). The supply of pistons to suit different stroke crankshafts is a further complication to piston choice!

Recording all the possible pistons that can be used in the Rover V8 could fill a small volume on its own when all the bore/stroke/connecting rod combinations are examined, but for the majority of engine builders it is not complex at all. There are only two main bore sizes, 88.9 mm or 94.04 mm (or possibly 93.5 mm). There are then the compression height/crankshaft stroke variables. If an engine is being built with a particular bore and stroke, it is down to the compression ratio required and whether cast or forged pistons are required. However, if one is going outside the OE cast piston or possibly Omega range of piston sizes, it would be well worthwhile sourcing a set of pistons before preparing the bores and connecting rods to suit. Some of the smaller USA manufacturers such as Jahns in Los Angeles will make a set of pistons to order from any number of basic blanks, without involving prohibitive costs.

CONNECTING RODS

There are now a considerable number of Rover V8 connecting rods to choose from, and there are a few principles that need to be considered. Like most things in engine building, choice is limited by cost and the intended use of the finished engine. As will be seen later, the Rover V8 does not need high rpm to produce adequate power, but the stresses and strains of racing do mean that high rpm reliability is essential. The standard connecting rods, suitably prepared, are capable of withstanding 6,500 rpm, but they have their limitations. Next to forged pistons, steel rods are arguably the most important insurance investment in a racing engine. Combine higher cylinder pressures with higher engine rpm and the adrenalin-charged heat of competition, and steel rods are a must for peace of mind when a rod breakage could completely wreck a valuable and lovingly built engine.

It is widely known that early Chevrolet small block con rods, actually from the 1964–67 327 Cu. in version, which have a 50.8 mm (2 in) big end bearing diameter, will fit the Rover engine with slight work, ie, about 0.254 mm (0.01 in) has to be removed from the offset side, and the small end internal diameter is the wrong size for a Rover wrist pin. At 144.8 mm (5.7 in) they are slightly longer than the Rover rod, which can either help the compression ratio or mean some machining of the piston. There seems little point in going to the trouble of using them now that such a good range of purpose-made Rover rods are widely available.

The standard Rover V8 rod can be retained in a competition engine, provided the revs are limited to about 6,500 rpm. They will of course have to be checked very carefully. They need to be crack-tested, checked for straightness, and checked to see that they are dimensionally correct in big end diameter, small end diameter and length. (See *Chapter 3*.) It is unlikely that anyone would trust the standard rod with a set of forged pistons, but if they did the small end diameter would have to be increased to suit the forged pistons floating pin, and a small hole drilled in the top of the rod to lubricate the pin.

The next step up from standard rods are known as Group A rods, manufactured for the racing days of the Rover SD1 saloon and later used on clubman spec Metro 6R4 engines. Visually they are identical to the standard rod, but they are made from stronger EN24 material. They are heavier too, weighing 540–46 g (1.19–1.2 lb) as opposed to the standard rods 501–509 g (1.10–1.12 lb and not cheap to buy, assuming a set can be located. The Group A racing engines were capable of sustained operation at 7,000–7,200 rpm, and rod failure was never a problem.

The best steel rod for the Rover V8 engine is the Carillo "H" beam connecting rod. These superb rods are precision-manufactured from SAE 4340 chromium/molybdenum alloy forgings, fully machined to remove all surface imperfections, heat treated, Magnaflux tested, and hardness checked. After machining to final size they are balanced and finally shot-peened. If the engine is being built for prolonged high rpm use, continuous rapid acceleration and deceleration in competitive all-out racing conditions, this is the rod to use. Of course you may not wish to spend the kind of money these rods cost, or you may feel that with the use the engine will be put it might be possible to get by with more modest rods. Fair enough, but anything less in an all-out racing Rover V8 will be a compromise.

There are Carillo pattern rods available. The Metro 6R4 engine in Clubman guise used Rover Vitesse Group A rods, but the full International engines used these Carillo pattern rods. They are still available and fit the Rover V8, and are an excellent if still expensive substitute. Unlike standard Rover production rods, Carillo rods have fully floating little ends. Therefore the pistons either have to have gudgeon pin buttons (to run against cylinder walls) or circlip piston retaining. Childs & Albert also make a steel rod for the Rover V8, and the Cosworth rod is actually a forging made for the Chevrolet Vega Cosworth engine, but apart from being 5 mm (0.2 in) longer than a Rover V8 rod it can be used. Remember that a longer rod can be utilized to raise the compression ratio of the engine depending on the piston used, but this kind of combination needs an experienced engine builder. TVR Challenge engines use a longer Carillo rod with a larger diameter wrist pin.

Excessive side clearance on con rods can lead to excessive cylinder wall oiling, making it difficult for the pistons rings to do their job and involving increased oil pressure/oil volume to maintain sufficient oil pressure during engine operation, so this is an aspect of rod installation that is well worth paying close attention to.

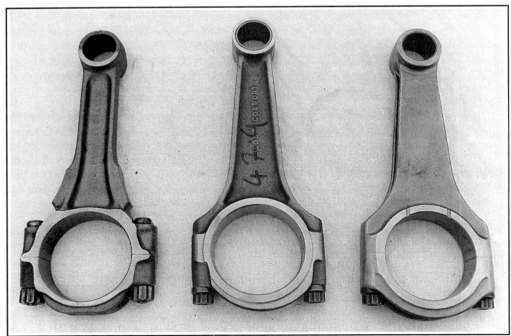

Connecting rods. Left to right: Group A, Cosworth Vega steel forging (5.08 mm longer than standard rod), Carillo pattern (Metro 6R4 International spec).

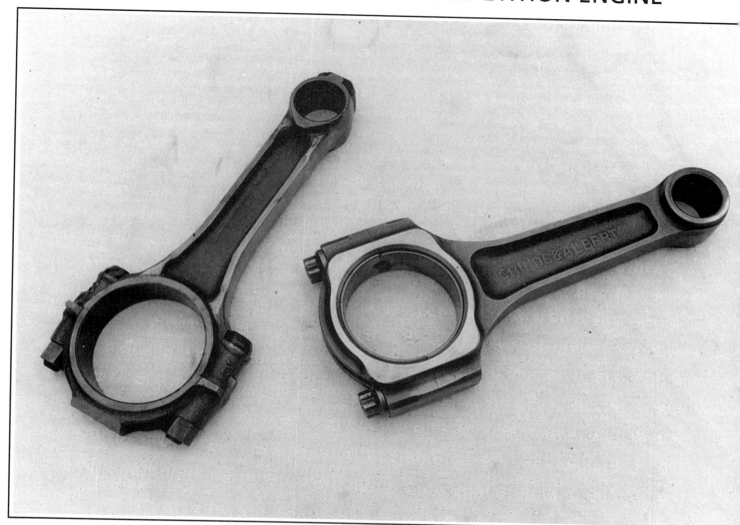

Connecting rods. Left: Chevrolet small block, Right: Childs & Albert custom-made Rover V8 steel rod.

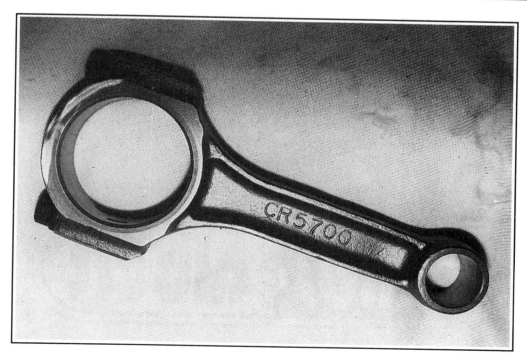

A J.E. Developments/Ian Richardson Racing steel rod, specially designed for Rover V8 applications.

95

ROVER V8

ALUMINIUM RODS

Rover V8 engine builders now have the opportunity to buy purpose-made aluminium rods for their engine made by Childs & Albert and available from Real Steel. These rods are ideal for a drag racing engine, and are worth considering for sprint and hill-climbing engines. They may also have a place in short circuit racing engines, but for longer "endurance" work a quality steel rod is the way to go. Aluminium rods certainly have no place in a road car engine.

It must be remembered, however, that aluminium rods are very sensitive to oil temperature and are better suited to use with pistons weighing 500–600 g (1.1–1.3 lb). They not only tolerate high rpm loads very well, but the light weight – 423 g (0.9 lb) as opposed to 500+ g (1.1 lb+) for a steel rod – also makes them easy on bearings and rod bolts, as well as significantly reducing the mass of the reciprocating assembly. The aluminium material does not transfer shock loads across the rod parting line as severely as a steel rod, making rod bolt failure highly unlikely. They have floating pin small ends.

They do have one well-known drawback and that is their low fatigue life, which unfortunately means that they have to be replaced at intervals. If installed and used in accordance with the manufacturer's instructions, they are almost a guarantee against rod failure.

For those engine builders who really wish to dwell in the rarefied atmosphere of exotic engine parts, it might be worth mentioning that Crower Research & Development in Jamul, California, manufacture titanium connecting rods for the Rover V8 (for which read Buick).

BEARINGS

The subject has already been touched upon when crankshafts were covered, and there is a limited amount to add. The standard Vandervell bearings are excellent and have

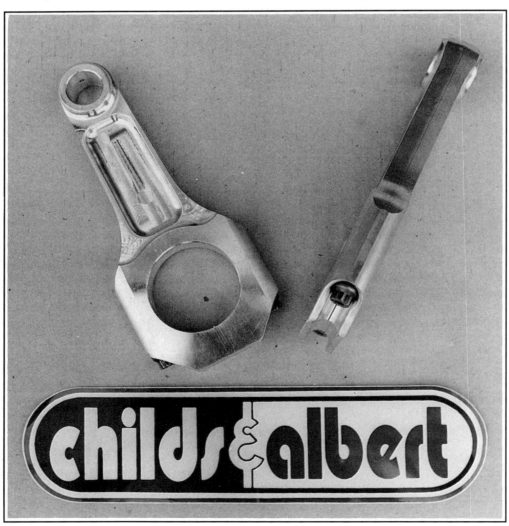

Childs & Albert aluminium connecting rods for the Rover V8, superbly crafted race engine pieces.

been used successfully in many different performance applications. When problems are encountered in this area it may be hastily concluded that an alternative should be sought, but this may not be the case. Bearing failure is very rarely due to the inadequacies of the bearing, but usually in the installation, contact surfaces or, most likely, in the lubrication system and one of these is almost always the culprit. So it pays to examine these areas before buying different bearings.

Having said that, there are alternatives available. TRW and Cleavite (77) manufacture heavy-duty bearings for the Rover V8, and both are eminently suitable for the job. They are available from the usual specialists such as John Wolfe Racing and Real Steel.

CAMSHAFTS

Increasing engine performance is all about cramming a greater amount of fuel/air mixture into the cylinders, compressing it and then igniting it. The greater the "explosion", the greater the power. Of course there are factors such as speed of burning, ensuring all the available mixture is burned completely, and exhaust gas pollution/reversion. This cylinder-filling process is not just down to the camshaft; it is achieved by the successful balance of the entire induction and exhaust system. However, the camshaft plays a vital part in opening the valves for long enough and lifting the valves high enough off their seats to fill the cylinders.

It is this lift and duration, increased over that of the standard production camshaft, that characterizes the "hot" or "wild" camshaft. Camshaft choice is even greater when building an engine for rally/race work or off-road applications, which means even more thought must be given to the matter. One very common error enthusiasts make is to choose a camshaft that is too wild. One sprint racer had built an engine for his sophisticated single-seater incorporating all the best parts and using one of the ultimate, full-race, solid lifter camshafts. As one would expect, there was an enormous amount of power available, but in a very narrow, high rpm range. It was taking what seemed like an inordinate amount of time for the engine to accelerate the car into that peak power band, and when the power came in it did so with a suddenness that the driver found very difficult to handle, resulting in a few spins. The answer was to install a milder camshaft, which marginally reduced the peak power output but flattened out the torque curve, bought in the power more gradually, and kept the usable power available over

a wider rev range. The result was a car that was much easier to drive and significantly quicker in competition. Camshaft choice is about optimizing torque and horsepower to suit a given combination.

There is a tremendous variety of camshafts currently available for the Rover V8, and there appears to be considerably more development to come in this area. Even roller cams may become a bolt-in reality in the near future. Manufacturers sometimes make specific claims for gains in horsepower if a particular camshaft is fitted, but these figures will vary according to the engine in which the camshaft is fitted, and what other modifications have been made to that engine. For instance, the use of fuel injection seems to soften the characteristics of quite radical camshafts, and properly tuned quadruple downdraughts appear to improve the driveability of some of the more radicals cams. This may have something to do with certain induction systems being less reliant on the weaker part throttle metering signals of these camshafts.

If the engine is being built to withstand higher rpm for longer periods, it follows that the camshaft selected should produce peak power at higher rpm; but beware of using a camshaft that produces that peak power in too narrow a rev range. The camshaft characteristics stated by the manufacturer are applicable to a 3.5 litre Rover V8, and it seems that larger-capacity versions of the engine will soften those characteristics somewhat, so it might pay to go for a slightly hotter camshaft than originally intended if building a 3.9 or 4.2 litre engine.

A decent competition engine can be built using hydraulic camshafts, and the rev-limiting characteristics of hydraulic followers can be beneficial on a budget engine, although it would be worthwhile to at least use hi-rev followers. Since hydraulic camshafts were discussed in *Chapter 3*, we will concentrate on mechanical camshafts in this chapter (valve gear will be discussed shortly). A Kent or Crane 238 is a good starting point on a balanced 3.5 litre engine built for 6,500 rpm operation, with the odd burst up to 7,000. A modest wet sump engine, with a pair of 50.8 mm (2 in) SU carbs, die-cast pistons, 11:1 compression ratio, and good cylinder heads should be good for 235 bhp (at the flywheel), while retaining reasonable road tractability. Sticking with the 50.8 mm (2 in) SUs but going up to 3.9 litres capable of operating at 7,000 rpm, and a Kent or Crane 256 camshaft should be good for 275–280 bhp and still be capable of being driven to and from a race meeting. Better carburation will push that bhp figure near 300!

ROVER V8

It is very difficult to generalize because there are a multitude of variables and results can vary. Mick Richards races a very successful 3.9 litre Rover V8-engined Triumph TR7 coupe. This engine uses a production-based fuel injection system and a Crane 248 camshaft which according to the specification is a high rpm camshaft with a power band between 3,500–8,000 rpm. This engine is powerful indeed, but produces its peak power of 260 bhp (at the wheels) at a very reasonable 5,600 rpm (peak torque of 270 lb/ft at 4,400 rpm), it does not need to be revved beyond 6,000 rpm, and the rev limiter is set at 6,750 rpm to allow for the cut and thrust of racing.

If a tried and tested combination is not being followed in an engine build, it is not a bad idea to try more than one camshaft in an engine, and if necessary do not be afraid to consult with the camshaft manufacturer for advice on camshaft choice. Swapping camshafts is not exactly a five-minute job, but it is relatively easy and enthusiasts should not be afraid to experiment with camshafts as a means of exploring an engine's potential.

Degreeing in a camshaft is a basic but essential procedure for installing a performance camshaft, and it will be assumed that this is within the capabilities of an enthusiast contemplating the building of his or her own engine. However, the simple procedure of phasing the camshaft, and installing it either 4° advanced for slightly increased low speed torque or retarding the camshaft 4° for slightly more high rpm horsepower, can be a useful indicator of possible alternative camshafts for the engine, depending on whether the driver finds either greater torque or bhp more useful in competition.

Before moving on there are one or two points relating to camshaft installation that should be considered. Camshaft valve lift will be important when building an engine, not least because high lifts will mean less valve to piston clearance. But it is not just opening valves higher that changes the relationship between the piston and valve, but also holding the valves open longer, so any change of camshaft needs careful clearance checks.

Valve lift is calculated by multiplying the camshaft lobe lift by the rocker arm ration (the Rover V8 has a 1.6:1 ratio) minus any clearances. However, the nature of the valve gear often means that the mathematical or theoretical lift is not achieved. To discover the actual lift, the valve gear should be assembled and the maximum lift measured with a dial gauge. If all the valves are measured, it is possible to calculate the average lift, divide this by the camshaft lobe lift and the result is the actual

rocker arm ratio. This kind of attention to detail is important in a racing engine. If an expensive pair of cylinder heads give maximum flow at a given valve lift but that lift is not being achieved at the valve, despite using the right camshaft, peak power will not be achieved. Also excessive effective rocker arm ratio may mean that the camshaft lobes designed acceleration rate is being exceeded, increasing the risk of valve gear component failure or premature valve float, which can adversely affect the relationship between piston and valve at high rpm.

ROLLER CAMSHAFTS

One of the limitations of the conventional camshaft is that the opening rate of the valve is limited by the diameter of the base of the follower/lifter. Make the opening ramp of the camshaft lobe too steep and the lifter base will have a tendency to try to dig into the ramp. Increase the diameter of the lifter and the ramp can be made steep, the opening rate of the valve quicker. There are limits to the size of lifter that will physically fit side by side in the lifter gallery of the engine.

Some early Rover V8 engines built for Formula 5000 racing used a Ford "mushroom" lifter, shaped like an inverted mushroom with a narrower body but a wide flat head to ride the camshaft lobe. The lifter bores were bushed to reduce their diameter to that of the Ford lifter, and the lifters themselves had to be installed with the engine inverted since the size of their heads made it impossible to drop them in from above as is usual.

The other solution is a so-called roller camshaft. The base of the lifter has a large diameter roller which rides the camshaft lobe, and the lobe shape itself is totally different with very steep opening and closing ramps, and a much more rounded peak. There are currently no roller camshafts available for the Rover V8, although at least one experimental engine has been built with a roller camshaft with good results, and it will not be long before roller camshafts become available.

TIMING GEAR

The fact that a camshaft can be installed either a few degrees advanced or retarded has been covered previously, but what should also be realized is that camshafts are often ground about 4° advanced to compensate for timing chain stretch, so that as the chain stretches it retards the camshaft timing. Whether or not it

Cloyes timing gear set with dual Reynolds pre-stretched chain and three keyways on the crank gear.

has been ground advanced will manifest itself when the time comes to degree in the camshaft. Since camshaft drive gear sets are not yet available for the Rover V8, anyone building a competition engine will have to use the best Duplex chain and gears. Timing chain stretch will tend to increase as rpm increases, advancing the cam at low speed (improving low speed power), and retards the cam slightly at high speed (improving top end power), but a good Duplex chain will do an excellent job.

As covered in the previous chapter, it is possible to uprate the standard timing gear considerably by taking a brand new standard chain and replacing the standard alloy/nylon cam gear. This can either be replaced relatively cheaply with a stronger all-steel version, or a more expensive steel vernier wheel which facilitates very accurate camshaft phasing. In either case a steel crank gear can also be substituted. Cloyes manufacture an excellent steel timing gear set with pre-stretched Reynolds chain (Duplex), with timing adjustments made by virtue of three alternative keyways in the crankshaft gear, ie, straight up, four advanced and four retarded. For full vernier adjustment of camshaft timing, Kent Cams have a vernier kit with rollchain, and Piper have a Duplex kit with vernier pulley, as do J.E. Engineering, all of which are well up to full race applications.

This might also be an appropriate juncture to cover a very contentious issue, that of

distributor drive gear wear. It has long been considered that the high rate of gear wear during high rpm operation is, for want of a better phrase the Achilles' heel of the engine, and there is no doubt that this phenomenon has caused many engine builders serious problems. It appears that the problem may be related to the use of a cam thrust button. The excessive wear is actually a result of the oil pump drive being taken from the end of the distributor shaft, which is itself driven by a pair of skew gears, one on the distributor shaft and one on the end of the camshaft, and it is the loading created by the oil pump at high rpm that causes the wear on the gear. Hardened gears are available – they were developed for Group A racing, made from EN36B nitrited material – but even they are no guarantee against the problem occurring. For some time J.E. Engineering have been taking an oil feed from the oil pump cover and, by drilling and tapping a small hole in the front cover, have directed a jet of pressurized oil directly on to the distributor drive gear. This simple modification is very sensible in any event, and in many cases may alleviate the gear wear problem. Racers who do not appear to experience the problem on their engines are those who do not use camshaft thrust buttons. A camshaft thrust button is used in place of the centre retaining bolt, holding the distributor drive gear in place on the end of the

99

ROVER V8

Kent Cams vernier timing gear kit allowing finite camshaft phasing (timing) adjustment.

Rover V8 post-SD1 front cover with external oil feed from oil pump cover to distributor drive gear.

Close-up of the oil feed showing the location and angle of feed to lubricate the distributor drive gear.

camshaft, and it has either a nylon or smoother steel face which acts against the inside of the front cover, restricting camshaft "walk" which can alter ignition timing. Normally the camshaft is held in place by the action of the lifters and the timing gears, but for positive location many engine builders consider a thrust button essential. With the camshaft, camshaft button and front cover installed, the end play is limited to 0.5–0.1 mm (0.002–0.005 in) by checking with a dial gauge on the rear of camshaft before the blanking plug is fitted.

Camshaft thrust button.

VALVE GEAR

High-performance Rover V8 engines have been pushed to 8,000+ rpm (and even higher), but the skills of the engine builder are sorely tested if these dizzy heights are to be achieved with any hope of reliability. In the Rover V8 field, valve lifts in the 14.7 mm (0.58 in) range are considered radical, but with some pretty long durations and fast opening rates there can still be considerable stress imparted on a Rover V8 race engine's valve train. As in all aspects of engine tuning, there is no definitive valve gear combination to apply to this engine; indeed the choice of components is bewilderingly wide. But there are some principles worth considering.

Assuming the short-block assembly has been buttoned up with properly prepared and machined block, checked and blue-printed crankshaft, steel rods, forged pistons and a camshaft has been selected, it is time to consider one of the most important aspects of high rpm operation and reliability. Valve gear failures can make an awful mess of an engine and cause damage far beyond the area of initial breakage, so it is vital that close attention is paid to component selection and installation.

Firstly, if a mechanical camshaft has been selected there has to be some means of setting the valve to rocker arm clearance, something that is not necessary with hydraulic camshaft followers/lifters. This can be accomplished by using adjustable push-rods. They

Standard production Rover rocker gear with alloy L & R rocker arms, alloy pillars and spring tensioners.

are less than half the cost of a set of roller tipped adjustable rockers, but they are awkward to use and are best utilized for adjusting preload on hydraulic followers. The Group A racing and works rallying engines used what has become known as the Group A set-up, which consisted of steel rocker pillars, larger 22 mm (0.9 in) diameter rocker shafts, and Volvo plain tipped rockers which have conventional adjustment. Some Rover V8 specialists can still supply these sets. But, while they may be a good set-up they were used with valves which had shorter stems, and rocker pillars of varying heights were utilized. Furthermore they cannot be used with Rover V8 push-rods because the Volvo rocker arms require a cup at the upper end of the push-rod (Rover push-rods have a "ball" at both ends). The Group A racing engines used special push-rods and camshaft followers compatible with this set-up, so if the Group A route is chosen make sure the correct push-rods and followers are supplied or can be sourced. This makes a good strong, well-proven assembly for use with camshafts of modest valve lift, but needs to be installed by someone with experience of valve train geometry, which will be covered shortly.

When using camshafts with valve lift over 12.7 mm (0.5 in), roller (tipped) rockers are a definite advantage. There are three main manufacturers of roller rocker for the Rover V8: Yella Terra (available from Rooster Racing),

Kenne Bell (available from Real Steel), and Crane (available from John Wolfe Racing), although Kent Performance Cams also list standard ratio roller rockers for the Rover V8. They all have conventional valve clearance adjustment and the precision roller tip, moving across the tip of the valve as it opens and closes, reduces friction loads and wear. Both the Crane and Kenne Bell type mount on the standard diameter Rover rocker shaft, although Real Steel can supply special thickwall tubing shafts that are far more expensive than standard shafts but worth every penny. The Yella Terra versions (YT 6025) come mounted on modular shafts. Roller rockers will not fit inside the standard rocker covers, and again Real Steel come to the rescue with an adapter plate which enables a range of small-block Ford rocker covers to mount on the Rover flange and provide ample clearance.

The Rover V8 rocker shafts each sit on four alloy rocker pillars. Identical steel versions were made, although they are in short supply. There have even been versions cast in titanium for Group A racing, although these are shorter to fit the variations of the Group A set-up. The final embellishment was the Group A split post, which facilitated the alignment of the rocker to the valve tip before clamping down the rocker shaft. J.E. Engineering manufacture their own billet steel versions, and these could be replicated fairly easily by any competent

A variation on the Group A theme, using Volvo rocker arms, solid spacers, 22 mm shafts and split billet steel pillars that allow fine adjustment to centralize rockers over valve tips.

machinist. The two outer rockers, at the extreme ends of the shafts sit unsupported. This has led to the manufacture of the so-called "outrigger" pillars machined from billet which support the extreme end of the shaft, overcoming the tendency of the rocker shaft to break through the centre line of the bolt.

The range of push-rods available to the Rover V8 engine builder is wide and varied. The first thing to do with any push-rod before

it is installed in the engine – and this includes a brand new one fresh out of the packaging – is to make sure it is straight. The simplest way to check is to roll it on a sheet of glass or possibly spin it in a lathe chuck. The OE push-rod is very good and provided it is absolutely straight will do sterling service in a tuned engine, but there are heavy duty alternatives such as chrome moly rods and the Crane lightweight push-rods. The OE items cannot be

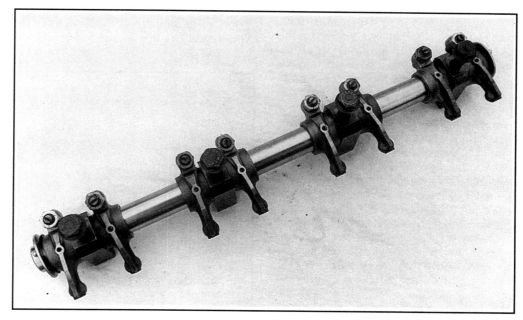

Group A racing rocker gear using Volvo L & R adjustable rocker arms, billet steel posts and 22 mm shaft.

used with adjustable rockers, so a set of push-rods compatible with the particular roller rockers being used will have to be obtained. A considerable range is available from specialists (eg, Real Steel, J.E. Engineering). For those having problems achieving satisfactory valve gear alignment, Real Steel can supply push-rods without the one ball end fitted which can be shortened to the required length (Part Nos. AZ500 and AZ1010).

Changing from an hydraulic camshaft to a mechanical one will involve changing from hydraulic followers (lifters) to solid followers. It is far simpler to use followers of the same length as the hydraulic ones they replace, although others such as the Volvo type do exist. Both Crane and Competition Cams supply solid lifters for the Rover engine, and they have been well proved in many competition applications

Having gone to the expense of using roller rockers, it is absolutely essential that the valve gear geometry is accurately set up for high rpm operation. This begins with the simple procedure of turning the engine over by hand and checking each and every push-rod and rocker to see that there is no interference between the push-rods and cylinder head castings, that the undersides of the rockers do not touch the valve springs or retainers, and watching the movement of the roller over the valve stem tip to see that it remains on the tip as the lift cycle occurs. A small hand grinder should see that all components have adequate clearance. Within reason no absolutely straight push-rod will fail unless it is coming into contact with the cylinder head casting or there is something wrong with the valve train, be that incorrect geometry or something obvious like the valve guide coming into contact with the valve guide at full lift.

So how can valve gear geometry be checked, and how can it be influenced if it is incorrect? Valve gear loads at low rpm are a product largely of the valve spring, and that load increases as the valve opens, peaks at the same time as maximum lift and then falls off as the valve closes. At racing speeds the load pattern differs considerably. The load peaks as the valve commences opening, decreasing rapidly as peak valve lift is reached. The valve gear has far greater inertia, loads falling off rapidly as the follower (or lifter) rides over the nose of the camshaft lobe, and under conditions of valve float the valve gear load is negligible.

So the valve gear has to be capable of withstanding wildly varying stress conditions and loads. Valve gear set up to minimize stresses at racing speeds will usually impart extra stresses on the valve gear at lower rpm. For high rpm the push-rod needs to be at 90° to the rocker arm, and the rocker arm angle should be 90° to the valve stem for between 30 and 50 per cent of the valve lift. The rocker

Alloy roller tipped rockers, with solid spacers and "outrigger" end rocker posts to support the very end of the rocker shaft.

Kenne Bell roller tipped rockers for the Rover V8, available from Real Steel.

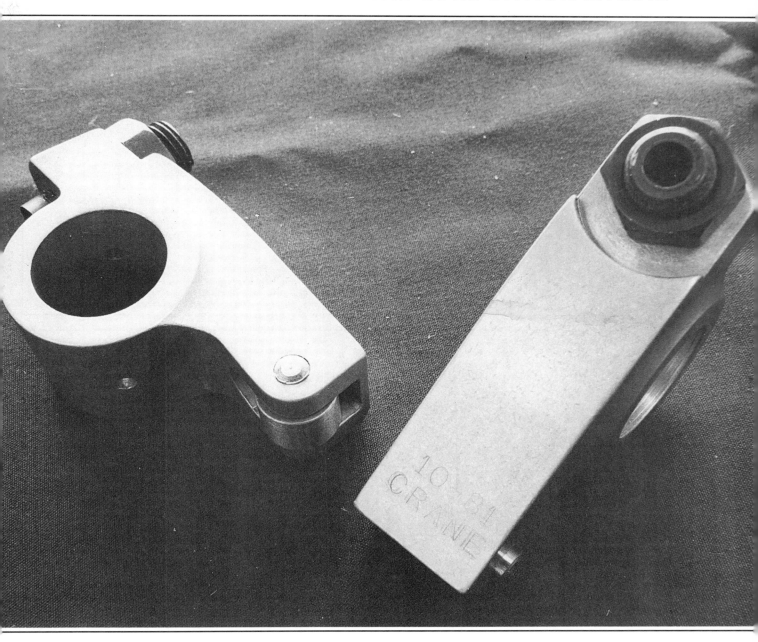

Crane gold anodized roller tipped rocker arms.

arm plane is taken as a line drawn through the centre point of the rocker shaft and the centre point of the roller tip of the rocker. So when the valve is fully closed, the angle between the rocker arm and the valve should be less than 90°, when the valve is at 50 per cent of its maximum lift it should be about 90°, and at full lift more than 90°. In addition, close attention needs to be paid to the relationship between the roller tip of the rocker and the top of the valve stem. At zero lift, the centre line of the roller needs to be just on the rocker shaft side of the valve stem, then as lift commences the roller tip should move away from the rocker shaft, reaching its farthest point at approximately 50 per cent lift. Then as lift

continues, the roller should begin to return towards the rocker shaft side. Such a motion minimizes valve stem loads and reduces wear on the valve stem and valve guide. Looking end on to the rocker, make sure the roller is centred over the valve stem. To achieve the optimum set-up you will have to vary the push-rod length (assuming there is insufficient adjustment), the height of the rocker shaft pillars (by shimming or machining), and possibly even the length of the valve stem. An adjustable push-rod for workbench testing can be made by cutting off the tip of an old push-rod and inserting a bolt with a nut on it. Cut the head off the bolt and grind the end into a ball shape. Rotating the nut will move the

head of the bolt upwards or downwards, altering the length of this crude push-rod. Once the correct length has been arrived at, a full set of push-rods can be made up.

It might be appropriate at this point briefly to discuss valve train weight, since there are some conflicting schools of thought. Obviously the valve train must be as light as possible without compromising reliability, because light weight equates to less stress and potentially higher engine rpm, but there are critical components to which special consideration should be given. Super lightweight carbon fibre push-rods, for instance, will have little or no effect on the rpm potential of the engine (and have a tendency to disintegrate if

the engine is accidentally buzzed to high rpm), nor will lightweight rocker arms or camshaft followers, but pay close attention to the weight of the valve and the spring retainer. That is one good reason why valves with oversized stems should never be considered for a performance engine.

CYLINDER HEADS

Assembling a good short block is essential to building a strong reliable competition engine, but the key to producing good power is the dynamic flow of intake and exhaust gases through the engine. Efficient cylinder heads

Top: Left to right: standard alloy rocker post, Group A steel post, early Group A titanium (alloy lookalike), J.E. Engineering steel billet post, and final version of Group A post in steel billet.

Above: Left to right: standard Rover P6B valve spring, standard EFi, J.E. Engineering double, and two different types of Group A racing valve springs.

Left to right: big valve retainer with three-groove collet (for 8 mm valve stem), Crane competition retainer, standard Rover EFi engine, standard SD1 and Rover P6B retainer (all for 8.73 mm valve stems).

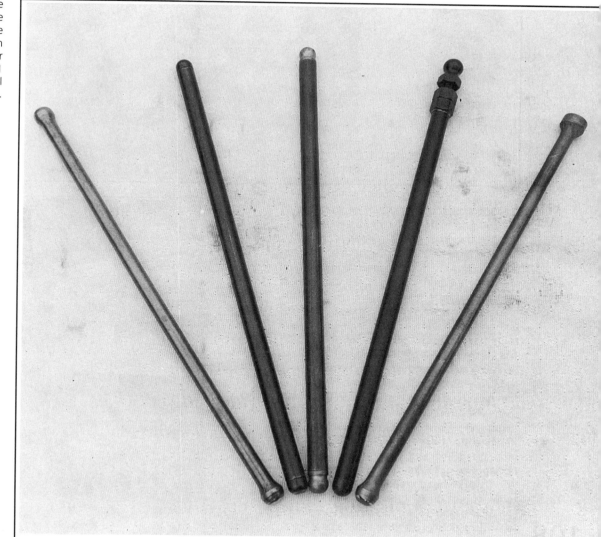

Push-rods. Right to left: standard Rover, Crane lightweight, J.E. Engineering for use with roller rockers, adjustable, Group A as used on twin plenum racing engines.

More push-rods. Left to right: standard pattern heavy-duty, adjustable chrome moly (semi-finished), adjustable chrome moly push-rod (finished), moly push-rod 209.55 mm with one ball not fitted (for custom length rod), as previous, but with oil holes, standard length chrome moly (for use with roller rockers) and TRW push-rod for use with Crane roller rockers.

Left to right: standard hydraulic lifter, solid Opel type, Crane hi-rev lifter, Group A Volvo lifter.

Fully ported and polished inlet ports showing the limits of the production castings.

are essential, and nowhere in engine building will you find more conflicting theories than in the preparation of cylinder heads.

The heads alone do not make an efficient dynamic flow path through an engine; there are other elements such as the carburettor venturi, the inlet manifold and runners, the intake ports, exhaust ports, exhaust manifolds and exhaust system, as well as the entire valve train assembly down to the camshaft itself. The whole process of engine breathing has to be balanced by matching the various elements as closely as possible, and careful consideration must be given to how changes to one element will affect the others. Alterations which might give a drastic increase in intake gas flow have to be matched by a corresponding increase in exhaust flow efficiency, if any horsepower gains are to be realised.

Cylinder head preparation, particularly in terms of port grinding and polishing, is a very specialized and skilled operation, requiring a lot of practical experience. The amateur can purchase the necessary equipment to do the grinding and polishing, even invest in or build his own flow bench, and do dyno testing if he is serious about his engine building, but he will ruin a few head castings and waste countless hours discovering for himself what many specialists have researched themselves years ago.

Selecting a specialist who really understands the theory of cylinder head airflow and who has really spent time on research and development with the Rover V8 heads is not so easy. Those to be recommended are Automotive Performance Engineering, J.E. Engineering Ltd, Rovercraft, Janspeed, and Real Steel. By all means discuss your requirements and ideas with whoever is preparing a pair of heads for you, and of course pay close attention to your overall budget, but unless you find this aspect of engine tuning particularly fascinating it is best left to experts.

The Rover V8 head castings as currently produced are little changed since the introduction of the Rover 3500 (SD1) in mid-1976, and they were never designed for use on a competition engine. However, they can be, and have been on numerous occasions, modified for use on some very powerful Rover V8 engines. One telling feature of the Rover heads is their inability to provide adequate higher rpm breathing to larger capacity versions (ie, 4.2 and 4.5 litre) of the engine, which are always characterized by fabulous torque outputs but disappointing peak bhp. Having said that, cylinder head work is critical to increased performance on this engine and warrants very close attention.

Cylinder head modifications for competition generally involve enlarging and polishing the inlet and exhaust ports to increase the sectional area to the maximum without compromising material thickness in any critical areas. The actual shaping of the ports, within the limitations imposed by the castings, is open to interpretation by the individual company or individual who grinds and polishes the ports, but there is little scope for excessive creativity. For example some theorists insist that the floor of the inlet port should not be lowered too much, but should give the incoming gases a smooth, large radius turn before it meets the head of the inlet valve. Others grind away as much as possible in this area, and claim worthwhile benefits from doing so.

The combustion chamber is also fully polished to remove any areas that may cause hot spots to develop (and so detonation) and also aid the smooth flow of inlet and exhaust gases within the combustion chamber. At the same time, the combustion chamber volumes should be equalized. The valve guides are usually bulleted, ie, the portion of the valve guide that

projects into the port is tapered to reduce its restriction on gasflow within the port. Some engine builders actually machine away the valve guide so that it does not project into the port at all, and remove the material inside the port which supports the guide at this end. Some consider that this reduces the support afforded to the valve by the guide and reduces the guides oil control capability, but bearing in mind the low mileage nature of a competition engine this does not seem to pose a problem in practice.

Also controversial in its treatment is the valve seat area, which has been the subject of some significant research in the search for performance. All gases entering and exiting the all-important combustion chamber must pass through this critical area, and unfortunately standard valve seats are designed for durability and not optimum gas flow. Modified three-angle valve seat grinds generally begin with a 60° angle for the first cut, marking the transition from port to the valve bowl. The next 45° cut is the actual valve seat and also involves reducing the actual value seat width – in the case of SD1 heads that is 62 thou – down to 50 thou on the inlet. The exhaust is usually slightly wider to aid valve cooling. The final "top cut" marks the wider radius of the valve bowl into the combustion chamber, and varies depending on the depth of the valve guide, etc. These three angles can be further refined by leaving the actual valve seat grind at 45° to match the angle of the seat on the valve itself and then skilfully smoothing the top and bottom cuts, but leaving the actual seat untouched, using a high speed grinder fitted with an abrasive roll. This leaves virtually no sharp edges to disrupt airflow.

Production cylinder heads use relatively small diameter valves because it gives good low and mid-range torque, which is where a road engine most needs it. This is because small ports and smaller valves (relative to engine capacity) give good gas velocity at these rpm. Gas velocity in the ports is an important factor to consider. If the ports and valves are too large for the engine capacity, gas velocity in the ports will be lost, losing mid-range engine response without any appreciable gains in peak power. For this reason the extent to which cylinder heads should be modified and the size of valves chosen has to be balanced against the operating rpm of the engine and its cubic capacity. Many successful competition engines have been built without increasing the valve size at all, although there seem to be definite advantages once the capacity goes beyond 4.0 litres.

Normal "big valve" heads for the Rover V8 are 41.4 mm (1.63 in) inlet and 35.5 mm

(1.4 in) exhaust. These are the largest valves that can be installed without requiring major machine work, but larger valves of 43 mm (1.69 in) inlet and 37 mm (1.45 in) exhaust valves have been fitted by J.E. Engineering of Coventry. As discussed earlier in this chapter, the weight of the valve gear is critical for high rpm operation, and the obvious conclusion to reach is that larger valves means greater valve weight. The standard inlet valve weighs 84.4 g (3 oz) and the standard exhaust valve weighs 80.1 g (2.8 oz). The usual big valve inlet will weigh 96.4 g (3.4 oz) and an exhaust 86.6 g (3.1 oz), but J.E. Engineering "super big" inlets weigh only 89.5 g (3.2 oz) for the inlet and 80.6 g (2.9 oz) for the exhaust. This is not, as it may seem, a blatant plug for the J.E. Engineering product, but an illustration that the obvious may not always be correct. The light weight for the much bigger valve was accomplished by using a thinner valve stem, and was done specifically to offset the weight disadvantage of a much larger valve. The standard valves have a stem 8.7 mm (0.34 in) while the J.E. Engineering super big valves have a stem diameter of 7.9 mm (0.31 in), a size shared incidentally with the equally light Group A racing engine valves (which were slightly shorter), so the integrity of the valve is not threatened.

Valve size is a very controversial area of Rover V8 tuning and the issue is further complicated by the different bore sizes of the 3.5 and 3.9 litre versions of the engine. There is no doubt that the larger 3.9 litre bore size of 94 mm (3.7 in) has a beneficial effect on the breathing ability of the engine when standard size valves are retained, because the bigger bore "un-shrouds" the valve in the area where the valve and cylinder wall are closest. Increasing the bore size moves the bore wall further away from the valve, improving airflow. Obviously any work done on the cylinder head will further enhance this. However, if you increase the valve size, the edge of the valve nearest to the cylinder wall will again become shrouded and the airflow disrupted. Likewise, the milling of the Rover V8 cylinder heads, either to clean up the deck mating surface or to raise the compression ratio, will move the valves closer to the edge of the cylinder bore with similar consequences.

A good port shape should work well with a smaller valve, and many Rover V8 tuning specialists produce heads that work well with standard or near-standard sized valves, and a great deal depends on the specific engine being built. Big valves are not an automatic ticket to greater bhp and can in certain cases have an adverse effect. Poorly shaped ports often need big valves to compensate, but that's not to say that big valves don't work on the Rover V8 because they most certainly have their place, especially when building an engine over 4 litres.

Unfortunately, the science of port contours, port wall texture, port cross-sectional area, valve size and airflow could quite easily fill this book and more besides. There are no hard and fast rules nor straight answers to the question of what cylinder head specification would be ideal for a particular engine, only opinions, and they are many and varied.

At the time of writing, an additional

Two views of the new Rover V8 cylinder head castings from Torque Developments. This is not a radical departure from the standard pattern, but promises a significant step forward in flow capability. Note the exhaust ports with their curved roof.

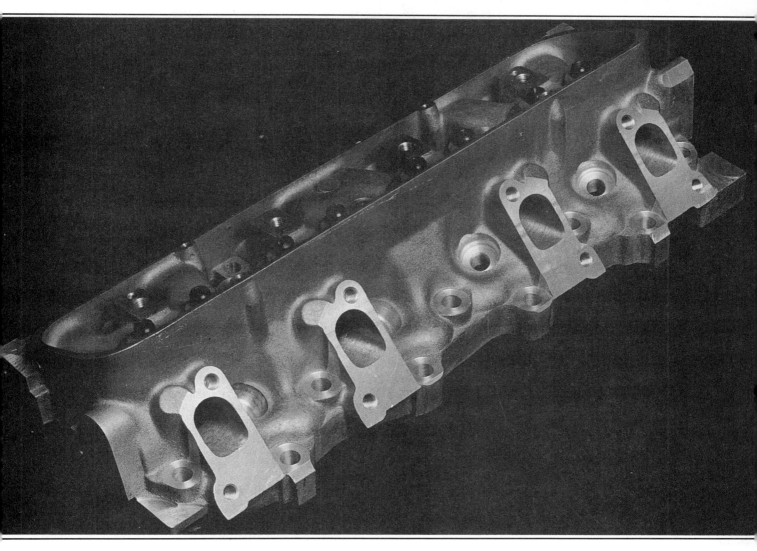

option became available to builders of Rover V8 engines, namely "new" head castings from Torque Developments of Barking. Since no independent data on these heads were available no objective opinion can be given, so the manufacturer's description and claims are all that are available. The heads are closely derived from the standard Rover castings but with special emphasis on improving the airflow coefficient well beyond the limitations imposed by them. It is claimed that out of the box these heads will out-flow and out perform fully modified standard castings. The intake throat area has been completely redesigned to increase the airflow, while retaining standard port runner volume for maximum gas velocity, although the volume can be easily increased. The heads will accept valves from 40.6 mm (1.6 in) to 45.7 mm (1.80 in) diameter inlet valves. A net increase in airflow of 33 per cent is claimed, with further increases easily attainable.

Probably the most interesting area of these heads is the redesigned exhaust port which incorporates a raised roof section which "dramatically increases airflow, without a reduction in gas velocity". Exhaust flow is increased by 60 per cent using a 35.6 mm (1.4 in) exhaust valve with further increases in flow easily achievable.

On paper these Torque Developments' heads seem the answer to many of the problems encountered when trying to build a performance Rover V8 engine using modified standard heads. Considering the cost of a pair of these heads, fully finished, and the present lack of corroborated data on their performance it might be more prudent to buy a pair of bare castings and take them along to a cylinder head preparation company (perhaps one you have worked with before) for evaluation, and if everything checks out have that company fully prepare them for use. They certainly seem to have considerable potential.

Virtually anything is possible with skill, time and the ability to weld aluminium! Willie Brown's supercharged Rover V8 has drastically altered cylinder heads with raised angle inlet ports, requiring the raising of the cover flange, a high-rise inlet manifold, and very rigid rocker gear.

Before moving on it might be interesting to mention another possible option for those who might have already dismissed the Rover cylinder heads as unsuitable for their particular project. Bruce Crower of Jamul, California, investigated the feasibility of building an Indy car using the Buick/Rover aluminium V8, using initially the '68 Buick 300 aluminium cylinder heads. Interestingly he considers that the Buick V6 Indy heads, which in Stage II form were produced in aluminium, could be cut and welded to produce a cylinder head for the Rover V8. These Stage II heads were especially redesigned from the original cast iron production version by Buick's Special Products Engineering Division, and had 51 mm (2.02 in) titanium inlet valves and Inconel 40.6 mm (1.6 in) exhaust valves. However, these turbo application heads are both rare and expensive, so whether anyone would ever have the inclination to start cutting and shutting them to fit a Rover V8 remains to be seen. Bruce Crower certainly never got as far as trying it because his Indy project faded due to the cost of operating a Lola or March chassis.

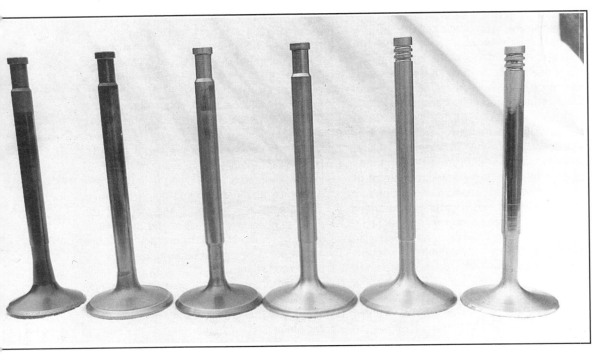

Inlet valves. Left to right: Rover pre-SD1, Rover SD1, Vitesse/EFi, J.E. Engineering "big" valve, J.E. Engineering "ultra big" (8 mm stem), and Group A with short 8 mm stem.

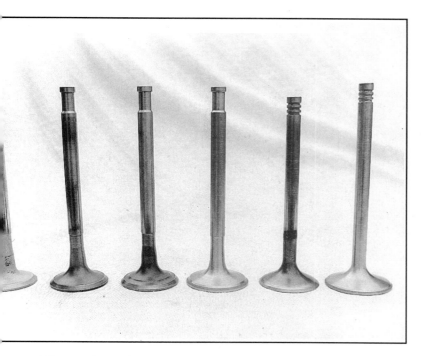

Exhaust Valves. Left to right: Rover pre-SD1, Rover SD1, Current 3.9EFi, J.E. Engineering "big" valve, Group A competition (8 mm stem), and J.E. Engineering "ultra big" valve (8 mm stem).

CYLINDER HEAD GASKETS

Since Land-Rover introduced the 3.9 litre version of the Rover V8, engine builders do at last have an easily accessible source of head gaskets for both the 88.9 mm (3.5 in) cylinder (3.5 litre) and 94.04 mm (3.7 in) cylinder (3.9 litre) bores. Fortunately the factory "tin" gaskets are very good, will stand up to most high performance applications and have a volume of 2.73 cc. The Felpro Permatorque gasket available for the 3.5 litre engine 88.9 mm (3.5) in bore size can be

Stainless steel (black coated) 35.6 mm exhaust valve (left) and 41.4 mm inlet valve (right) from Real Steel.

used on non-factory 3.9 litre engine conversions using a 93.5 mm (3.6 in) bore size. These gaskets have a volume of 6.82 cc.

J.E. Developments have composite head gaskets with 95 mm (3.7 in) bore for use with 94.04 mm (3.7 in) cylinder bores, and also a gasket with a 97 mm (3.8 in) bore for bore sizes in the region of 96 mm (3.7) which will be of interest to engine builders wanting to stretch the bore size to the upper limit. These have a volume of 8.5 cc. The Buick 300 head gasket can theoretically be used with 96 mm (3.7 in) bores, but it does not have enough holes for the cylinder head bolts, nor does it seal against the inlet manifold gasket. (For more information on increasing the capacity see *Chapter 5*.)

For anyone having cylinder head sealing problems, perhaps because of exceptionally high compression ratios or forced induction, it might be worth mentioning that TVR Power in Coventry, who build all the TVR Tuscan Challenge engines, machine the cylinder heads to accept soft copper wire "O" rings, a drastic but very effective method of containing high cylinder pressures.

INDUCTION SYSTEMS

Anyone building a Rover V8 for competition has a reasonable range of inlet manifolds/induction systems to choose from, assuming competition regulations allow, but those which are more widely available are probably more practical. However, for those wishing to use one of the Holley four-barrel carburettors on a competition engine may find their choice rather restrictive.

THE HOLLEY CARBURETTOR AND MANIFOLDS

In the previous chapter we looked at the popular Holley 4160 390 cfm four-barrel carburettor with vacuum secondaries. For a road-driven competition vehicle this carb can have its uses, but there are better alternatives if the vehicle is used exclusively for motor sport. For enthusiasts contemplating the building of an engine on a restricted budget, the Holley four-barrel carb is difficult to beat in terms of value for money. It is not expensive and can be set up for a particular engine easily, but it does have its limitations.

Those limitations are to a great extent caused by the available inlet manifolds, but to understand why it might be worth considering the special requirements of the inlet manifold, which is required to feed the fuel/air mixture

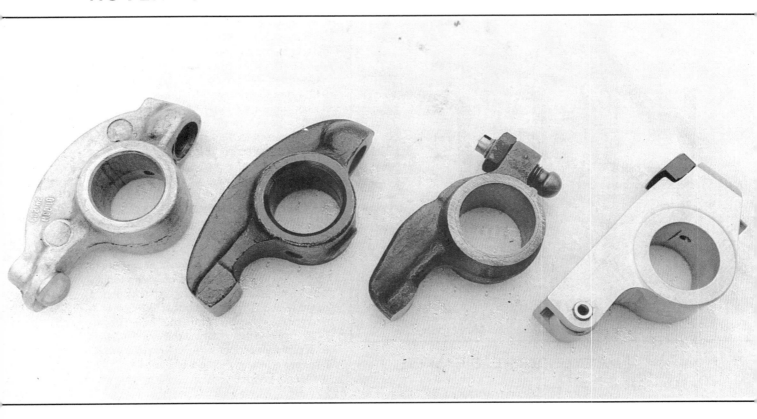

to the eight cylinders of the Rover V8. For instance, the layout of a V8 engine makes it impossible for a single plane design to have equal length runners. Those leading to the four corner cylinders are longer than those leading to the centre cylinders. However, despite such drawbacks this design does mean that in open throttle/high rpm conditions all the cylinders are able to draw fuel/air from all four carburettor venturi, the mixture being drawn into the plenum, and then diverted towards each runner when called upon to do so by the opening of the inlet valve. However, the mixture entering the plenum is constantly

being forced to change direction as the mixture is diverted into the runners and pressure pulses feed back via the runners straight into the plenum. These disturbances can cause a great deal of turbulence which in turn causes fuel metering problems for the carburettor.

Design limitations aside, the best performance manifold currently available on which to mount the Holley carburettor is the Huffaker, which is a single plane design, having a large central plenum immediately beneath the carburettor with reasonably straight, manifold runners leading from the plenum to the entrance of the inlet port in the

Left to right: upper view of the same rockers. Standard alloy, steel replica, Group A/Volvo and alloy roller rocker.

Left to right: standard production alloy rocker arm with steel inserts for push-rod and valve contact. The GKN replacement steel rocker arm needs the oil hole welding up before installation, as this hole will squirt oil directly at the valve guide. Group A/Volvo rocker arm needs larger diameter rocker shaft, and finally an alloy J.E. Engineering/Titan Motorsport roller tipped arm (fits standard size shaft).

cylinder head. It has no provision for water heating so is not suitable for street use, and it is considerably taller than the more popular Offenhauser 360° dual plane manifold.

There are other manifolds that can be used in conjunction with the Holley. We have already discussed the use of a modified standard Rover manifold, the Offenhauser 360° and the Offenhauser/JWR Dual Port Design, but none offers any advantage over the Huffaker design for all-out competition applications, and the Offenhauser 360° would best be considered if the Huffaker creates insurmountable under-bonnet clearance problems.

There are four distinct versions of the Holley four-barrel carburettor currently used on the Rover V8, and they are rated according to the flow capacity in cubic feet per minute. Thus we have the Holley 390 cfm, the 390 cfm "double pumper", the 465 cfm and the 600 cfm. The larger the venturi (the cfm number), the greater the peak horsepower (all else being equal), but at the expense of mid-range engine response. Small venturi can react more quickly under acceleration to the engines fuelling needs and provide more efficient mid-range metering.

There are two particular features of the Holley carb that should be explained at this stage. The Holley four-barrel describes the four distinct venturi in the carb body which have their own individual throttle butterflies. If the carb is described as having vacuum secondaries, the mechanical accelerator linkage only operates two of those four venturi butterflies. The vehicle is for most of the time driven on the two primary barrels or venturi of the four, with all the resultant advantages of strong metering signals at low rpm and high flow velocity through the venturi for good response and economy. When additional acceleration is required and the flow range of the two barrels becomes insufficient to provide the engine with the fuel air volume, it needs the low inlet manifold vacuum present in such circumstances to open the butterflies in the second two carb venturi, doubling the carb's capacity to flow fuel and air. In performance/competition versions of the Holley carb, the primary and secondary barrels are mechanically linked and operate in unison, but with this system comes a trade-off in street driveability.

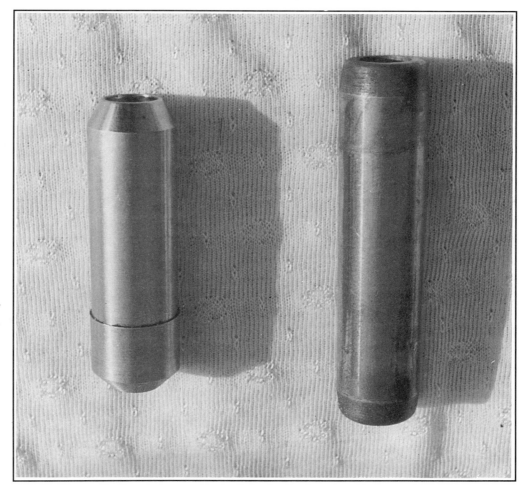

Standard valve guide on the right and J.E. Engineering bronze guide on the left. Note how the bronze guide has a small stop to aid correct height installation and also prevent the guide dropping into the port should it come loose in the cylinder head. If a guide does drop, it invariably jams the valve open with dire consequences!

McCord Permatorque cylinder head gasket.

There is also the "double pumper' feature which again needs some explanation. On a normal street-applicable Holley four-barrel with vacuum secondaries, the accelerator pumps work only on the primary side of the carb. When the primary and secondary sides of the carb are mechanically linked, separate accelerator pumps are provided for the secondary side of the carb too, giving improved response when the throttle is opened quickly from low rpm when the metering signals are weak. The extra fuel enrichment of the double pumper is ideal for lighter cars using wilder camshafts, higher final drive ratios and higher rpm engine use.

The Holley 4160 390 cfm (as distinct from the double pumper) is the popular street carburettor for the Rover V8. It has vacuum actuated secondaries and electric choke. This carb is used extensively on the Rover V8 engine and has been pretty well sorted now for using on the equally popular Offenhauser dual plane manifold. This Holley used to be criticized for having a serious mid-range flat spot, but this was mainly caused by a delay in the vacuum secondaries opening as the flow limit of the primaries was approached.

The Holley 390 cfm double pumper is a competition version of the above, having mechanically operated secondaries, double accelerator pumps and no choke. It can be used on a road-driven car, but it really is an excellent competition car carburettor and very good value for money.

The Holley 465 cfm has vacuum secondaries and divorced choke. Its great flow capacity means that it should produce greater peak power, but will have reduced mid-range response. It is perhaps a better choice for engines over 4.2 litres for a more balanced response.

The Holley 600 cfm is available with mechanical or vacuum secondaries, single or dual accelerator pumps. Since this carburettor would only be used in competition it is the mechanical secondaries and dual accelerator pump version that would be applicable, and should make an excellent choice for either high rpm smaller capacity engines or the bigger 4.2 or 4.5 litre versions of the Rover V8.

WEBER/DELLORTO CARBURETTORS

The Huffaker inlet manifold. This single plane, raised runner design is possibly the best competition piece for four-barrel carburettors, but can cause under-bonnet clearance problems. It has no facility for water-heating.

A quadruple set of Weber or Dellorto carburettors immediately stamps the symbol of "serious performance" on a Rover V8 engine. Their performance potential can be in no doubt and they have found success in many applications. They can and have been used on many road cars, but their cost and potential justifies their examination in this chapter.

The Weber version is available in both downdraught and sidedraught configuration. The popular 48IDA comes with a bore diameter and throttle plate size of 48 mm (1.9 in), while the IDA means high performance downdraught. Sidedraught carbs all carry DCOE suffixes with bores from 38–55 mm (1.5–2.1 in). Webers have the ability to change the choke or venturi, varying the cfm flow rate of the carb to suit differing applications. Selecting the cfm flow rate to the engine size is essential for good driveability and performance. Unusual rules apply, ie, smaller flow rates give better mid-range response, higher flow rates greater power at peak rpm.

The Weber has three basic circuits. The idle circuit is controlled by the idle jet and jet carrier, which controls the fuelling from idle all the way up to about 3,000 rpm, with fine tuning via the idle mixture screw. The main circuit consists of the main jet, the emulsion tube and the air corrector, and tuning should under most circumstances be limited to the main jet itself, which will affect the whole rpm range. Finer adjustments, especially at the top of the rpm range, are done with the air corrector. The accelerator pump circuit, like any carburettor, eliminates "bog" under sudden acceleration. There are two main elements, the pump jet and the pump exhaust valve, which is actually a bypass valve and regulates the fuel available for the pump shot: the smaller the valve orifice the more fuel. The duration of the shot is varied by the size of the pump jet.

Performance is one the more obvious benefits of using the quadruple downdraught or sidedraught induction system, but another is the exceptionally smooth idle and low rpm driveability, even when using fairly radical camshafts, not unlike fuel injection. In fact, on road-driven cars it is quite reasonable to use more radical "fast road" camshafts without the characteristic poor driveability under normal road conditions. The performance and driveability are a product of the independent runner manifolds, feeding each cylinder equally from an independent carburettor barrel. There is no interconnection of cylinders via a plenum chamber.

This independent runner set-up makes accurate synchronization of all eight carburettor barrels to all eight cylinders an absolutely vital part of proper installation and tuning. All four carbs have to be connected by a solid, well-designed and mounted throttle linkage, but once they are set they are good for many thousands of hard, reliable motoring miles.

The manifolds for mounting these carburettors start with a single sidedraught or

117

ROVER V8

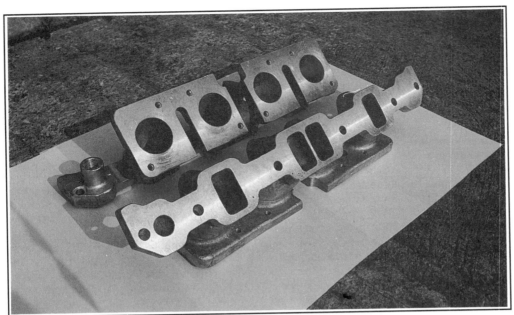

Cast alloy manifolds (one pair) for mounting quadruple downdraught Weber or Dellorto carburettors.

Works style "swan neck" inlet manifold mounting quadruple sidedraught Webers. Fabricated in steel, the welds can be susceptible to engine vibration....

... and thus enter the brand new cast alloy version from J.E. Developments.

Quadruple downdraught Dellorto carburettors mounted on a Rover V8 in a Cobra replica kitcar.

downdraught on a modified standard Rover twin SU carb manifold, which requires the pent roof mounting to be machined off, and either a flange for a single downdraught or a small cast alloy adaptor for the sidedraught. A pair of sidedraughts can be mounted on any Holley four-barrel flange using a cast alloy adaptor, as used by the early works Triumph TR7 V8 rally cars, but this set-up was not very successful due to distribution problems and excessive fuel consumption. The most well-known use of Weber sidedraughts is quadruple with either steel "swan neck" or steel cross-over manifolds, although the manifold runner length on the less common cross-over type is a little too long. The swan neck manifolds are now available in cast alloy from J.E. Developments. The most common mounting is quadruple downdraught on cast alloy manifolds, but the principle drawback here is under-bonnet clearance, which either means a decent set of air filters protruding through the bonnet (covered by a bonnet bulge), or no filters and very short ram pipes.

There is no doubt that a set of Weber or Dellorto carburettors is probably the ultimate induction set-up for normally aspirated Rover V8 engines, and they are capable of providing the fuelling requirements of virtually any state of tune. Properly installed they will also prove reliable and simple to maintain, but of course they are not cheap.

EXHAUST SYSTEMS

The previous chapter covered the principles of performance exhaust systems in some detail

and some manifolds available for the Rover V8.

The majority of systems depend more on the limitations imposed by the vehicle than on arriving at an optimum system for the particular engine and its requirements. Not so much a question of what system to design as what system will fit? However, there are one or two important principles to bear in mind before taking out the tube stock, putting it in the bender and getting down to welding. Longer primaries will usually produce more high rpm power, while shorter primaries will help the mid-range. Large-diameter primaries will give greater peak power, while smaller-diameter primaries will help the mid-range. So a large-diameter, long length primary is good for high rpm, peak horsepower. For the Rover V8, primaries are usually 41.3 mm (1.6 in) or 44.5 mm (1.75 in) diameter for larger capacity performance engines.

It is also important to try to keep the primary pipes all the same length as far as possible, and this must be combined with equal flow through each primary pipe: that is, the tubes must have bends of equal radius, no sharp bends in any one pipe, and pipes with more bends will flow less efficiently than the ones with few. Also, try to keep the header pipe straight immediately after the cylinder head, so that as the exhaust gas pulse leaves the exhaust port and enters the primary header tube it does not encounter any sharp bends. Exhaust gas velocity at this point is relatively high, and the tendency with most tubular exhaust manifolds is to turn sharply downwards immediately in order to clear inner wheel arches or chassis members. One important but

This Rover EFi installation in a GT40 replica illustrates a good competition cross-over exhaust system. The system should link alternate cylinders into a 2 X 4 pipe connector.

Fuel pump blanking plate from Real Steel, for use when the standard mechanical pump is being removed from the engine and replaced by purely electrical pump(s).

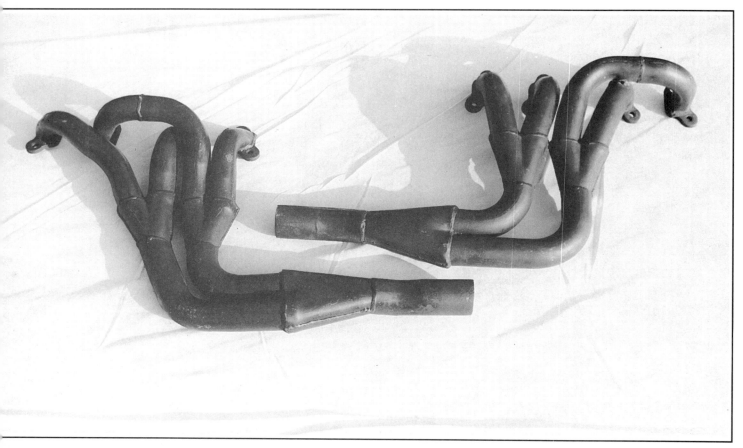

Left A hillclimbing and sprint single-seater with equal length 4 into 1 exhaust system. Finding chassis clearance for this kind of installation is not a problem.

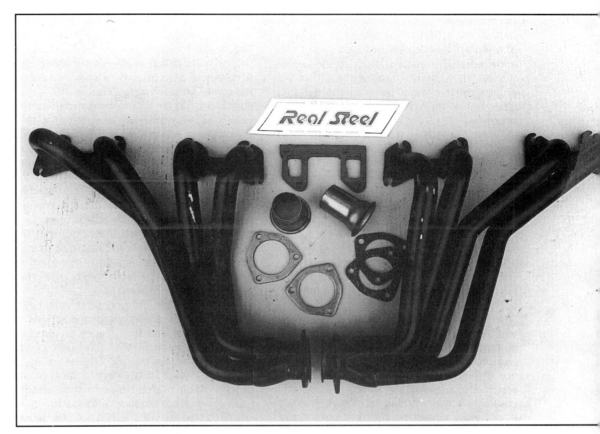

Hedman 4 into 1 tubular exhaust manifolds (or headers) in 1½ in. tubes, good for big capacity engines as well as 3.5 litre engines, but will not fit all vehicle installations.

This is a big bore tubular stainless steel header as used on racing Morgan Plus 8's.

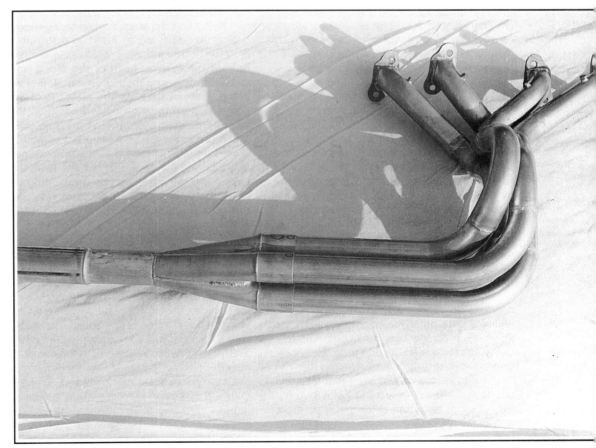

Left Big bore Range Rover tubular headers of 4-2-1 design as used on the Paris-Dakar vehicles.

difficult feature to incorporate into a system is to have the collectors (or tailpipe in the event of using a full-length exhaust system) exit into a low pressure area beneath or to the rear of the vehicle. This will reduce the effort the engine must expend pushing the exhaust gases out of the system and into the atmosphere.

Noise abatement regulations in most areas mean that the majority of competition vehicles now have to carry some form of silencer as part of the exhaust system, and low-restriction silencer boxes are available from specialists.

OIL SYSTEMS

The standard Rover V8 wet sump oil system has a gear pump which feeds oil at a pressure of 35 psi at a nominal 2,400 rpm. The later SD1 engines had an improved skew gear drive to the oil pump and more rigidly supported pump shaft to avoid binding. The sump was also provided with a simple baffle in anticipation of higher cornering forces. Obviously it is essential to overhaul the standard pump and ensure that it is working to maximum efficiency before considering further uprating of the system.

The Rover V8 engine does not like modern lightweight oils such as 5W–50 because it cannot be pumped in volume in the same way as heavier oils, although oil pressure will be maintained. The system is a high-volume system not high-pressure, and since oil is the lifeblood of an engine both for lubrication and cooling it must be treated with respect. For competition use the engine needs SAE 30 or 40 oil, and it helps to increase the capacity of the sump by adding sections to extend the sump out to the sides and to the rear, with some simple internal baffling to control the oil's movement within the sump during vehicle motion.

Controlling the oil in a wet sump system is never easy in a competition car, and the ultimate wet sump was developed for Group A racing which has regulations excluding dry sump systems. Some of these sumps still exist, but the complex system of baffles and trapdoors would be very difficult and expensive to replicate. The other major problem with the Rover V8 in competition conditions is its tendency to retain a lot of oil inside the rocker covers and lifter gallery, and anything that can be done to recover the oil from that area and return it to the sump is a big help. Two 6.4 mm (0.25 in) holes can be drilled in the front wall of the lifter gallery where oil tends to collect, allowing oil to drain into the front cover,

not only giving oil an alternative route to the sump but also aiding timing gear lubrication. The works Triumph TR7 V8 rally cars had a pair of holes drilled in the rear of the gallery from where pipes routed oil straight back to the sump. Mick Richards' Triumph TR7 V8 circuit racer has an interesting modification worth passing on. His car is fitted with a pukka Group A wet sump which has large side extensions or "wings". Into the top of one of these wings is a large diameter pipe routed to an ordinary 12 volt electric water pump, the sort used in caravans. A micro-switch attached to the throttle bracket of the fuel injection system is tripped when full throttle is used, turning on the pump which draws oil from the rear of the rocker covers and returns it straight to the sump. The pump does not seem to have suffered any ill effects from pumping hot engine oil instead of water!

If the engine is being built with roller rockers, it is possible to restrict the oil feed to the rocker gear and thus reduce the amount of oil that collects in the upper part of the engine. Oil reaches the rocker gear via an oil feed hole in each of the deck surfaces of the block, which match holes in the cylinder heads, with a corresponding hole in the cylinder head gaskets. NB The P76 4.4 litre engine is unique in that valve gear oiling is via hollow push-rods as per small block Chevrolet engine.

Restricting the amount of oil to the rocker gear is accomplished by inserting a threaded plug (small carb jets work well) in the oil feed hole of the cylinder head or the block, and drilling a small hole about 2.38 mm (0.094 in) in the centre of the plug. The exact size of the hole may need to be varied depending on the oil system being used, the oil pressure, etc. When restricting top end oiling in this way, it should be remembered that the oil does not only lubricate the valve gear but also cools the valves and the valve springs. High rpm can cause the valve springs to get quite hot, and the exhaust valve will obviously need more cooling than the inlet.

Controlling the temperature of the oil in a competition engine is absolutely vital to engine reliability. An oil temperature gauge should be installed, preferably a capillary type, provided the tube can be routed safely into the vehicle. The oil temperature can then be monitored and an oil cooler added, preferably with a thermostat, if the oil temperature is not satisfactory. Within reason, oil temperature is not critical to performance with the Rover V8, but ideally should be maintained at no more than 10° C hotter than the water temperature.

Oil pressure can be increased to 55 psi by fitting the pressure relief spring used on the

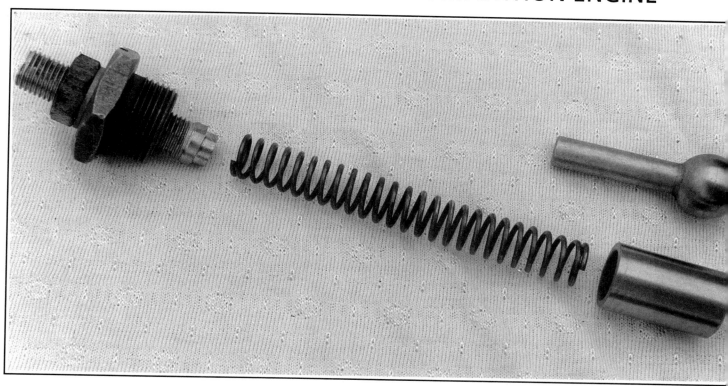

Adjustable oil pressure relief valve with standard cylinder alongside a J.E. Engineering "tadpole" non-stick valve.

MGB V8. This is a popular cheap tweak, but the standard oil pressure is perfectly adequate for most applications unless the engine is to be taken beyond 7,000 rpm, and besides, excessive oil pressure or volume beyond the requirements of the engine consumes horsepower. Excessive pressure will also contribute to high oil temperatures. Adjustable oil pressure regulators are available, which work by altering the tension of the relief spring. If the relief valve plug is removed from the oil pump, the relief valve spring can be removed, followed by the relief valve itself which is a plain steel cylinder. This cylinder can stick in its bore in the oil pump cover, and J.E. Engineering have designed and manufactured a replacement "tadpole" valve. Instead of being a cylinder, the valve is spherical with a small rod on which the relief spring is located – hence the tadpole name. It is virtually impossible for it to seize. The oil pump on all pre-SD1 engines will certainly benefit from an uprating or "high volume" kit which consists of deeper pump gears and a housing extension, available from John Wolfe Racing and Real Steel. Both increase the volume of oil the older pumps can circulate, but they are not recommended for use with post-SD1 engines.

Wet sump systems have their limitations with the Rover V8 because of the oil pump drive being taken from the end of the distributor shaft, and anything that increases the load on this shaft aggravates the distributor drive gear problem experienced by many engine builders operating this engine at relatively high rpm. The obvious, although expensive, answer is to install a dry sump system, but some racing classes exclude this option. In competition classes where wet sump systems are mandatory it is possible to install an external single-stage pump belt driven from the front pulley. The pump takes oil from the wet sump and reintroduces it into the block via a modified front cover, feeding oil into the main oil gallery. The standard Rover V8 oil pump cover is removed, along with the gears and shaft and the flange covered with a blanking plate.

Dry sump systems are the ultimate for competition engines, and with the high cornering forces possible with modern slick tyres and sophisticated chassis it is almost impossible to retain oil control with a wet sump. Not only is there the problem of the oil pump pickup remaining sufficiently submerged in oil, but also the crankshaft will be subjected to oil being thrown against it. It is possible to get by with a wet sump system – indeed some class regulations stipulate it – but it depends on the competition involved. A dry sump system will allow the engine to sit closer to the ground, thus reducing the vehicle's centre of gravity, the total oil capacity carried on the vehicle can be increased, within reason the oil tank can be positioned to suit the vehicle, and it will theoretically liberate a small horsepower increase. It also completely eliminates distributor gear wear problems.

The heart of a dry-sump system is the

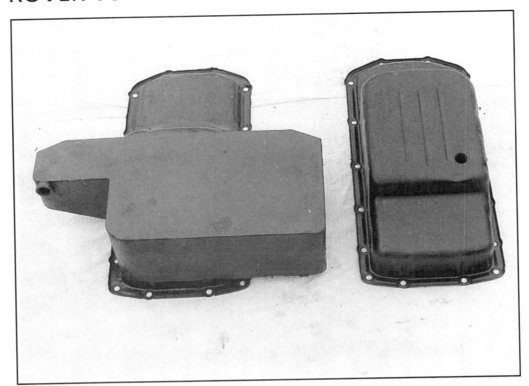

On the right is a standard Rover P5B/P6B sump and on the left is pukka Group A "big wing" racing sump.

Turn over the Group A sump (on the left) and put it alongside a production Rover SD1 sump (on the right) this time and the complexity of its design and construction are plain to see.

Thermostatic sandwich plate with inlet/outlet to oil cooler with current oil filter (ERR 1168) mounted. These filters are superior due to better non return valve in base.

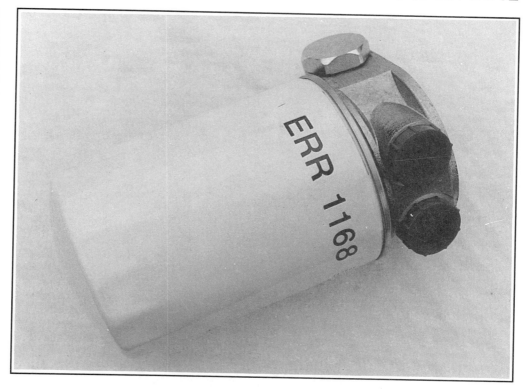

Early type thermostatic take off with non threaded pipe fittings.

127

externally mounted pump itself which is modular, ie, it consists of sections which are individual pumps themselves, each section being a gear pump which works on the same principle as the standard oil pump. Usually two scavenge sections recover oil from the shallow oil pan and pump it into the remote oil reservoir, while one pressure section draws oil from the reservoir and pumps it into the engine's oil passages. The width of each section determines its volume capacity and the pressure section has an adjustable pressure bypass. The pump itself is belt driven usually at 0.7 or 0.5 engine speed, and remote oil filters are positioned so that scavenged oil is filtered before it goes into the oil tank. In fact it is a good idea to have another remote filter between the tank and the pressure pump, before the oil goes through the oil cooler after which it enters the engine. The front cover of the engine has to be modified to allow oil pipes and fittings to connect into the two main oil galleries which can clearly be seen in the front of the block, on the left side, when the front cover is removed.

Unfortunately it is not a simple matter to remove the standard oil pump gears and oil pump cover and fabricate a new flat cover with a couple of oil entry holes welded in, because a vast amount of oil would shoot up the hole where the oil pump drive shaft used to sit. It can be done this way, but a blanking plug for the drive shaft housing would have to be fabricated first. Also, take the line for the oil pressure gauge from a point very close to where the oil enters the engine, so that the oil pressure can be adjusted and set as near as possible to the actual engine. Filters and sharp bends in the pipe fittings can cause significant pressure drops in the system, which will require increases in oil pressure to compensate. Take the pressure reading from some point too remote in the overall system, and it is possible to have a much lower oil pressure actually in the engine itself.

Although the basic layout of these systems is the same, most installations have to be individually designed and plumbed to suit the chassis of the vehicle. There are one or two areas that should be carefully considered. The

Basic non-thermostatic oil cooler take-off.

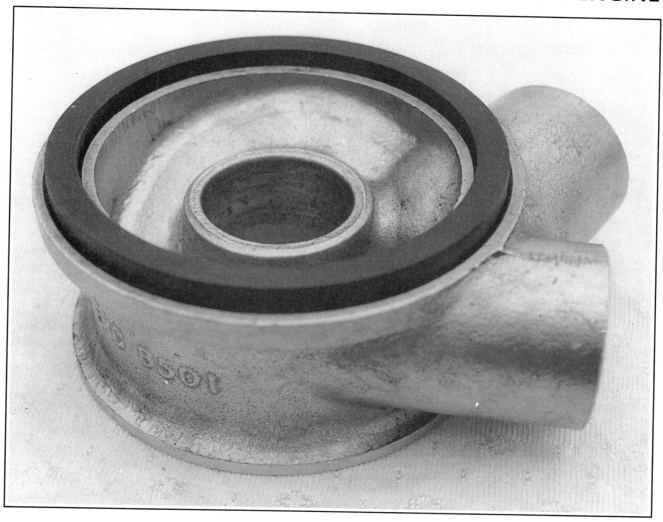

MGB V8 pattern (re-cast by J.E. Engineering) adaptor for remote oil filter. Bolts direct to the block, does not require O ring sealing.

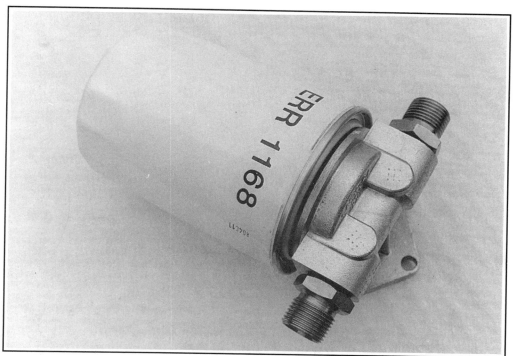

Remote filter housing fitted with latest factory oil filter.

Thermostatic sandwich plate with blanking plate for use with remote oil filter housing.

Single stage oil pump used to replace standard internal oil pump in engine where comp. regulation stipulate dry sump not allowed. The pump takes oil from wet sump, curing distributor drive gear wear common on engine using 5500+ rpm for sustained periods.

pumps are expensive and on most systems oil drawn straight from the oil pan enters the scavenge pump. If there is any kind of component failure, it is possible that particles (or worse) can fall into the oil pan and be drawn straight into the pump, so it is a good idea to try and incorporate some small high-capacity screen-type filters in the lines to protect the pumps. Obviously, with a dry-sump system the standard sump is not retained, and J.E. Engineering manufacture a substantial cast alloy oil pan which is designed to add rigidity to the bottom end on the block casting. However, it is possible to fabricate a dry sump pan using the pressed steel flange of the original sump as a basis, removing the rest of the sump and cutting and welding in steel sheet. Oil pan design is a subject worthy of its own volume, but it is certainly a neglected area of future development, as anyone who has studied some American designs such as the Moroso dry sump pans will testify. The oil tank is also worthy of some thought and can again be fabricated, although aluminium is probably a more suitable material. The tank needs to be tall and round, rather than squat, with two entry fittings in the top for the lines from the scavenge sections entering at a tangent, so that oil entering the tank swirls against the side of the tank rather than gushing out into fresh air before falling into the tank. A couple of perforated horizontal baffles are needed inside the tank to enable the oil to settle gently to the bottom of the tank with the minimum of aeration. The outlet at the bottom of the tank for drawing oil off to the pressure section must sit higher in the car than the inlet of the pressure section so that the pump is always primed by gravity. The oil carried should be between 6 and 10 litres (10.6 and 17.6 pints), but the tank capacity should be about 30 per cent higher than the volume of oil you intend to use in the system.

IGNITION

Having gone to the expense of carefully selecting all the components and assembling a high-performance Rover V8, it would be foolish not to pay close attention to the ignition system. After all, if the system is not absolutely 100 per cent perfect, it follows the engine cannot produce its absolute peak horsepower. For high performance Rover V8 engines the contact breaker point ignition is really not suitable, except perhaps for a mildly tuned road engine. That means an electronic, capacity discharge, breakerless ignition system.

It is surprising just how many high-performance/competition Rover V8 engines retain the standard distributor, albeit one of the more recent electronic versions, usually backed up with a powerful ignition amplifier and high quality plug leads. The best OE distributor to use on a performance Rover V8 is the Lucas 35DM8 electronic distributor, introduced on all engines in 1982 to replace the Lucas 35D8 which had mechanical contact breaker points. The Lucas 35DM8 has the control unit (amplifier) mounted separately and therefore more remote from engine heat (the cooler the better). After 1986 the amplifier was incorporated in the distributor body, so units manufactured between 1982 and 1986 are the best OE units to use.

What is needed on high-performance engines is enhanced spark duration to initiate the combustion reaction under a wide range of combustion chamber conditions. A good basic boost for the standard electronic system would be an Accel coil and Lumenition ignition module, together with a top-quality set of performance plug leads. The same kind of additions can boost the performance of the earlier contact breaker points distributors.

High compression engines demand high energy sparks for efficient combustion and clean running. There are numerous high output ignition coils and ignition amplifiers available to the engine builder; MSD (Multiple Spark Discharge) by Autotronic Controls is probably one of the best-known, but Lumenition and Micro Dynamics also have a range of products designed to enhance the spark quality of the ignition system.

There are aftermarket distributors available from Mallory (available through John Wolfe Racing and Real Steel), and these can be particularly useful for pre-SD1 engines which will not accept OE distributors from post-SD1 engines because the distributor drive is different. To fit, for instance, the Lucas 35DM8 distributor to a pre-SD1 engine you would need to fit the oil pump gears from a post-SD1 engine, but these gears will not fit the pre-SD1 housing (ie, front cover) because the gears are deeper. So either the gears need to be machined down (shortened) or the front cover from a post-SD1 engine would need to be fitted too! So Mallory very conveniently produce an electronic distributor with or without vacuum advance for the pre-SD1 engine at a very reasonable price. For those who prefer the familiarity of a set of points and a condenser, Mallory also manufacture dual point distributors, which are better able to cope with higher rpm on eight cylinders. They are available for pre-SD1 and post-SD1 engines, with or without vacuum advance.

It might be relevant at this point to clarify the whole question of ignition advance. The

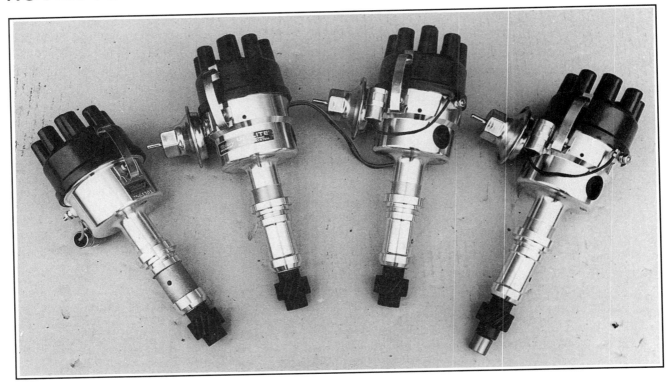

Mallory performance distributors. Left to right – Dual point, no vacuum advance (pre-SD1 only), Unilite electronic with vacuum advance (pre-SD1 only), dual point with vacuum advance (pre-SD1 only) and post-SD1 dual point with vacuum advance and adjustable advance curve.

Aluminium bronze alloy distributor drive gear prevents damage to camshaft gear under high load conditions.

Rover V8 has static ignition timing of 6° BTDC (before top dead centre) with maximum advance of 32° BTDC reached at 4,000 rpm. The vacuum advance senses the throttle position via the manifold vacuum. On a high-performance engine it is actually needed because tuned engines are less efficient at low rpm, but in fact usually have no provision for vacuum advance because they produce very poor manifold vacuum at low rpm. Hence the Mallory performance distributors are available with or without the facility.

So many high-performance Rover V8 engines rely entirely on centrifugal ignition advance, and as a rule of thumb the less ignition advance the engine needs to optimize peak power, the more efficient the engine is. At low speed on a light throttle the engine should need a lot of advance, but at full load it should need less. So when tuning the ignition advance the key should be to limit the amount of maximum advance, and this is done by introducing stronger springs to the distributor's centrifugal weights. Of course, depending on the engine combination used – camshaft, compression ratio, actual cylinder pressures, fuel/air

mixture – the principles may not always apply, and the ignition curve should really be established on the dynamometer.

High energy ignition systems need controlling to ensure that that energy is delivered to the spark-plug gap and does not leak away to ground once it has left the coil. It will always seek to take the path of least resistance, and if it finds an alternative the result will be an annoying misfire. There is little that can be done about the design of the distributor, except perhaps ensure that the cap is in perfect condition. Ideally the plug wires should be routed to keep them well apart and as isolated as possible, and high-performance engines should ideally use spiral core plug leads (Moroso), or at least a good set of silicone leads (Accel).

A very popular spark-plug for tuned Rover V8 is the NGK B7EV, or the Champion N6Y for engines of moderate power outputs. Next up the scale is the Champion N2G, and for high power engines possibly the Champion N84G. If the engine has the pre-SD1 cylinder heads which use shorter spark-plugs, the Champion L82Y of L64Y are a good starting point.

This little Moroso kit is actually for GM vehicles but the selection of springs work well with Rover distributors for fine tuning mechanical advance.

ROVER V8

Dry sump pump with two scavenge and one pressure elements. Note toothed belt drive off crankshaft but also poly-V belt drive to water pump.

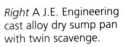

Right A J.E. Engineering cast alloy dry sump pan with twin scavenge.

Right Inside view of J.E. Engineering cast alloy dry sump pan. Cast pans such as this can add strength to lower cylinder block area.

Another dry sump pump installation but in this case the alternator moved over to the left hand side of the engine and the dry sump pump on the right. All drives are by toothed belts.

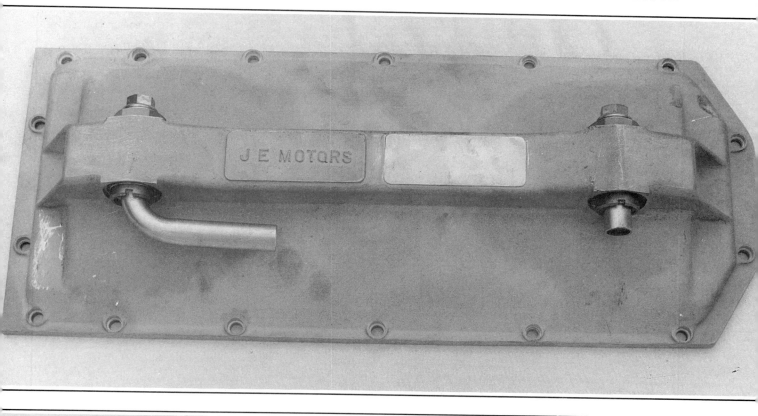

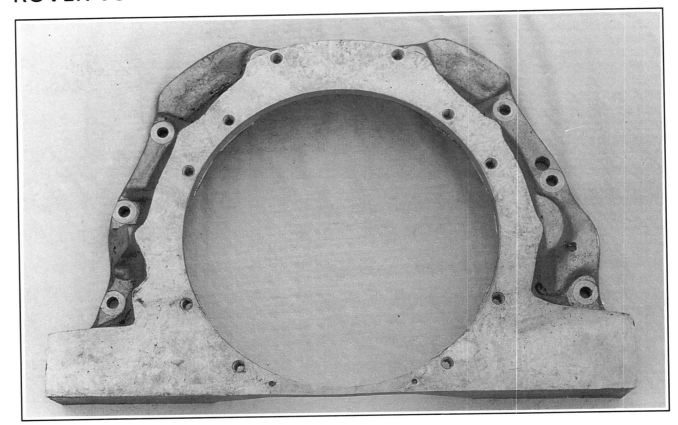

A Rover V8 to Hewland gearbox adaptor makes single seater racing car installation a snip!

McLeod 10.5 inch clutch with matching steel flywheel. This competition clutch can be used wih the standard Rover flywheel but the outer ring of bolts have to be redrilled to match the McLeod cover.

The McLeod all steel twin plate clutch which has road use applications but is also suitable for nitrous oxide and high output engines.

Possibly the ultimate. The McLeod "Magnum Force" twin plate race clutch with aluminium flywheel capable of handling up to 500 lbs/ft of torque. If you are lucky enough to produce over 1000 lbs/ft of torque you will need a double diagram version!!!!

ROVER V8

CONCLUSIONS

The Rover V8 engine has considerable potential as a power unit for any number of competition applications. But given a reasonable budget and engine building ability, what are the power output realities? It is very difficult to be specific, but there are examples of normally aspirated engines that give a good indication of what can be expected.

Few people looking for greater power persist with the 3.5 litre unit, but it is capable of nearly 300 bhp in full race form, albeit with a corresponding loss of mid-range torque and very peaky power curve. A more realistic output would probably be 250-260 bhp for competition work. The cost of building such a 3.5 litre engine, with reliable high rpm operation would make going to 3.9 litres a more sensible approach, since the bigger capacity means lower rpm and greater torque.

Most engine builders go straight for a 3.9 litre unit which has the potential for 330 bhp at 6,250–500 rpm and very healthy torque of around 300 lb/ft at 4,500–750 rpm. This would probably involve a Kent 256 (full-race) camshaft, quadruple downdraughts, big valve heads, dry sump lubrication, and steel con rods with forged pistons. It is fair to say, both in road and race engines, that the 3.9 litre offers the best value for money in terms of power and torque.

As the capacity increases from 3.9 litres towards 4.2 and 4.4 litres, we encounter diminishing returns as the gains in power against cost involved begins to slow down. But having said that, the rpm at which the power and torque are produced is lower with the bigger capacity units. For instance, a good 4.5 litre engine will produce over 300 lb/ft of torque at 3,500 rpm, and 300 bhp at probably 1,000 rpm less than the 3.9 litre unit. Rover 4.4 and 4.5 litre engines can, depending on specification, produce close on 400 bhp in full race form, but the cylinder heads will need a lot of work to achieve the flow these big engines need.

Chapter Five

Increasing Capacity

There is now a tremendous amount of interest in big capacity versions of the Rover V8, the 3.9 litre conversion being almost standard as step one in the search for more power, and now it is possible to build an engine with virtually any capacity required right up to 5.2 litres!

At 3,531.6 cc (or 215 cu. in.), the Rover V8 is not by any means a large capacity V8, and since the Buick/Oldsmobile days people have contrived to increase it. Not until 1989 when Land-Rover publicly introduced the 3.9 litre version of the Rover V8 in the Range-Rover had the engine being manufactured in anything other than its 215 cu. in. form. In September 1992, Land-Rover unveiled the even bigger 4.2 litre Rover V8 to power the considerably revamped Range-Rover LSE. The Leyland Australia 4.4 litre version is the exception, and this will be covered later.

Early research by enterprising speed shops in the USA centred on increasing the bore size to accept certain Chevrolet small block pistons (both cast and forged) and certain Ford V6 pistons, as well as the installation of the Buick 300 crankshaft, which is still used today for increasing the stroke beyond the 71.12 mm (2.8 in) of the standard Rover crankshaft. Apparently even the Chevrolet small block crankshaft has found its way into the Rover block!

The mostly straightforward method of increasing the capacity of the Rover V8 is to increase the cylinder bore from the standard 88.9 mm (3.47 in), although this invariably means replacing the cast iron liners in the aluminium block. Recently Land-Rover themselves have produced an effective solution with their 3.9 litre version of the engine which has a 94.04 mm (3.7 in) bore, giving an actual capacity of 3,951 cc.

One obvious and simple method of building a 3.9 litre Rover V8 is, of course, to obtain a brand new 3.9 litre short engine assembly, or even just buy a block and a set of factory 94 mm (3.7 in) pistons from the spare parts department of a Land-Rover dealer. This is an expensive route to take, although the 3.9 litre blocks will be stronger because they have been cast with more aluminium material around the cylinder liners to accommodate the larger bore. If you bore a 3.5 litre block to take a larger liner, for a 94.04 mm (3.7 in) bore, you are taking some strength out of the block, and although this has never been a problem in practice, the 3.9 litre factory block is stronger in this respect. However, some engine builders like to base an engine build on a used and therefore seasoned block, and obviously it will take time for these new 3.9 litre blocks to become available in this condition (ie, used). The real benefit of the factory 3.9 litre blocks is their ability to take bores larger than 94.04 mm (3.7 in) because of that greater inbuilt strength margin.

There are also better alternatives to the OE 94.04 mm (3.7 in) pistons, although they are perfectly adequate for mild tuning applications. Parts for those engines manufactured for production Land-Rover vehicles are made and costed on different criteria to parts made for more specialist (ie, performance) use, and are therefore not necessarily the best option when selecting parts for performance use.

Since 3.9 litre engines are relatively new on the market, the main interest still centres around what can be done to the original 3.5 litre version with its 88.9 mm (3.47 in) bore. A normal rebore on this engine with the usual 0.5 mm (0.02 in) oversize piston gives a bore of 89.41 mm (3.48 in) and a marginal increase in capacity to 3,572 cc. From this point on, the original cast iron cylinder liners are bored out of the block completely, along with some of the aluminium block material surrounding the bores. New cylinder liners are pressed into the heated block and machined to take a variety of aftermarket or replacement pistons. Such a procedure results in what is universally regarded as the 3.9 litre (or 4.0 litre) conversion, although the exact capacity depends on the bore size used by the particular company which undertakes the conversion, and this in turn depends on which pistons they elect to use. J.E. Engineering, for instance, originally used a 93.5 mm (3.65 in) bore which with a standard stroke crankshaft gave a capacity of 3,906 cc. Their first oversize rebore from this was 94.04 mm (3.67 in), which coincidentally became the size of the Land-Rover 3.9 litre Rover V8. So now J.E. Engineering have standardized their conversion to the same 94.04 mm (3.67 in) bore size (3,951 cc). Other conversion specialists may use slight variations on bore sizes, depending on the piston they elect to use.

The exact bore size varies because the crucial factor from the converter's point of view is the source of the pistons. There are a number of major piston manufacturers who produce both cast and forged pistons in a multitude of dimensions. Some converters simply select a piston that has the required dimensions from one of these catalogues, perhaps necessitating some minor machining in the gudgeon pin to small rod end dimensions, and having the cylinder liner bored to suit. The use of certain Chevrolet small block pistons is a perfect example.

How big the cylinder bore can be "stretched" before the block is seriously weakened is another contentious issue, and opinions vary as to where the outer limits lie. The fact of the matter is the larger the bore the larger outside diameter of the new cylinder liner, and therefore the more material has to be machined from the block. The cast aluminium surrounding the cast iron liner gets thinner as the bore size gets bigger, eventually compromising block rigidity and ultimate strength. The only other alternative is to reduce the thickness of the liner wall itself, and this again involves compromises. Stretching the bore size to extremes can be very much a balancing act, and while some engine builders prefer to err on the side of caution, some see no reason for concern.

Incidentally, when Vandervell built the engine for GKN47D, the Lotus-based special designed to be a rolling showcase of GKN products, they bored out the standard 3.5 litre block by 1.575 mm (0.062 in) for a bore size of 90.47 mm (3.528 in) on the standard liners! Even they admitted this was marginal, but they did not encounter problems afterwards. Such an overbore results in a capacity of 3,658 cc, although Vandervell combined the overbore with a longer stroke Buick 300 crankshaft. Exactly which pistons they used is unclear, except that they were "Alcoa slipper-type".

To give some idea of the enormous variety of possible hardware combinations, here are some – but by no means all – of the ways of adding more cubic inches to the Rover V8. If the replacement liner is bored to 94.89 mm (3.7 in), it is possible to use a Chevrolet 305 cu. in. L69 small block piston, to arrive at a capacity of 4,014.8 cc, but this requires the use of Buick 300 con rods with the small end honed from the standard 23.55 mm (0.927 in) to 23.88 mm (0.94 in). Alternatively a Chevrolet 265 cu. in. flat-top piston will fit in a bore of 95.25 mm (3.75 in), with an early 50.8 mm (2 in) big end journal small block Chevrolet con rod, to produce a capacity of 4,047 cc.

The oldest crankshaft associated with Rover V8 capacity increases is commonly known as the Buick 300 crankshaft (manufactured 1964–7), which has a stroke of 86 mm (3.36 in). This crank has been used successfully in the Rover block from the earliest Buick/Oldsmobile days for road and racing engines. However, the Buick 300 crank has a longer rear overhang and has larger main bearing journals, so it is certainly not a bolt-in replacement. (It is also externally balanced.) Obviously the main bearing journals have to be turned down to 58.4 mm (2.3 in), but the important work is in the rear main oil seal area, which requires the fabrication of a labyrinth-type seal arrangement using an adapter plate. The most common method of accomplishing this, and used widely in the USA, involves sealing the adapter plate to the block using the front pump "O" ring gasket from a General Motors Turbo Hydro 350 automatic transmission, and to the crank with a Chevrolet big block neoprene rear main seal.

There is a range of engine capacities available when using the Buick 300 crankshaft that is worth noting. If the crankshaft is installed but the standard 88.9 mm (3.47 in) bore is retained, it is possible to produce a capacity of 4,293 cc by using pistons from the Chevy Vega 140 cu. in. engine on an early 50.8 mm (2 in) journal Chevy small block con rod, or for a slightly lower compression ratio the 267 Chevrolet small block piston with 1.27 mm (0.05 in) machined from the crown.

If the 88.9 mm (3.47 in) bore is taken 0.76 mm (0.03 in) oversize, then pistons from

Different stroke crankshafts require pistons with different compression heights. On the right is a piston for a 71 mm stroke crankshaft and on the left is a piston used with a 77 mm stroke crankshaft.

a 170 cu. in. Ford six-cylinder engine (US) in 0.76 mm (0.03 in) oversize can be used to produce 4,358 cc. The standard Rover con rod can be used by the small end, but must be honed out from 22.23 mm (0.875 in) to 23.16 mm (0.912 in) which can potentially weaken it.

To go any larger in capacity it is necessary to fit larger cylinder liners, but there are still a number of options. With a bore of 93.47 mm (3.65 in) and the standard Rover con rod (again honed to 23.16 mm/0.912 in), it is possible to fit pistons from the Ford 255 cu. in. engine to arrive at 4,736 cc. Increasing the bore slightly to 94.5 mm (3.69 in) and using the previously mentioned 50.8 mm (2 in) journal Chevy rod gives a capacity of 4,785 cc. The pistons for this must be Ford 2.8 litre V6 with a compression height of 38.5 mm (1.516 in) (they are available in a range of compression heights) and 1.53 mm (0.06 in) oversize, with the gudgeon pin holes in the piston honed to take the Chevy gudgeon pin. Bigger still at 4,883 cc are Chevy 305 dished LG4 pistons with the 50.8 mm (2 in) Chevy rods in a 94.89 mm (3.7 in) bore. In addition to the above, there are still more bore sizes/pistons/rod variations, but the ultimate combination with the Buick 300 crank is a 96 mm (3.7 in) bore to take Ford 2.3 litre Turbo 4 cylinder engine pistons on 50.8 mm (2 in) Chevy rods for a capacity of 5 litres (305 cu. in.). These Ford pistons have especially thick crowns 10.16 mm (0.4 in) because of their turbo application, so

can be machined to arrive at a range of compression ratios.

The pistons available for use in these larger bores can be bewildering if one were to insist on having all the possible options – there are in fact over 30 capacity variations based on available bore/stroke combinations – but nowadays the optimum combinations have pretty much been worked out already by the principle Rover V8 specialists who carry out these conversions.

The largest "factory" capacity Rover V8 to make it into volume production has become known as the P76 engine, actually a 4.4 litre version of the basic Rover V8 developed by Land-Rover at Solihull for potential use in a new Rover saloon. The Rover car was stillborn, but the 4.4 litre engine design, along with sufficient production tooling, was sold to what was then Leyland Australia. It was produced in volume for the Leyland P76 saloon and the Leyland Terrier truck until 1976 when production stopped, and Leyland Australia eventually closed down.

The basis of the engine was a special version of the Rover V8 block with a standard 88.9 mm (3.47 in) bore and a crankshaft of 88.9 mm (3.47 in) stroke, which was deemed by Land-Rover engineers as the largest stroke crankshaft that could fit inside the crankcase and still have sufficient clearance between the crankshaft counterweights and the camshaft lobes (without compromising the crankshaft design). The longer stroke was

141

used in conjunction with longer connecting rods, requiring a cylinder block that was taller (deck heights) than the 3.5 litre Rover version by 17.46 mm (0.69 in).

The P76 engine differed in many other details, too. The heads are simply not worth discussing except to say that top end oiling was via the hollow push-rods, the rockers were paired on a single stud (as per the Chevy small block), and they had absolutely no performance potential or compatibility with the Rover V8. The inlet manifold was also a poor performance piece, and because of the P76 having a taller block the heads were slightly further apart, so the inlet manifold was unique to this engine.

The number of P76 engines in the UK must be extremely small, and when they were imported many years ago their performance potential was deemed to be poor, although they produced tremendous torque. Also, at the time they were available Rover V8 engine tuning in general was only just beginning, and the number of performance parts to choose from was very small. To a certain extent the engine has been rediscovered in recent years, and Australian tuners are building engines for SD1 and Range-Rover conversions based on the 4.4 litre block because they are, of course, a bolt-in replacement. In their 4.4 litre form they are virtually a straight swap for the 3.5 litre Rover, and by substituting the Rover SD1 cylinder heads and using spacer plates to allow the fitting of any 3.5 litre Rover inlet manifolds, or quad downdraught manifolds which are obviously unaffected by the heads being slightly further apart, some very respectable engines can result.

The one important point about the P76 4.4 litre engine is that by fitting the now commonplace 94.04 mm (3.67 in) pistons and liners (the liners have to be slightly longer but that is not a problem) used in the popular 3.9 litre conversions, the result is a Rover V8 with 4,939 cc, and by offset regrinding the big end journals on the crankshaft to take oversize big end bearings the stroke can be made a full 90 mm (3.51 in), which with the 94.04 mm (3.67 in) bore results in a capacity of 5000 cc's. This is the absolute maximum achievable without resorting to a one-off billet crank.

Before we leave the subject, it might be worth mentioning that the P76 crankshaft can be fitted into a normal 3.5 litre cylinder block, but that it has 63.5 mm (2.5 in) main bearing journals. The easiest course of action is to have the P76 main journals machined down to 58.4 mm (2.30 in), but it is considered wise with a "stroker" crank such as this to keep the main bearings big, ie, the original 63.5 mm (2.5 in) and have the block line bored to 63.5 mm

(2.5 in). It also saves on machine work, getting the crankshaft's main bearing surfaces treated and polished back to the necessary finish. Rovercraft use a 63.5 mm (2.5 in) main bearing journal on their 82 mm (3.2 in) stroke crankshaft, so presumably can do the machining and have the bigger main bearings that this swap would require. However, physically putting the P76 crankshaft into the 3.5 litre block is not the end of the problem, since the longer stroke with standard length con rods and standard dimension pistons will push the pistons above the block deck surface at TDC. Using shorter con rods to correct the problem will result in interference between the crankshaft counterweights and the underside of the pistons as they approach BDC. Assuming the crankshaft is going to be used in conjunction with a 94.04 mm (3.67 in) bore, then pistons with a shorter compression height must be used, together with possibly some piston crown machining to get the pistons flush with the block deck at TDC. Of course, depending on the pistons used, this will result in a high compression ratio if normal Rover P6B/SD1 cylinder heads, with their 36 cc combustion chamber volumes, are used. The Buick 300 heads have a more acceptable 54 cc volume for this application, or perhaps Turbo Technics might be persuaded to put SD1 heads on their milling machine and opening up the chambers to a greater volume, since they do this work as matter of course with the Range-Rover turbocharger conversion.

Since the P76 4.4 litre engine, with its long stroke crankshaft, has to all intents and purposes passed into the history books, the source of longer stroke crankshafts is limited, although Land-Rover themselves have recently introduced their 4.2 litre version of the Rover V8 with its 77 mm (3.00 in) stroke. At present two companies (other than Land-Rover) manufacture a factory specification cast crankshaft with a larger stroke: Rovercraft with their 82 mm (3.2 in) crankshaft, and J.E.Engineering with their 77 mm (3.00 in) and 81 mm (3.16 in) cranks developed from Land-Rover tooling. The Rovercraft 82 mm (3.2 in) crankshaft differs from the J.E.Engineering versions in one important respect; the main bearing journals have intentionally been made 63.5 mm (2.5 in) (the Rover normally has 58.4 mm/2.3 in), so the block has to be line bored to the larger size before the crankshaft will fit, with, of course, larger bearings.

The J.E.Engineering crankshafts were developed from Land-Rover cranks built for the stillborn Iceberg Rover V8 diesel engine project which used a 71 mm (2.78 in) stroke (as standard) crankshaft, but a bigger big end bearing size, principally to increase the overlap

A Rovercraft cast 82 mm stroke crankshaft also has a larger 2.5 in main bearing diameter, requiring line boring of the block.

In the background is a standard Rover crankshaft, in the foreground is a Buick 300 crankshaft. Note the longer rear overhang and the totally different shape. The Buick crank will fit the Rover block, but not without machine work.

and make for a stronger crankshaft, which diesel engines need. When the project was cancelled, remaining stocks were bought by J.E.Engineering, who offset machined these larger big end journals to the standard (petrol) big end journal size but a longer stroke. Initially this was 77 mm (3.00 in), but eventually they modified the tooling to produce a crank with an 81 mm (3.16 in) stroke. This is however, about as far as the casting could be stretched.

As mentioned before, longer stroke crankshafts require either shorter rods or pistons with a lower compression height, that is pistons that have less distance from the centre of the gudgeon pin bore to the piston crown. If these critical dimensions were not altered, the longer stroke would result in the piston sticking out of the top of the block at TDC. It is more practical to use pistons with a lower compression height than shorter con rods and

as the stroke is increased the compression height must be decreased by 50 per cent of that increase because the piston has to move further down the bore as well as up. This means that an increase in stroke not only involves a new crankshaft, but also a new set of pistons, and that is the case regardless of the bore size. So if you have already gone to the expense of a 3.9 litre conversion and decide at a later date to go for the full 4.5 litres, remember it not just a case of buying a stroker crankshaft; you will have to buy new pistons again as well!

To go over 5 litres for a Rover V8 is "mountain" motor territory, but it is possible and many such engines have been successfully built. Achieving the necessary combination of cylinder bore and rod/piston to suit the crankshaft with the required stroke is not so easy. One such option is to increase the bore beyond the accepted limit of 94.04 mm (3.67 in). Bore

The J.E. Developments/Ian Richardson Racing 5.2 litre cylinder block, converted from a new 3.9 litre casting.

The J.E.Developments/Ian Richardson Racing 5.2 litre cylinder block again, with a close-up of the billet four-bolt main bearing cap and the block machining to accommodate it.

The J.E.Developments/Ian Richardson Racing 5.2 litre cylinder block from the front, with billet main cap precision machined to fit exactly the machined block and form a very strong structure.

sizes of around 96 mm (3.74 in) are considered the absolute sensible maximum that can be achieved in the Rover V8 block, and only then if the block is sonic tested to check adequate and uniform material thickness around the bores before any machining is attempted. Obviously the newer 3.9/4.2 litre factory blocks are better in this respect, because they have more aluminium material around the cast iron liners. Incidentally, to use significantly larger bore sizes than 96 mm (3.74 in) involves removing all the block material from around the cast iron liner so the coolant actually circulates around the outside surface of the liner itself – so called wet liners – but this seriously weakens the block, as well as giving rise to sealing problems between the liner and block. In one instance of this being tried, the block did not even survive having the cylinder heads torqued down before it split. It is definitely not an option worth investigating.

J.E.Developments acting as sole distributors for Ian Richardson Racing currently have a mighty 5.2 litre version of the Rover V8 available which uses a 96.21 mm (3.75 in) bore and an 88.9 mm (3.47 in) stroke billet steel crankshaft. The block is converted from a brand new standard 3.9 litre factory casting to four-bolt mains (ie, not a factory cross-bolt casting) with massive billet main bearing caps, and can be built for heavy duty road or competition use.

To increase the capacity of the Rover V8 still further can only be accomplished by increasing the stroke even more. Crankshafts with greater stroke than the 88.9 mm (3.47 in) of the Australian P76 4.4 litre version of the engine are not available unless one resorts to having a one-off billet crankshaft manufactured. The largest capacity Rover V8 engine known so far is 5.5 litres, built using a billet crankshaft and requiring some fairly involved re-routing of an internal block oilway to clear the crankshaft counterweights. But if that were not enough, Crower Research & Development in Jamul, California have manufactured billet cranks for the Rover/Buick engine with a stroke of 96.5 mm (3.76 in) which with a 94 mm (3.67 in) bore would mean a capacity of 5,403 cc or 329 cu. in., and with a 96 mm (3.74 in) bore would mean – wait for it – 5.6 litres! Whether any such engine has been successfully built and what pistons/con rod combination would need to be used is not known.

There are a multitude of combinations and options for bigger-capacity Rover V8 engines, and even more than one way to arrive at a given capacity based on the bore and stroke variations available to the engine builder. For instance, engines of 3.9 litres have been built by retaining the standard 3.5 litre engine bore of 88.9 mm (3.47 in) and fitting a longer stroke crankshaft. The logic may seem questionable, but the engine's performance is quite simply staggering (not necessarily as a direct result of utilizing this combination of course), so the relative merits and potential of all these combinations is worth exploring.

If you wish to play around with the various bore/stroke combinations the calculation you will need in order to arrive at the capacity is: 0.7854 x 8 x stroke x bore x bore. You might also bear in mind the following facts. The standard 88.9 mm (3.49 in) 3.5 litre bore does shroud the valves somewhat, so to increase the capacity by going to a bigger cylinder bore will not only increase the engine's capacity, but will also help the engine's breathing by moving the cylinder walls away from the valves. The limitations of the bore are already apparent. Only so much of the aluminium material around the cylinder liners can be removed before the block structure becomes terminally weakened. The extent to which the stroke can be increased is limited by two factors. One is the maximum size of crankshaft that can physically rotate within the confines of the Rover cylinder block or crankcase; opinions here vary. The other major limitation of stretching the capacity of the Rover V8 is the breathing ability of the cylinder heads, one reason why bigger Rover V8s have often been praised for their outstanding torque outputs, but often disappointing in horsepower. The potential of the Rover V8's cylinder heads is the subject of much controversy, but at the moment there are few alternatives.

Whatever the extent to which the cubic capacity of the Rover V8 is increased, there are appreciable power gains to be had from the undertaking, a 3.9 litre engine will produce about a 15 per cent increase in power over a 3.5 litre. As the capacity increases further, the power gains become progressively more expensive to yield, but bigger vehicles such as Land-Rovers and Range-Rovers benefit greatly from the increase in torque at lower rpm. In fact a 4.2 or 4.5 litre Rover V8 will literally transform the Range-Rover into a vehicle no longer burdened by its size and weight, but sharp and responsive to the point that older versions might need some uprating in the suspension and brakes' departments. The larger capacities do not necessarily mean higher fuel consumption either. The engine needs less rpm to achieve the required performance; lower rpm translates equally into lower fuel consumption and far more relaxing transport, as the engine works nowhere near as hard.

There is still some way to go yet before the full performance potential of the bigger capacity engines show themselves in competition, although the 4.4 litre Tuscan Challenge engines have demonstrated that these big engines are potent indeed and able to deliver power in abundance. With the promise of engines of 5 litres or more available to the competitor, who knows what new heights the Rover V8 will reach in the future?

Chapter Six

Supercharging, turbocharging and nitrous oxide injection

SUPERCHARGING

One method of giving a 3.5 litre Rover V8 engine the power of one of the bigger capacity versions is to supercharge it. How much power depends on the pressure at which the supercharger is geared to operate, even though operating it actually absorbs engine power, within the limits of cylinder pressures, combustion chamber temperatures and detonation. The key to the equation is the *efficiency* of the supercharger itself. Supercharging instantly increases the power output of the engine right across the rpm range, without an increase in engine "temperament", and provided the engine is in good condition before the conversion requires no additional performance parts.

One of the most interesting superchargers for the Rover V8 is the Sprintex, a simple but effective screw compressor available through DPR Engineering. They have developed an installation specifically for the Rover V8 which is available as a conversion (not a bolt-on kit) for either carburetted for fuel injected (EFi) engines.

The Rover V8 engine layout is particularly well suited to supercharging by virtue of having all the inlet ports grouped closely together. The Rover Vitesse/EFi fuel injected version is particularly convenient; with its plenum chamber drawing air from one side of the engine, the supercharger can blow into it via relatively straightforward trunking. Mounting the Sprintex unit is also easier as it normally sits alongside and slightly above the engine, either flat or on its side, depending on the particular engine compartment involved. Traditionally supercharged V8s have usually had the supercharger mounted directly on top of the inlet manifold, which adds greatly to the height of the engine.

The Sprintex supercharger on a Range-Rover EFi engine only absorbs about 15 bhp to drive it, but produces an additional 75 bhp at the flywheel, with the maximum boost not exceeding 6 psi. The power absorption at light throttle is minimal so that any fuel consumption penalty is offset by the reduced tendency to depend on lower gears to obtain satisfactory performance. The engine is left virtually standard, except for the fitting of a slightly thicker cylinder head gasket to reduce the static compression ratio and ensure freedom from detonation under load. The drive for the Sprintex is via a pulley off the crankshaft and a drive belt. On a 3.5 litre Range-Rover engine, the power is boosted to 240 bhp at 4,750 rpm and 280 lb/ft of torque at 3,200 rpm, allowing the Range-Rover to exceed the performance 0–60 mph of the current 3.9 and 4.2 litre versions quite comfortably, which of course could also benefit from a Sprintex installation!

There was some publicity recently concerning B & M Performance Products in California offering a supercharge kit for the Rover V8 which promised much. B & M are one of the most respected names in supercharging, and in particular bolt-on kits for the enthusiast, so the news was greeted with some excitement. Unfortunately the kit never appeared, and only minimal development work was done before the concept was handed over to B & M's UK agents, Real Steel. The

A Rover 3.5 litre engine fitted with a Sprintex S102 supercharger develops 270 bhp at 5,500 rpm and 290 lb/ft of torque at 3,500 rpm. The TVR 350SX it is installed in accelerates from 0-60 mph in 6.3 seconds, and does the standing quarter-mile in 14.7 seconds.

The Sprintex twin screw supercharger consists of a pair of helical screw gears which are geared together but do not actually make contact with each other. The intake charge is compressed between the rotors as it moves through the case.

A vane-type supercharger installed in a rallycross MGB GT. This is the traditional position for a V8 supercharger installation and required some fabrication of mounting flanges and ancillary brackets.

In this B & M supercharger installed in a Range-Rover, the long drive shaft snout can be seen, pushing the supercharger drive well forward and clear of the ancillary drive pulleys and belts.

recession has slowed the remaining development work needed to produce and test a fully functional kit ready to go on to the market, but it *will* happen. That is not to say that it is impossible to fit a B & M supercharger to the Rover V8 engine, because of course it is. The supercharger can be bolted to any Holley four-barrel carburettor flange, which will mean mounting it directly on top of the engine and devising a belt drive from the front of the crankshaft. The belt has to be kept in tension, which will involve some sort of tensioning device, and the belt drive and other engine ancillaries, such as the alternator and water pump, also have to be maintained. The supercharger will then accept either fuel injection, American four-barrel carburettor, or even a pair of sidedraught Webers.

TURBOCHARGING

It is interesting to note that the GM aluminium 215 cu. in. engine in one of its original forms, the Oldsmobile version, was one of the very first engines to be used in a series production turbocharged car.

In April 1962, Oldsmobile introduced their Turbo Rocket V8 version of the engine. The first year of Oldsmobile F-85 sales had been disappointing (the Studebaker Lark outsold it by a couple of thousands!), but had it not been for the F-85 Cutlass in the model range, sales would have been much worse. The Cutlass, introduced in May 1961, was sporty and it was ideally suited to a performance version of the engine, hence the "Jetfire", a unique turbocharged version of the aluminium V8.

In this press release photograph of the prototype B & M supercharger "kit" the superbly finished components look very attractive, but there are obviously problems still to be sorted with pulley drives to the alternator and water pump, etc.

151

ROVER V8

As far back as October 1959, GM engineers had been extracting greater power from the engine, but in production terms, with the technology of the day, they felt the engine had limitations. So the Oldsmobile engineers began their own tests with various commercial turbochargers, but they found them all lacking in some respect.

It is normal practice in forced induction engines to lower the compression ratio, but on the Jetfire it was left at 10.25:1, and a special carburettor and injection system were designed. The special Rochester carb was a sidedraught without a throttle plate. In its place were two butterfly valves between the carb and the turbo inlet. One of the valves acted as a throttle, while the other restricted the compressor inlet in case it ran out of "Turbo Rocket Fluid". This was in fact a 50/50 mix of methyl alcohol and distilled water. It was stored in a reservoir, pressurized by the inlet manifold vacuum, and under conditions of high manifold vacuum, when the turbo was not really working, the fluid was prevented from being sucked into the engine by a check valve. Under open throttle when boost pressure reached 1 psi, the valve opened and the pressure in the reservoir forced the fluid through the discharge nozzle into the engine. This kept consumption of the precious fluid to a reasonable level, allowed several thousands of miles of normal driving but effectively suppressed detonation.

The turbocharger itself was driven from the right-hand cylinder bank only, and consisted of a radial inflow turbine wheel and shaft made of Stellite steel with an aluminium centrifugal compressor wheel on the other end of the shaft. Both were less than 63.5 mm (2.5 in) in diameter and spun at up to 90,000 in the Turbo Rocket V8 engine. It was equipped with a wastegate, bleeding off excess pressure into the exhaust system, limiting the boost to 5 psi maximum, which with atmospheric pressure equal to 14.7 psi gave a total boost pressure of 19.7 psi.

The new engine was given the go-ahead for production in December 1961, and produced 215 bhp at 4,600 rpm, with 300 lb/ft of torque at 3,200 rpm. It appeared in the Oldsmobile Jetfire at the New York International Auto Show in April 1962. With an automatic transmission (a four-speed manual was standard), it could accelerate from 0–6 mph in 8.9 seconds, and with 3.36:1 rear axle achieve a maximum speed of 177 km/h (110 mph). This from a vehicle with a kerb weight of 1,300 kg (2,865 lb)!

The turbocharger is an exhaust-driven air pump which forces air into the engine's cylinders. Hot exhaust gases drive a turbine which is connected by a common shaft to a compressor, which compresses the fuel-air mixture and forces it into the engine. Although the turbocharger is a relatively simple piece of equipment it has to withstand extraordinary conditions – for example, the exhaust turbine may endure temperatures as high as 982°c (1,800°F) – and extraordinary rotational speeds of perhaps 100,000 rpm. This necessitates the use of high-quality materials and precision assembly techniques, which of course are expensive.

To work properly, the right turbocharger has to be correctly installed by someone competent in its application. Common sense, yes, but not so easy to achieve in practice. There are no commercially available turbocharging DIY kits for the Rover V8. Janspeed, who still produce turbocharger conversions for the Rover V8 (mostly for Range-Rover applications), did at one time market such a kit, but problems with customer installation, despite very comprehensive instructions, forced them to insist on selling fully fitted conversions.

Interestingly, Janspeed turbocharger conversions for the Rover V8 engine were available for the Rover 3500 (SD1) at a time when this saloon was regarded as a rather respectable luxury car, and lacked the performance image bought about by the touring car racing programme and the introduction of the Vitesse version. Available initially as a kit, it involved fitting twin Roto-Master turbochargers. The standard air filter box was retained, as were the twin SU carburettors, which were mounted so that the turbos were drawing the air through them (as opposed to blowing through them). The fuel/air mixture, after being pressurized in the turbos to a maximum of 7 psi, was blown into the standard inlet manifold via short pipes. Standard pistons with a 9.35:1 compression ratio were used, which limited the amount of boost that could be used (and the cost involved), but the performance was impressive. 0–60 mph came up in a mere 7.5 seconds, and 0–100 mph in 19.7 seconds (maximum 211 km/h/131 mph), with an abundance of additional torque in the mid-range. Janspeed have not forsaken the Rover V8 installation, but nowadays it is more usually applied to the Range-Rover, where their twin turbocharger conversion boasts 220–240 bhp and over 250 lb/ft of torque at a mere 2,700 rpm with a 3.5 litre engine.

Turbo Technics in Northampton began turbocharging the Rover V8 in 1981, using pressurized twin Strombergs (so-called blow-through), and later experimented with a single, twin choke down draught Weber version. But they could never completely cure hot start problems caused by rapid build-up of under-bonnet

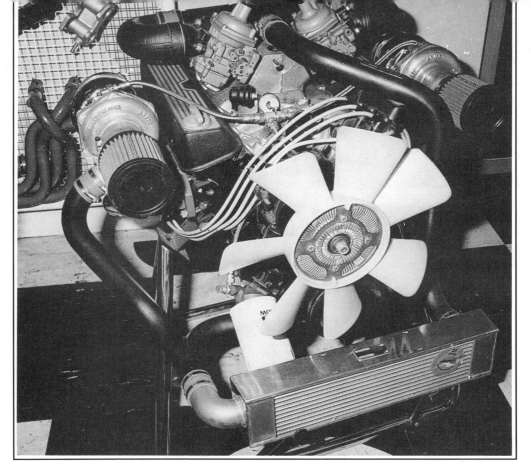

A Janspeed twin-turbocharger installation on a Rover V8 with an intercooler will produce around 260 bhp on a 3.5 litre engine.

The single turbocharger installation built by Nic Mann for his Morris Minor hillclimb car. The power of this 3.5 litre engine has never been accurately measured, but the car could accelerate from 0–60 mph in 3.1 seconds, 0–100 mph in 6.9 seconds, and once did the standing quarter mile in 11.1 seconds!

153

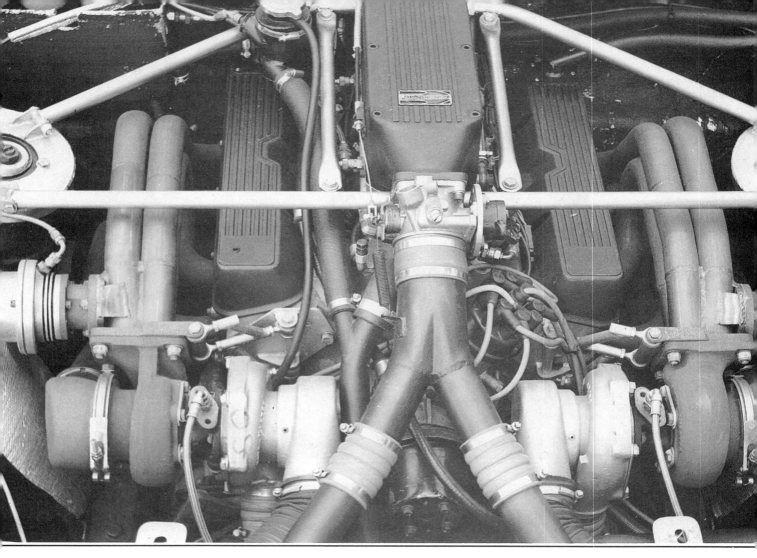

heat when the engine was switched off after a hard run. The heat would cause fuel vaporization in the carb and make the engine very difficult to restart. This, of course, was unacceptable for an expensive road car conversion of a luxury vehicle such as the Range-Rover.

The almost universal use of the fuel injected version of the 3.5 litre and 3.9 litre Rover V8 in production vehicles has made the whole engineering of turbocharging of this engine much simpler. Two of the most powerful Rover V8s ever built – Nic Mann's legendary Morris Minor and the Janspeed Le Mans Turbo TR7 V8 – use the manifold hardware of a Land-Rover production fuel injection system, albeit much modified, effectively to manage the fuel requirements of these turbocharged engines, particularly on-boost enrichment, which is probably the most critical area.

The fact is that turbocharging needs the sophistication of fuel injection to provide satisfactory fuel/air delivery, and the key to a good turbocharger installation is that it should drastically enhance the engine's performance with no trade-off in fuel economy, driveability and

power delivery. In short, no disadvantages, only advantages. Turbo Technics retain the standard ECU (Electronic Control Unit) which retains engine management under part throttle conditions, but their own supplementary electronic "injection modulation processor" gradually takes over as boost increases. The current Turbo Technics' installation results in a Rover V8 engine that delivers 258 bhp at 5,000 rpm and a massive 330 lb/ft of toque at 2,500 rpm! That is sufficient to give a Range-Rover a 0–60 mph time of 8.1 seconds!

Modifications to the actual engine are minimal, except for one very sophisticated operation on the cylinder heads. The combustion chambers are machined on a CNC milling machine to reduce the compression ratio to 8:1, which involves subtly reshaping the combustion chamber so that cylinder head material thickness remains constant around the combustion chamber. The operation is so precise that no hand finishing is necessary after the milling operation has been completed. A stronger cylinder head gasket is also substituted which coincidentally is slightly thicker.

The Janspeed Triumph TR7 V8 Le Mans project twin turbocharged, intercooled 3.5 litre engine. Power output has never been accurately measured, but the car was timed at 311.34 km/h on the Mulsanne Straight at Le Mans. Nuff said.

SUPERCHARGING AND TURBOCHARGING

A new offside exhaust manifold cast in nickel iron has been designed specifically for the Range-Rover installation, and receives the exhaust gases from the other cylinder bank via a stainless steel connecting pipe which goes under the sump. There is also a stainless steel large bore exhaust system to reduce back pressure.

The turbocharger itself is a Garretts T3 unit (or a T3/T4 hybrid on 3.9 litre engines), fully assembled by Turbo Technics from castings, with a balanced shaft and water-cooled bearings. Turbochargers are not particularly complex and are capable of lasting the life of most engines. Their weakness is the bearings which carry the central shaft, and failure of these bearings probably accounts for 90 per cent of turbo failures.

The secret to reliable turbochargers is the correct and precise balancing of the central shaft which carries the turbine impeller on one end and the compressor impeller on the other. The other development has been water-cooling of the shaft bearings. After a turbocharged engine has had a hard run and got exceptionally hot it has always been necessary to let the engine idle for a few minutes before switching it off. This was to enable the oil to continue circulating through the turbo via the engine's oil pump to draw heat from the turbo body, and if this was not done the oil in the turbo could carbonize due to the terrific heat. The thick black carbon/oil mixture thus produced would eventually clog the oil ways to the bearings, and once the bearings were starved of oil they were quickly destroyed, requiring a new or reconditioned turbo. Turbochargers now have water-cooled bearing housings, which enables the temperature around the central shaft to be much better controlled, and when the engine is switched off the natural thermal water circulation continues around the engine, carrying excess heat away, stopping the oil around the bearings reaching critical temperatures and preventing carbon build-up.

Detonation is the limiting factor of ultimate turbocharging power; the higher the static compression ratio of the engine, the less boost pressure can be applied before detonation occurs. However, if you lower the static compression ratio excessively, the engine will have very poor response at low rpm when turbo boost is low. The norm is around 8:1. How much boost the turbocharger is capable of delivering depends on the turbine impeller to turbine housing clearance, and the amount of boost delivered to the engine during operation is controlled by a wastegate. The wastegate senses inlet manifold pressure and via a diaphragm-operated lever diverts boost pressure into the exhaust pipe, downstream of the turbo. Greater boost requires greater cylinder head to block face contact, and a strong bottom end is essential. Bearing in mind the fact that boost pressures will make little impression on engine performance until at least 2,000 rpm, the Rover V8 lends itself well to turbocharging because of its good low rpm torque characteristics, and when building specific engines it is important to choose the right turbocharger for the intended application, which needs specialist knowledge.

It is impossible to give detailed turbocharger installation instructions for the Rover V8 engine, because there are so many variables involved. For instance, the size and layout of the engine compartment will dictate turbo positioning; and there is also the type of induction system used, simple carburation or electronically controlled fuel injection road or competition use, single or twin turbochargers, engine displacement, etc, to be considered.

However, for the knowledgeable enthusiast, designing and building a turbocharger installation is a realistically achievable option. Indeed it may be the only option, since to take your individual requirements to one of the major turbo specialists and have a one-off installation done would be extremely expensive because of the fabrication and tuning time involved. Companies prefer to invest in a conversion which they can reproduce and market, offsetting the development costs against the sale of a number of units. If you do not wish to turbocharge the engine in the particular vehicle involved in the conversion, or it cannot be easily adapted to your application, then you have no option but to seek specialist assistance or tackle the job yourself.

It is possible to give some worthwhile guidelines to designing a one-off turbo system for a Rover V8, and these should be carefully considered before embarking on such a rewarding venture!

There are various items of plumbing essential to the operation of the turbo. First to consider is the exhaust gases into the turbine, or the "exhaust plumbing". With the Rover V8 having one manifold on either side of the engine, it makes the fitting of a single turbo slightly more difficult than twin turbos (one for each cylinder bank), but what is required is an exhaust system that retains as much exhaust pressure, exhaust gas velocity and heat as possible, and provides the most direct route from the exhaust port outlet on the cylinder head to the turbo. Considerations of smooth exhaust flow and tuned pulsing, which are so important in a normal non-turbo performance engine, are of no importance with a turbo. The high exhaust temperatures encountered with a turbo will put great demands on the material used to fabricate a tubular system, so normal thinwall tubing will not do. The same demands will be made of the exhaust manifold flanges too, which must be thick enough to avoid warping, and thus remain completely leak-free. Stock cast manifolds can be cut, ground, and arc-welded, with the turbo mounting flange cut from good quality steel 19 mm (00.75 in) plate. Some turbo specialists can supply ready-made flanges to match particular turbochargers. If a manifold is fabricated from tubing, then good quality thickwall tubing or even stainless steel will have to be used, if any kind of durability is to be expected.

If you are going to build a twin turbo installation with a turbo mounted on separate manifolds either side of the engine, you should consider a balance pipe connecting the two manifolds, in order to equalize pressure. If a single turbo is used, the exhaust manifolding will have to be designed so that all eight cylinders are routed into the turbo, and of course the turbo or turbos must be mounted conveniently, with due consideration given to interference with other engine ancillaries, the effect of turbine heat on surrounding components and bodywork, and other plumbing involved, which we will now examine.

Once the combined exhaust gases have been routed into the turbo or turbos, these same gases then have to exit from the end of the exhaust turbine and into the atmosphere via an exhaust system. The turbocharger will itself drastically reduce exhaust noise, but the exhaust system should still include a silencer, which must have as little restriction to gas glow as possible, whilst still retaining sufficient muffling. The exhaust system after the turbo should also be of a generous diameter around 63.5 mm (2.5 in) so as not to restrict exhaust gas flow.

The airflow into the compressor is probably the most difficult aspect of turbo installation to consider, depending on how the turbo is plumbed into the induction system (draw-through or blow-through). In a typical Rover EFi system, the turbo sucks fresh air through a large low-restriction filter, compresses (and heats) the air in the compressor, and then blows the air into the plenum chamber (so-called blow-through), which forms a convenient pressure equalization chamber for all eight cylinders. The ECU of the EFi system has to be suitably modified to provide boost enrichment. A turbocharged engine requires more fuel under boost conditions than a normally aspirated engine, because the cylinders are receiving a greater volume of air. However, this is made more complex by the fact that turbo boost is a product of engine load more than rpm, so the engine's fuel requirements increase with load/boost more

than rpm. This is one reason why fuel injection is so much more compatible with turbocharging than carburettors. Fuel injection systems are more expensive and require sophisticated ECU management, but they already utilize high fuel pressures (needed to overcome boost pressure on blow-through systems) and can be "mapped" more precisely over a wider rpm range, albeit needing expensive dyno time. The ECU used on standard Rover V8 EFi systems is not mappable – see *Chapter 7*.

That is not to say that effective turbocharger installations on the Rover V8 cannot be built using carburettors. However, a blow-through system using a single Holley carburettor mounted on a conventional Edelbrock manifold will involve enclosing the car in a box capable of being pressurized, into which the single or twin turbos blow. Fuel lines and the throttle links have to be routed through the wall of the box, which must remain airtight.

More straightforward for carburettors is a draw-through installation. Carburettors can be mounted downstream of the compressor inlet, so the turbo draws fuel/air mixture through the carb, into the compressor, and then blows it out of the compressor under pressure into the inlet manifold. The carburettor is able to function as it would for a normally aspirated engine, and does not have any special fuel pressure requirements. It is possible to design an installation that would involve a carburettor for each turbo, a pair of SUs, for instance, or a pair of turbos drawing through a single four-barrel Holley. If the Holley is mounted above a plenum from which the turbo (or turbos) draws, it might be necessary to provide water heating for the plenum base to aid fuel vaporization and avoid carb icing. The choice of carburettor will be critical to the overall performance potential of the installation. The greater the boost used, the greater the carb will have to flow, or it will act as a restricter to potential boost. However, under conditions of low boost the carb has to retain the same response, driveability and economy as it would on a normally aspirated engine. This is one reason why a four-barrel Holley with vacuum secondaries would be ideal, but it has to be tuned to give a smooth transition when the secondaries open under boost, and this requires careful selection and testing of diaphragm springs.

The main turbocharger bearings need a constant supply of clean oil (the main reason why the turbo will suffer when engine maintenance is neglected). The most convenient and most often used source is the oil pressure warning light or gauge sender unit, which can have a "T" piece inserted from which can be taken $\frac{1}{4}$ or 5/16 in braided line to the turbocharger. The drainback of oil from the turbo can be simply welded or brazed into the sump, but care must be taken to ensure that it is above the oil level to avoid back-pressure.

INTERCOOLERS

Intercoolers have been marketed in the turbo era as a further addition to a hi-tech, high-performance power unit. Whether they should be included in a system is determined as follows: if the power outputs required can be achieved without using intercoolers, they should not be used. They are expensive and add to the complexity of the installation, as well as requiring further under-bonnet space.

The function of the intercooler is simple. It is an air to air heat exchanger, mounted between the turbo compressor and the inlet manifold, which lowers the temperature of the fuel/air charge before it enters the combustion chamber. As the intake charge is compressed (by turbocharger or supercharger), its temperature rises. Cooling the charge means lower combustion chamber temperatures, allowing more boost and more ignition advance before encountering detonation. In fact, any means of lowering the temperature of the intake charge is worth considering. For instance, the Rover V8 already has a metal sheet (part of the inlet manifold gasket) separating the lifter gallery from the underside of the inlet manifold, but the Huffaker inlet manifold for the Rover V8 has the manifold runners raised well clear of the hot engine, which in theory should mean a cooler intake charge.

So much for the turbocharger. What about the Rover V8 engine to which the turbo is going to be applied? What needs to be done to the engine to ensure it is able to cope with the additional power and operating conditions? A healthy engine can be turbocharged to moderate boost levels with little internal alteration, but if the engine is going to be built for high boost levels and high rpm, perhaps for competition use, then many of the rules of engine preparation for normally aspirated engines apply.

Firstly, the compression ratio needs to be lowered to around 8:1. This is low enough to allow a reasonable amount of boost, but not so low that the engine will have no response at low rpm when the turbocharger is hardly having any effect on engine performance. For instance, the Turbo Technics conversion for the Range-Rover is designed not only to be efficient and give a worthwhile performance boost, but also to allow the turbocharger installation to be carried out with the minimum expense. That means that if the engine is new or low mileage, the conversion can be almost bolt-on. Hence they avoid going to the expense of stripping the engine in order to fit low compression pistons, but instead only go as far as removing the cylinder heads and opening up the combustion chamber volume with a programmed milling machine. For the enthusiast building an engine, perhaps for competition use, the lowering of the compression ratio can best be accomplished by replacing the pistons, which may have to be machined to achieve the desired compression ratio. High boost pressures require good quality forged pistons with a relatively thick crown. One other effect of turbocharging that may require piston modification is excessive piston crown heat which may cause the top part of the piston to expand and reduce piston to cylinder wall clearance, causing scuffing. The cure is to machine the piston above the first compression ring so as to reduce the piston diameter in this area by a few thousandths of an inch.

Likewise Turbo Technics retain the standard camshaft, and in this respect they have no reason to change it. "Wild" camshafts with a lot of overlap, essential for high rpm operation, have no place on a turbocharged engine, since efficient cylinder filling is the function of the turbo, not holding the valves open until the last possible moment. With forced induction it is important to get the inlet valve open as far as possible, as quickly as possible, but too much intake duration can mean excessive fuel/air mixture being forced into the engine, and it is important to get the exhaust valve closed as soon as possible in order to avoid the incoming charge of fuel/air being literally blown out of the exhaust pipe!

Stronger head gaskets are desirable, as is ensuring that the cylinder heads are firmly attached to the cylinder block. Nic Mann, with his turbocharged Rover V8-engined Morris Minor, found that the heads were lifting under high boost conditions, so he had the heads and block machined to take larger diameter head bolts, while retaining the standard Rover head gaskets. Janspeed found it necessary to "O" ring the heads for extra insurance. This involves machining a groove around each combustion chamber, into which was inserted soft copper wire, which crushed when the heads were bolted down to the block, forming an extremely tight seal.

Accurately machined, wide valve seats (2.032 mm/0.08 in intake; 2.54 mm/0.1 in exhaust) are also important for two reasons. Firstly this allows a good valve to seat seal which is needed under high cylinder pressures, and secondly the wider seats will allow better heat transfer from valve to cylinder head,

Detail of a draw through, twin turbocharger installation on the March F2 of Roy Woodhouse. The 3.9 litre Rover V8 could power the car through the standing half-mile in just under 16 seconds at over 240 km/h.

The Rovercraft 4.5 litre Rover V8 engine is claimed to produce a massive 720 lb/ft of torque at 3,000 rpm, but peak power was not quoted. Its twin turbochargers with intercoolers make this car a top contender in hillclimbing and sprint competition.

Kev Jenkins sits on the start line at Avon Park Raceway waiting for the 3.9 litre Rover V8 with nitrous oxide injection to launch the car down the quarter-mile in under 10 seconds!

which will help to control combustion chamber temperature in this critical area. The valve springs also have more work to do. The exhaust valves have to fight against back-pressure, which builds up between the backside of the valve head and the turbo, and the inlet valve spring has to push back against the boost pressure, which will try to keep the valve open under boost. These pressures can also wear the rocker arms rapidly too, so it might be wise to replace the standard aluminium Rover items with steel or roller rockers.

One point to consider is the retention of the hydraulic cam followers on a turbocharger installation, even in a high-performance engine. The additional plumbing of the installation invariably limits access to the rocker covers and the valve gear, so the low maintenance requirements of hydraulic followers is ideal in this situation, particularly on a road vehicle.

Rovercraft have built a full race 4.5 litre turbocharged Rover V8 which probably represents the current state of the art. The engine is the power unit of the "Rovercraft", a specially built, March-based, hillclimb and sprint car, jointly owned and campaigned by Tony Marsh and Simon Law of Rovercraft. In this branch of motor sport, real torque is important, and this engine produces 720 lb/ft at

3,000 rpm. The engine was originally 3.9 litres, and it produced excellent power between 3,000 rpm and 7,000. Since going to 4.5 litres the engine has upped the torque, but there is still work to be done in pushing the engine for more top end rpm, since there is no power gain about 5,500, and the chassis now has problems putting the power to the track surface. Increasing the boost just increases the torque.

Rovercraft were entirely responsible for this unique twin turbo (with intercoolers) installation, which uses Garrett turbos specially built for this application by Turbo Technics. The engine has oil-cooled, ceramic-coated pistons, and full Motec electronic ignition. At the Brighton Speed Trials in 1991, the car ran a best time of 16.61 seconds at 249 km/h (155 mph) over the classic half-mile course, its top speed being limited by not having large enough diameter rear tyres to raise the gearing for ultimate top speed. Roy Woodhouse was running a March in the same event using a 3.9 litre twin turbocharged (non-intercooled) Rover V8 with larger rear tyres, and therefore better gearing, for a long half-mile straight, and achieved 15.92 seconds at 246 km/h (153 mph), and ran 265 km/h (165 mph) earlier in the day. The turbocharged Rover V8s were running two seconds faster than the non-turbo

159

ROVER V8

Rover V8-engined racing cars in the Over 2,000 cc class, which was good enough for sixth (Woodhouse) and eighth (March), right there behind full race Cosworth DFV and Judd-engined cars.

NITROUS OXIDE

Nitrous oxide and nitrous oxide systems for use on the Rover V8 are of great interest to anyone involved in drag racing, and can make for an extremely interesting road car, too! It is now banned in nearly all forms of mainstream motor sport, and most recently was excluded from hill-climbing and sprinting, mainly through safety concerns about having a pressurized bottle of gas on board a car should it crash.

However, in drag racing nitrous oxide is used to lift the quarter-mile performance ability of the Rover V8 to truly spectacular levels, as demonstrated in the Custom Car/Real Steel Rover V8 Championship. At the time of writing, a 3.9 litre Rover V8 with nitrous oxide assistance had propelled a car down the quarter-mile (from a standing start) in a mere 9.7 seconds. On another occasion it went through the timing beams at the end of the quarter mile at 239.69 km/h (148.97 mph)! The car in question, a Ford Pop built specifically for drag racing by Bob Nixon is driven by Ken Jenkins, and has a Rover V8 engine built by Peter Pinion of Real Steel around an ex-TWR Group A block with standard 88.9 mm (3.47 in) bore and steel 77 mm (3 in) stroke crankshaft. The engine was fitted with a partial girdle plate, but the main bearing caps still fretted (ie, loosened) at high rpm, although fixing them with a stud kit cured the problem. The big valve cylinder heads prepared by Real Steel have also been attached to the block using studs. The steel crankshaft carries Childs & Albert aluminium connecting rods and Ross forged pistons. The camshaft is a mechanical Crane 266 (out and out power, high rpm) with Kenne Bell roller rockers. Induction is by Holley four-barrel on a Huffaker manifold, with a 175 bhp kit from the American company Nitrous Oxide Systems, an MSD 7L2 ignition, and wet-sump lubrication. This relatively unsophisticated engine is coupled to a two-speed Powerglide automatic transmission, which changes gear at 7,000 rpm, and when the car crosses the finish line it is pulling 7,300 rpm! Drag racing machines in these "Pro-Rover" and "Street Rover" classes really are performance marvels, and without wishing to detract from the abilities and innovations shown by the competitors, it is nitrous oxide that has really enabled these cars to produce such staggering performances from engines which, although a credit to their builders, are not ultra sophisticated or indeed expensive, considering their performance.

So what is this magical substance, and how does it have such a dramatic effect on engine performance? Nitrous oxide (or laughing gas) was discovered in 1772 by the same man who discovered oxygen, Joseph Priestley. It was first experimented with in relation to internal combustion engines during the Second World War as a means of boosting aero engine performance for short periods, but the introduction of the jet engine made such work redundant.

American hot-rodders and drag racers dabbled with it in the early years, but found methanol and nitro methane easier to understand and develop. In fact, it has been suggested that nitrous oxide resumed its development as a clandestine means of giving competitors in petrol-only racing classes an unfair advantage. It is now in widespread use for all sorts of high-performance engines, but its properties and its use are still looked upon by many as slightly oddball.

Whatever its reputation, nitrous oxide has enormous potential as a performance booster for the Rover V8 engine. It is possible to drive the vehicle when required with a mild, economical power unit, but when called upon to do so the touch of a button can add 75-150 bhp for short durations. The nitrous oxide will add to the engine's power output by a given amount, regardless of whether the engine has been otherwise modified to increase its performance.

Nitrous oxide is a gas, but it is used in liquid form. It is not a fuel, and cannot be burned in a combustion chamber by itself. Rather it is an oxidizing agent, which when heated breaks down into nitrogen and oxygen. The freed oxygen will then support the combustion of additional petrol which must be introduced with the nitrous. However, the ability of nitrous oxide to support combustion is equalled by its ability to lower intake charge temperature, hence its other reputation as a detonation suppressor. Nitrous oxide has a high latent heat of evaporation – it absorbs a tremendous amount of heat as it changes from a liquid into a vapour – and an extremely low boiling point. So as the pressurized liquid is released into the intake manifold its pressure and temperature drop rapidly, it absorbs heat as it vaporizes, and absorbs still more heat as it tries to rise from its low vaporization temperature to something equal to that in the combustion chamber. The lower the temperature of the induction charge of fuel/air (or in this case fuel/air/N_2O), the denser the charge. The denser the charge, the greater the power as a

The innocuous looking 3.9 litre Rover V8 engine has steel crank, aluminium rods, forged pistons, Huffaker intake manifold, and single Holley four-barrel. The NOS nitrous oxide system supplies an additional 170 bhp at the touch of a button.

The engine in Martin Cowell's MG "Mighty Midget" is nitrous oxide-injected and runs in the Street Rover class of drag racing. It covers the quarter-mile in just over 12 seconds at over 176 km/h.

result of more being able to be packed into the cylinder prior to compression. It must be understood at this point that a nitrous oxide injection system, when activated, will endow a given engine with an increase in power (actually torque) of, say, 100 bhp, and this increase remains constant as engine rpm increases. So like turbocharging and supercharging, nitrous oxide injection allows more horsepower to be produced without increasing engine speeds by increasing the thermal efficiency of the engine.

While nitrous oxide has the ability to suppress detonation in turbo/supercharger installations, one of the main problems encountered when using nitrous oxide on a normally aspirated engine is detonation caused by exceptionally lean mixtures. Since nitrous oxide is not a fuel but merely supports combustion, it must have additional fuel added to the cylinder to use the additional oxygen liberated from its breakdown. Not enough fuel can have the same effect as an exceptionally lean mixture, ie, rapidly increasing combustion chamber temperatures. Matching the correct

amount of additional fuel with the "dose" of nitrous oxide is critical. The correct ratio of nitrous oxide and fuel has been established by those currently leading the field in commercial systems.

The nitrous oxide supply carried by the vehicle is stored in a pressurized bottle, usually carried in the boot. The actual pressure at which it is stored varies according to the temperature, so for safety the 5 lb or 10 lb bottle cannot be located where it may be exposed to exceptional heat. Also a bottle may not last all that long if the system is activated regularly, so it has to be conveniently placed for refilling.

There are two basic types of installation system: plate systems and individual port systems. Any system involves a very simple assembly of components, the actuating valves being the only moving parts. From the bottle the nitrous oxide runs to the engine compartment through a high-quality steel braided line, while a second line is taken from the fuel line immediately after the fuel pump (4.5–5 psi is needed). Both lines require good filters to keep the system absolutely clean.

This Rover V8, installed in an MGB GT is interesting. It is nitrous oxide-injected and runs in the Pro-Rover class, but has a fabricated tunnel ram intake manifold mounting a pair of Weber carburettors. The car has run low 12 second quarter-miles at over 185 km/h.

With a plate system, the two lines run to a plate similar to a carburettor flange, and nozzles in the plate spray the fuel and nitrous oxide into the inlet manifold. The mixture is then distributed to the cylinders in the same way as the fuel/air mixture from the carburettor. Nitrous Oxide Systems produce a plate kit for a Holley carburettor flange pattern at quite a modest price, which is suitable for the Rover V8 and would be capable of delivering a 100+ bhp punch to a road engine.

With an individual port system the nitrous oxide and fuel lines run to distributor blocks on the engines and individual steel lines run to nozzles tapped into the individual inlet manifold runners. The fuel and nitrous oxide are mixed at the point of injection. Some systems will have a pair of nozzles in each manifold runner, one for nitrous oxide and one for fuel, while others, such as the NOS system use a so-called fogger nozzle which takes both into a single nozzle. Individual port systems are slightly more complex and are more involved to install, as well as more expensive, but they are also more efficient.

Multistage systems are the most sophisticated. In competition, particularly drag racing, there can be problems with launching a car from rest with a particularly powerful system. Available traction and the shock loads on transmission and drive line components can make full-power launches difficult, so rather than reducing the overall nitrous oxide use to a more controllable level or activating the system once the vehicle is moving, nitrous oxide system builders have come up with the two-stage system. The car leaves the start line with a proportion of the system's total capacity, and the second stage is activated later to power the car towards the finish line.

The Rover V8 in good condition can be run with a nitrous oxide system installed, but most systems will be added to modified engines, in which case certain principles need to be adhered to. A performance engine using nitrous oxide will need to be built with the same care and attention to detail as any other. The higher the state of tune of the engine, the less power that can be added by nitrous oxide before the mechanical limitations of the engine are reached. High compression ratios should be avoided and attention should be paid to the exhaust side of the engine, particularly the exhaust manifolds and system. Serious engine builders should pay particular attention to the exhaust valve and port, not easy on the Rover V8, but installing a bigger exhaust valve and drastic exhaust port work with large-diameter primary exhaust manifold pipes will pay dividends in high-power systems. As power outputs are increased the engine's compression ratio can eventually become a limiting factor as detonation occurs. Nitrous oxide systems usually have the fuel to nitrous oxide ratio as much as 50 per cent rich in order to cool the intake charge and help suppress detonation, but as an engine is built to produce maximum power on nitrous oxide, then the static compression ratio can become a limiting factor and may need to be reduced. A nitrous oxide camshaft, used on an engine with a relatively restricted exhaust port, will need a wide lobe centre line with the exhaust 15–20° longer than the intake, and the cam will need to be set in the engine advanced. A good ignition system is important, with slightly cooler running spark-plugs, and the timing may need rethinking. Nitrous oxide increases the oxygen content of the mixture which tends to increase the speed at which the combustion flame travels through the combustion chamber, thus requiring less ignition advance.

One of the leading suppliers of nitrous oxide systems in the UK is TMS (Automotives) Ltd, who manufacture Highpower systems, designed, produced and developed in the UK. Trevor Langfield, the company's founder, has been involved in developing systems for the Rover V8 and successful engines have been built for racing and road cars. They quote a standard Rover SD1 3.5 litre saloon with a quarter-mile standing start time of 17.8 seconds with a terminal speed of 124 km/h (77 mph) having that reduced to 13.5 seconds at 165 km.h (102 mph) by the installation of a Highpower system. Systems can be assembled from a range of components, with varying degrees of sophistication and power output depending on the application. Because the engine does not have to achieve high rpm levels to produce high outputs, a typical competition engine may have die-cast pistons, standard blueprinted con rods, cross-drilled standard crankshaft, mildly prepared cylinder heads with the emphasis on improving the exhaust side and with the appropriate nitrous oxide system produce upwards of *450 bhp* for short duration bursts such as drag races. Truly remarkable.

Chapter Seven
Fuel Injection

With today's fuel-efficient, low emission petrol engines being as much a requirement of Government legislation as customer demand, the use of electronic fuel management is becoming evermore widespread. Witness the ever-growing number of new often mundane cars now carrying the "i" badge. Until such demands were brought to bear on the motor industry the carburettor had always remained prevalent, despite the development and specialized use of fuel injection systems, because of cost. Mechanical fuel injection systems have been in existence and had limited production applications for decades, but it was the enormous advances made in microchip technology, its reliability and its cost that made electronically controlled systems practical in recent years. Electronic fuel injection combines the mechanical advantages of a fuel injection system with the enormous processing power of the computer enabling such a system to provide the engine with near optimum air/fuel ratio's under virtually any operating conditions.

The Rover V8 engine was not exempt from meeting strict efficiency standards and fuel injection was applied by Land-Rover in the 1980s to export versions of this engine, for emission purposes only, when the Rover 3500 (SD1) was chosen for the North American export market. In order to comply with the market's demand on emissions and other parameters, the Rover V8 had to have fuel injection, and the development of this so-called "Federal" system was carried over to the Triumph TR8 and vehicle sales in the Australian markets. Because these early systems were required to meet the demands of emission legislation, power production was not a high priority, but this does not mean

that they do not have good performance potential.

It was October 1983 with the Rover Vitesse that the Rover V8 engine got fuel injection to enhance performance, and all the basic components of the earlier system were applied to a newly designed performance inlet manifold and plenum. The Vitesse's 190 bhp provided a significant improvement over the Federal version's 150 bhp and the UK carburetted version of 155 bhp. The Vitesse system was rapidly developed during the racing programme, culminating in the so-called "twin plenum" system, perfected with the aid of Lotus, which saw limited application on the showroom Rover Vitesse towards the end of its production life. Development of the more familiar single plenum system continued, appearing in the Range-Rover in 1986 with altered ECU (Electronic Control Unit) parameters to take into account greater fuel efficiency and the softer characteristics of the Range-Rover camshaft. This system is found on all EFi engines up to 1986 when a second-generation system, currently in production at Land-Rover, introduced a "hot wire" airflow meter and detailed ECU alterations to accommodate it.

The introduction of the hot wire system coincided with the launch of the Range-Rover in North American, and once again the ability of the engine to meet emission standards held sway in the development process. The restrictive nature of these standards led to the introduction of the 3.9 litre Rover V8 which eventually became available in the UK market, where without certain power-sapping additions it produced 185 bhp. Well run-in 3.9 litre engines (UK versions) are reputed to be capable of giving over 200 bhp. As Range-Rover

Later production inlet manifold from 3.9 litre Range-Rover.

On top of this...

...goes the trumpet base. Shown here is the fuel rail in the later 14CU/14CUX type with "O" ring injectors. On top of this...

...goes the final component, the standard production plenum cover with the throttle disc orifice facing the camera.

got 3.9 litre engines, so Discovery V8s became available with EFi engines, utilizing the new hot wire technology to give improved fuel efficiency and cleaner emissions but no more power. An interesting feature of the 3.9 litre hot wire injection system is that the ECU contains software that limits maximum speed to just below that of the maximum of the S rated tyres, ie, 182 km/h (113 mph).

The standard Rover Vitesse/EFi fuel injection engine is still a fairly expensive proposition for the enthusiast to purchase (compared with older, more plentiful carburetted versions), but it has now had widespread production use, being fitted first in the Rover Vitesse, then the

This is the bigger "twin plenum" trumpet base with its larger diameter...

Rover SD1 Vanden Plas, the Range-Rover EFi, Vogue and Discovery. More recently the EFi unit is being used in an increasing number of specialist vehicles such as the Morgan, Marcos and TVR sports cars. The availability of second-hand engines is fairly limited, but as the years go by this situation will change, and the performance potential of the unit is thus becoming of greater interest. Unquestionably the electronically fuel injected Rover V8 does have enormous performance potential. In its heyday of production saloon racing, which has more restrictive regulations than the frequently referred to Group A, the best Rover Vitesse engines were squeezing out 218 bhp, but this did not even allow a change of compression ratio. A single throttle plenum (ie, the normally available type) was good enough to fuel the

300 bhp+ Group A racing engines in the Rover Vitesses. The "twin plenum" injection system used on the 1986 Group A racing Rover Vitesses is even better, the racing engines producing well over 300 bhp, but it was really too much of a compromise on a road engine, actually giving too much flow at lower rpm with a 3.5 litre engine. This twin plenum system is extremely rare, original production probably being only about 200, and thus very expensive, although more have been cast, so availability (at a price) has improved.

Many enthusiasts are intimidated by the electronics of the Rover EFi system, and its "black box" ECU module, but there is no need. Much of the mystery surrounding electronic fuel injection has been cultivated and nurtured by manufacturers, no doubt to

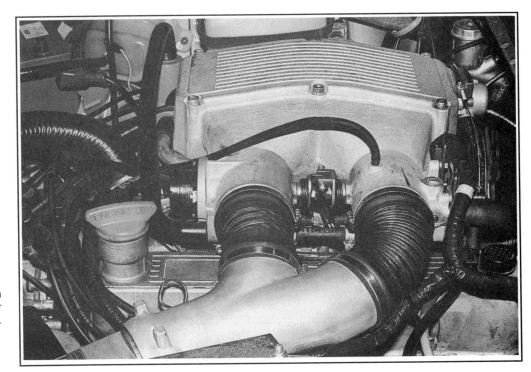

...and this is the "twin plenum" top with its pair of throttle discs.

167

Early prototype race version of the "twin plenum" trumpet base, with very short trumpets...

...and this is its unique plenum top made by welding two single plenum tops together. Research such as this led to the pukka "twin plenum" limited production design.

"Twin plenum" trumpet base modified by J.E.Engineering to accept slightly shorter but standard diameter aluminium trumpets...

...then those same aluminium trumpets squeezed on to a production single plenum trumpet base.

ROVER V8

ensure that vehicles so equipped are always returned to franchised dealers for servicing and repairs.

The Rover V8 engine uses multipoint or port fuel injection, which uses one injector per cylinder. Multipoint injection allows near perfect cylinder to cylinder fuel distribution, promoting superior fuel atomization (more efficient combustion) because fuel is injected at high pressure through a small orifice directly into the manifold airflow close to the inlet port. Although such a system uses a throttle body to regulate airflow, it should not be confused with throttle body fuel injection, which not only regulates airflow, but also flows fuel through the throttle body butterfly (or butterflies).

The superiority of multipoint fuel injection as a means of delivering the correct fuel/air mixture over a wide range of engine requirements has as much to do with the inlet manifold design as the technology of microchips. A typical V8 inlet manifold with twin SUs or single Holley has to distribute a wet mixture of air containing atomized fuel droplets to eight cylinders, and the manifold design has to ensure that as little fuel as possible drops out of suspension on its way to those cylinders. The multipoint fuel injection system on the Rover V8 has only to guide air efficiently to the port entrance, where the fuel is added, in precisely metered doses, by the injector nozzle.

With the obvious exception of the induction system, the Rover V8 EFi engines are mechanically identical to the normally aspirated engines, apart from one or two details. The inlet and exhaust valves introduced for the Rover Vitesse in 1982, are of the same size as the SD1 valves, but have waisted stems and material removed from the back of the valve head to aid gas flow with *slightly* different machining to the ports immediately behind the valve seats.

Apart from these very minor cylinder head changes the difference with the Vitesse/EFi Rover V8s is centred entirely around the induction system, ie, the inlet manifold with its plenum chamber, airflow meter, fuel rail, injector nozzles and attendant "black box", the ECU.

The current inlet manifold, as introduced on the Rover Vitesse, was designed by Land-Rover engineer Richard Twist and is made up of three basic parts. The inlet manifold lies between and is bolted to the cylinder heads in the conventional manner and has eight individual runners. Each one of these runners has an injector nozzle located close to the inlet port of the cylinder head. On top of this manifold is the plenum base, a flat alloy casting

The one-piece plenum of the early "Federal" injection systems, designed with emissions, not performance in mind, but still capable in tuned applications.

Underside view of the "Federal" injection system plenum. The row of eight ports matches an identical flange in the inlet manifold, with injectors in the manifold runners.

which has eight steel flared unequal length trumpets. Entirely enclosing this base is the cast alloy plenum chamber which has a single throttle butterfly on one side.

There was an earlier Federal/emission injection system fitted to Rover V8s for certain export markets, eg, California. The vehicles involved were mainly Rover SD1s and Triumph TR8s, and none of these engines was officially available in the UK, although some of these injection systems have found their way into the hands of enthusiasts. The injection system itself is still Lucas "L", like the Vitesse, but the inlet manifold and plenum chamber are very different. It is made up from only two castings and the manifold itself has the runners congregated into a straight row of eight square orifices, which match the underside of the one-piece plenum casting. While not designed for performance, this earlier manifold/plenum design is perfectly adequate to meet the needs of a good road engine's requirements.

The Lucas "L" system owes much to the well-tried Bosch L Jetronic, to which it bears some resemblance, using a similar flap type airflow meter as the main sensor. Later versions use a hot wire airflow meter. The ECU, however, is more closely related to the Lucas 6CU "P" system used until recently on the Jaguar V12 HE.

The whole system can be divided loosely into three groups:

1. Air flowing components begin with the air filter, a vital engine component which too many abuse or even eliminate to their cost. Next in line is the airflow meter. The Bosch flap type airflow meter is quite simple, although many of its functions are rather subtle and not immediately apparent from observation. It consists of a specially profiled channel containing a pivoted and spring-biased flap which is deflected by air passing through to adopt an angular position where the spring force is balanced by the force of air against the flap. The angular position of the flap is converted to a voltage via a sophisticated potentiometer, and this voltage signal is converted within the ECU to a digital code.

With the introduction of the 3.9 litre EFi Range-Rover, the flap-type airflow meter was replaced with the Lucas 13CU hot wire airflow meter which has no moving parts. Instead of a flap and potentiometer it functions on the simple principle that air passing over an electrically heated wire will cool the wire, changing its resistance. In the hot wire airflow meter, air enters via an air cleaner and passes over two wires, stretched across the internal air passage with the meter. One wire is controlled by an amplifier circuit which varies the current passing

171

Collector's item. A "twin plenum" production Rover Vitesse installation. J.E.Engineering carry all the spares and service these rare machines.

Unique "Costello" low profile plenum for installation in MGBs retains standard bonnet line, and fits the standard manifold.

FUEL INJECTION

through the wire in order to maintain it at a set temperature. More mass airflow means more current to maintain the temperature, and this information is passed to the ECU. The second unheated wire acts as a control, and enables the meter to compensate for variations in incoming air temperature.

The hot wire airflow meter has nothing to restrict the path of the incoming air. Instead a small bypass port in the meter carries just a small proportion of the air passing through the meter and over the two wires.

Three views of a one-off fabricated sliding throttle injection system built by Ray Woodcock for use in brother Reg's Westfield 11 race car. Based on a pair of downdraught Weber/Dellorto cast manifolds, the system has zero airflow restriction, tuned length trumpets and sophisticated Lucas electronics. Cost to replicate? Don't ask.

2. Engine control components centre around the ECU. The ECUs used on earlier flap-type airflow meter systems are not interchangeable with those used on the later hot wire systems because the earlier systems use analogue computing principles while the hot wire system uses digital. The digital systems are far more accurate, being capable of being tailored much more closely to the very detailed requirements of the engine, as well as having greater long-term stability and reliability. While the later system is better, the earlier system is still an excellent performer.

The ECU has a memory in which the basic fuel requirements of the engine are stored. In order for the ECU to respond to these requirements the ECU needs data from various sensors fitted to the engine. There are two main sources of data, airflow from the airflow meter and engine speed from the coil in the form of pulses (or via a flywheel or crankshaft sensor from the front crank pulley on some systems). The digital code from the airflow meter in combination with a crank speed signal from the ignition coil is applied to a "look-up table" type of memory in the ECU which determines the required pulse duration, for the injectors, driven by an oscillator or clock. These basic fuel requirements are just that, basic, and take no account of engine temperature, acceleration, deceleration, cold/hot starting or emissions. These are known as correction factors and data for coolant temperature, air temperature, battery voltage, throttle position and cranking enrichment are added by further analogue circuitry which modulates the clock frequency to extend the pulse as required. All "L" type ECUs are identical in appearance, apart from the Lamba sensing emission type, and are more or less interchangeable, although there are some differences according to engine specification.

3. Fuel flowing components. Fuel is drawn from the tank to a high-pressure fuel pump and the pressurized fuel is then passed to the engine compartment and the fuel rail (injector feed pipe). Connected to the fuel rail are the injectors (one per cylinder) which are solenoid operated valves sitting in the inlet manifold and pointed towards the inlet valve. A fuel pressure regulator maintains the fuel pressure in the fuel rail to a predetermined level.

The fuel pressure regulator has a spring-loaded diaphragm valve covering an overflow port, the spring pressure keeping the port closed. As fuel pressure rises it will, at a certain level (normally 36 psi), compress the spring and open the bypass part. Excess fuel will then return to the fuel tank, thus maintaining the fuel pressure in the fuel rail at a constant pressure.

The spring pressure in the regulator will only maintain the required fuel pressure at atmospheric pressure, but inside the inlet manifold the pressure can fluctuate considerably with changes in throttle position. The EFi system requires constant fuel pressure at the injector tip for accurate fuel metering, so the fuel pressure must also alter with changes in the inlet manifold pressure.

To achieve this a small bore pipe connects the inlet manifold to the fuel pressure regulator. The changing manifold pressure acts on a diaphragm which alters the spring rate, which in turn changes the fuel pressure in line with manifold pressure changes in exactly the same way as the vacuum advance mechanism operates within a distributor. The function of the fuel pressure regulator and its effect on the injection system when tuning an engine is something that should be fully understood.

SELECTION AND INSTALLING A SYSTEM

Obtaining a second-hand production system is not simply a case of buying all the obvious hardware, such as the manifold, ECU, injectors and some wiring, bolting them together and starting up. The complete system requires more extensive installation and careful setting up if the results of this considerable investment do not end up being a disappointment.

The cost of a second-hand system will depend primarily on whether an airflow meter or a hot wire system is chosen, and whether the system offered is complete. A fully functional airflow meter system from a Range-Rover is probably one of the best options in terms of value for money. This system has advantages over the Vitesse single plenum system which more readily appears in second-hand sales columns. Firstly, the age of the system – any Range-Rover system is bound to be newer than that from a Vitesse – and secondly, for some reason the Vitesse systems carry a price premium, despite the fact that the only effective difference is in the mapping of the ECU. Changing an ECU is no more complicated than unplugging one and plugging in another.

The current hot wire system will be more expensive being relatively new. However, the hot wire system does have the advantage of being the current production system and is mapped for the 3.5, 3.9 and 4.2 litre engines, which gives greater scope for further modifications, and thus the potential to produce more power than the airflow meter systems.

So having found a system available for purchase, what components should be on

Standard single plenum trumpet base with shortened trumpets for use with 3.9 litre conversions (greater airflow capability).

Standard single plenum trumpet base with very large diameter trumpets, hence the notches in the bell mouths.

view to convince the prospective purchaser that the system being offered is complete? An airflow meter system should consist of the following:

1. Manifold assembly (including the plenum and throttle body).
2. Airflow meter and connection pipe to throttle.
3. Injection wiring harness.
4. Fuel pump.
5. Two injector relays and a steering module (diode pack).
6. Power resistor pack.
7. ECU.

The manifold assembly should come with the following components attached:

8. Eight injectors (grey harness connectors).
9. Cold start injector (blue connector).
10. Coolant temperature thermistor (white connector).
11. Thermotime switch (brown connector).
12. Extra air valve.
13. Fuel rail.
14. Fuel pressure regulator.
15. Throttle potentiometer.
16. Throttle mechanism.
17. Breather pipes.

If the system being offered for purchase is missing any of the above, price up a replacement. In the case of major items, prices of at least three figures are the norm, so if any are missing it is best to continue looking for a complete (or *more* complete) system.

If you have located a complete system, try and get some information on its history and if possible some sort of guarantee that it is in working order. Testing of major components would be advisable, either via a specialist or Rover dealer. The cheapest alternative would be a friendly Range-Rover or Vitesse owner whose vehicle could have the main plug-in units fitted to see whether they are working.

In the case of the hot wire system there are fewer components than the airflow meter system. The complete list should read:

1. Manifold assembly (including the plenum and throttle body).
2. Airflow meter (hot wire version) and connection pipe to throttle.
3. Injection wiring harness.
4. Fuel pump.
5. Two injector relays.

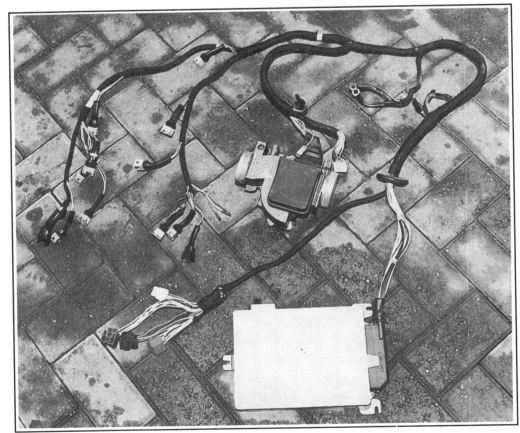

This is how the "electronics" of a second-hand system might look when offered for sale, with the wiring harness connected to the ECU (in the foreground), the airflow meter in the centre, and injector nozzles arranged on the upper left.

6. Road speed sensor.
7. ECU.

The manifold assembly should come with the following components attached:

8. Eight injectors.
9. Coolant temperature thermistor.
10. Stepper motor.
11. Fuel rail.
12. Fuel pressure regulator.
13. Throttle potentiometer.
14. Throttle mechanism.
15. Breather pipes.

Again, any missing parts need to be individually priced to check the viability of buying the system offered. Prices for major components are expensive if bought new.

In addition to the above lists there may well be additional items, depending on the source of the system. There will be extra solenoid valves and relays for the airflow meter system and Lamba (oxygen) sensors for both, if the engine has catalytic converters fitted. As well as these, both systems will have been fitted with a high-capacity, high-pressure fuel filter and a small (6.8 k ohm) resistor, fitted into the engine speed input wire to the ECU.

Again, when considering a system for purchase try to obtain some history, and if possible some guarantee from the vendor. Testing as much of the system as possible is beneficial, but finding a friendly Range-Rover (3.9 litre) or Discovery owner will be that much more difficult, so it is probably down to specialists or Land-Rover agents for testing.

Once obtained, the major task confronting you will be fitting the system to the engine and wiring it into the vehicle. Whatever vehicle the system is going to be fitted to, the principles remain the same, and the base rule is to mimic the fitting of the system to its original application, especially in the fitting of components that do not fit on the inlet manifold.

The fuel pump has to be a high-volume, high-pressure (4 bar/60 psi) pump intended for fuel injection applications. It can be submersible (Range-Rover and Rover 800) or external mount (Vitesse and Maestro/Montego injection). Whichever is used, modifications will have to be made to the tank in order to ensure an adequate fuel supply and prevent the pick-up from becoming uncovered, which would cause the engine to die immediately.

Most original equipment fuel tanks are built with special internal baffling to prevent excessive fuel surge, and there is often a special bowl known as a swirl pot which is designed to provide a constant reserve of fuel for the pick-up and to act as a point where the

returned fuel from the pressure regulator is collected. Ordinary fuel tanks can be successfully modified with components sourced from breakers' yards, with the obvious caution when using heat on any fuel system components, but a better solution is to change the tank for a fuel injected version, or modify the tank to injection specification.

The fuel pipe dimensions are also very important. For all pipe feeds to the high-pressure pump an internal bore of 13 mm (0.5 in) is required, while all delivery (pressure) pipe needs to be of 7 mm (0.27 in) bore. Additionally, all flexible hoses need to be of a type specifically made for high-pressure fuel injection systems, and all clips have to be of a similar standard.

Whilst dealing with the fuel supply, another point of note is that all the Bosch-type external injection pumps must be mounted at or very close to the line of the fuel tank base. This is because they do not draw fuel very well and need all the syphoning assistance they can get. They can also be very noisy in operation, and many applications include a separate fuel pump resistor to reduce voltage and therefore pump speed during operation. The wiring is exactly the same as a ballast-resisted coil.

The wiring harness for the Rover V8 injection system is very helpful to would-be transplanters as it is completely separate from the main vehicle harness and covers the complete injection system. For the airflow meter system there will usually be one multi-plug which connects to the main vehicle harness and two further connection points. The easy one to work out is the collection of earth connectors which must be bolted to the engine. There is a further single wire going to the negative side of the coil for providing the engine speed information to the ECU. This is applicable to both airflow meter and hot wire systems.

The main multi-plug will provide connections to the main wiring harness for battery voltage, ignition switched voltage, fuel pump feed and starter solenoid connection for the airflow meter systems. The hot wire system has the first three plus a number of other connections, which include input from the road speed sensor, air conditioning and automatic transmission. There is also likely to be another plug for the dealer diagnostic function, too.

Other points to note include the mounting of the airflow meter, which in both systems is mounted on rubber bushes to isolate it electrically from the vehicle body/chassis, and this must be done when transplanting a system. The air filter assembly in standard form is not ideal. For instance, the system as applied to the Rover Vitesse is reputed to gain up to 10 bhp by fitting a larger capacity filter unit. If this is true, slightly less could be expected from the standard Range-Rover spec 3.5 litre system, but about the same from the 3.9 litre unit.

Bolting on the injection system should present no problems, but if the cylinder heads on the particular engine chosen are from a non-injected engine, a slight angled grind in the roof of the inlet port is needed to provide injector clearance. In addition, the inlet manifold gasket (the "valley" gasket) has to be of the injection type, which also has small reliefs to clear the injectors. The gasket can be used for reference when relieving the roof of the inlet ports, but care is needed to ensure the gasket line is not undercut.

Finally, when fitting an injection system to any vehicle not previously equipped, it is best to leave everything else as standard or not disturbed from a previous working situation. This will make injection system fault identification and rectification much easier.

MODIFICATIONS AND TUNING

Fuel injection systems cannot in isolation be modified to produce more power in the same way, for instance, as a turbocharged engine can have a performance chip inserted into its ECU. A simple and effective way to gain 8–10 bhp on a standard Rover V8 EFi engine is to remove the standard factory air cleaner and replace it with a high-capacity, low-restriction design, such as one manufactured by K & N Filters (Europe) Ltd. However, they can be modified in a variety of ways to meet the fuelling needs of an engine that has been modified to produce more power. What has to be stressed is that the standard Rover V8 fuel injection system is perfectly capable of handling the fuelling requirements of a tuned engine. Remember that if the breathing ability of the engine is enhanced by, for instance, the addition of a good pair of cylinder heads and tubular exhaust manifolds with a free-flowing exhaust system, the injection system via the airflow meter will measure the superior breathing of the engine and supply a fuel/air mixture to suit.

The vast majority of modified engines are equipped with the digital "L" 4CU system, referred to throughout as the airflow meter system with its flap-type airflow meter (as opposed to the hot wire system). This system is capable of meeting the fuelling needs of modified engines to a certain extent because there is a 25 per cent correction factor built into the standard system to cope with variations in production engine power outputs. Above that correction factor, it is very much

A Lucas 4CU ECU. This one has a simple fuel enrichment module attached to the right-hand side, but this enriches right across the rpm range.

down to the individual system as to whether it is adequate. For instance, the injectors can have a 15 per cent flow variation due to production tolerances which with the current hot wire system, at the standard 2.5 bar fuel pressure, can mean a fuel flow through the injectors of anything between 160 and 180 cc per minute. To give an example, the MBG V8 Roadster owned by enthusiast Roger Parker has a carefully built but relatively standard 3.5 litre Rover V8 engine fitted with an unmodified early Federal-type injection system, with its flap-type airflow meter and a standard Range-Rover ECU. The engine is fitted with Automotive Performance Engineering modified cylinder heads, with standard size valves and a pair of tubular exhaust manifolds. The engine produces no less than 190 bhp *at the wheels*, which represents a 40 per cent increase over standard without even a change of camshaft.

It is only when the fuel flow rate of the injectors or, less likely, the air flowing capability of the inlet manifold is exceeded, thereby restricting the engine's performance in the higher rpm ranges, that we have to look at serious modifications to the system. However, given that the system can cope with the additional fuel demands of a tuned Rover V8 EFi to a certain (albeit limited) extent, engines modified to increase the power output seriously will eventually have to have the injection system adapted to provide extra fuelling. As with most things, there are easy and difficult ways to solve problems, and the costs of possible solutions vary considerably. The best solution will always be expensive. Tuned road engines operating beyond the capacity of the original system usually present more of a challenge than race engines, because road engines are driven most of the time at part throttle openings. Not surprisingly, this is the most difficult area of an injection system to map.

The problems that usually occur are lean mixtures at full throttle and in the upper engine speed range. There is a simple and inexpensive cure. The first step is to change the standard fuel pump for one with greater capacity, then the simplest method of providing the extra fuel is to increase the fuel pressure to suite the maximum power requirement. Higher pressure regulators are available to set values, eg 3 bar, and adjustable regulators are available from various sources. This crude but effective approach is not very satisfactory, however, because considerable compromise must usually be accepted over much of the operating range, and safety margins deteriorate as the pressure increases.

Raising the fuel pressure in the fuel rail in this way will raise the maximum fuel delivery rate through the injectors to 180–200 cc per minute. The drawback is that this 10 per cent increase is right across the board, ie, at tick-over (giving a lumpy idle) and at cruise rpm (effecting economy). It has less effect at full power since the injector will be working on or near capacity anyway. There is also a pressure limit above which the injector nozzles will fail to perform correctly, and increasing the fuel pressure can damage catalytic converters. There are special regulators, known as rising rate regulators, which are designed to increase the fuel pressure when full throttle is used, whilst retaining the standard pressure at all other throttle positions. In many cases this will provide the extra fuel needed without damaging fuel consumption too much.

It is also possible to increase the fuelling by fiddling with the sensor signals. For instance, if extra resistance is added to the coolant sensor circuit, the ECU will provide extra fuel (ie, a richer mixture), thinking the engine is running cooler than it actually is. Some modified "adjustable" ECUs have just such a device to fool the circuitry into thinking the engine coolant is actually at a lower temperature than it really is and delivering more fuel to compensate. The overall effect on driveability is most unsatisfactory, since enrichment will be present throughout the whole engine operating rate, aggravated by the "L" system having the unusual characteristic of triggering acceleration fuelling with sharp changes in sensor voltage. Hot wire systems are more sensitive to sensor input change, the

ECU having much finer control over the engine, and often provide the drive for the temperature gauge. Small changes in input will lower the gauge reading, while larger changes will not only cause greater changes, but also trigger the idle speed control circuit, giving the engine a very fast idle!

When a significant power increase is planned, the standard injectors may be unable to flow the required quantity of fuel because as the engine speed rises the time available for the injection process becomes less. At 6,000 rpm, for instance, the available injector time is 10 milliseconds, and if the pulse duration is of the same magnitude the injectors will be continuously open and the fuelling limit will have been reached. On large displacement or high revving versions of the Rover V8 engine, it is therefore usual to find that black or green injectors with higher flow rates have been substituted for the standard light grey type. Again, however, the fuelling will be enriched everywhere, and if part load performance is not to be compromised the fuelling must be weakened at such times.

An alternative solution is to provide an extra injector or two squirting into the inlet tract, usually on to the throttle plate, so that the contribution is distributed equally to the eight cylinders. This method can be arranged to function only at full throttle or under boost in the case of forced induction, but the additional complication, increased risk of failure and general difficulty of obtaining smooth progression from a system that is unavoidably of a step change nature, is unattractive to most engine tuners.

If satisfactory performance across the whole engine performance spectrum is required, changes to the ECU are necessary. The main fuel memory chip in the production ECU is custom made and can neither be replaced with an alternative nor reprogrammed, but it is possible to replace the standard ECU with a specialist item. There are a number of possible options with cost, ease of programming and, most important, results being the primary considerations. Certainly we are moving into an expensive area, but that has to be balanced against the excellent potential this aspect of tuning fuel injection offers.

Most specialist ECUs eliminate the restriction caused by the airflow meter, which as we have discussed is worse with the Bosch flap-type airflow meter than the latest hot wire type. The power gain possible by removing this restriction from the standard Rover EFi engine is about 8-10 bhp, but larger displacement versions of the engine can gain twice this amount. A simple solution adopted by

179

The fuel memory chip in the ECU is not reprogrammable, but by removing the standard chip and substituting a chip carrier the ECU can have these interchangeable memory chips for instant upgrades.

some has been to fit the larger airflow meter (flap type) from the Jaguar V12, but this is only a partial solution involving a number of compromises.

Obviously to remove the airflow meter entirely is not a simple matter. Until recently, the only answer when omitting the airflow meter was to replace the ECU with an expensive programmable alternative. However, through J. E. Engineering it is now possible to obtain a relatively inexpensive ECU conversion to sense engine load from inlet manifold pressure, thereby eliminating the restrictions of the airflow meter. It is available with adjustment via several micrometer dials or to a fixed specification. When first tested on a Sprintex supercharged 3.5 litre Range-Rover, a power increase in the region of 18 bhp was achieved. Another alternative is becoming available. At the instigation of J. E. Engineering, and exclusively for them, Lucas have developed a programmable system which uses throttle angle and engine speed as the main parameters (the so-called N Alpha principle) on a 16 x 16 site matrix with added correction for air temperature and barometric pressure. This is designated 14CU and is based on the hardware for the 13CU system. A portable PC computer is used with a development aid to map the engine fuelling requirements from dynometer tests

and final road testing, the resulting data being burnt into an EPROM (external programmable read only memory) chip. The standard production chip is carefully removed from the production ECU and replaced with a chip carrier into which the EPROM chip can be inserted. Such a fuel programme can easily be stored and reproduced for other engines of the same specification. For security reasons the programme will partially corrupt if an unauthorized attempt is subsequently made to copy it from the ECU.

Almost all the replacement ECUs available require a considerable amount of computer hardware and software, not to mention dyno time, to map correctly. Rovercraft have become distributors for the Australian-made Motec ECU which can be calibrated on a rolling road or dyno using a CO_2 exhaust gas analyzer in a relatively short time. The Motec ECU allows the setting of the engine's fuel supply in a sequence of 500 rpm steps, with nothing more technical than a screwdriver, making the mixture leaner or richer by varying an LED reading displayed on the ECU. In this way, the engine's fuel supply curve can be calibrated from the top to the bottom and refinements are taken care of by the ECU's internal programming. The ECU takes its cue from induction manifold pressure, engine rpm, air

J.E. Engineering have experimented with many variations, amongst them this "billet" trumpet base which has individual throttle discs for each trumpet. Linkage on right-hand side.

A large capacity Rover V8 undergoing dyno tests to evaluate its fuelling requirements over its complete rpm range. Optimum fuel delivery equates with maximum performance.

J.E. Engineering cast throttle bodies mounted on modified downdraught Weber/Dellorto manifolds displaying range of trumpets used.

J.E. Engineering in collaboration with Mangoletsi developed this twin plenum system which used a standard inlet manifold. It suffered from poor distribution due to the inner tracts taking more air than the outer.

This cross-over manifold is probably best associated with the Pierburg-injected Triumph TR7 V8 rally cars, but this manifold was also used with Lucas/Kinsler/Fuerstenau injection by the Group 44 Tullius racing TR8 in the USA.

temperature and engine coolant temperature, while compensating for ambient temperature, fuel density, atmospheric pressure and battery voltage fluctuations.

As we develop both the injection fuel system and the ECU to control it, the actual manifold hardware begins to become more of a potential area of inlet flow restriction. This is the main reason why the legendary "twin plenum" injection was developed in the heady days of TWR Group A Rover Vitesse racing and was good for 300+ bhp on the 3.5 litre engines in full race tune. The term twin plenum is actually misleading since this system used a larger plenum base and a larger volume plenum chamber with a pair of throttle butterflies instead of the usual single. As stated earlier, these twin plenum manifolds were available on a limited number of production Vitesses (about 200), but the design has now been recast and is therefore still available. It does provide a big increase in inlet flow, most desirable at higher rpm, and has been put to excellent use on larger capacity Rover V8 engines, but it is an expensive route.

There is scope to increase the airflow capability of the standard type single throttle butterfly plenum. The early Federal injection systems used an elliptical throttle disc which varied in diameter between approx 63.5 mm

(2.5 in) and 61 mm (2.4 in). The Vitesse and Range-Rover 3.5 litre round throttle disc is approximately 63.5 mm (2.5 in) while the 3.9 litre Range-Rover system uses a disc of approximately 67.31 mm (2.65 in). The throttle disc from a 4.2 litre Jaguar system is a convenient source for a still larger throttle disc which should fit the Rover casting with some machining of the orifice. Rovercraft produce a 71 mm (2.769 in) throttle body conversion, and J.E. Engineering can also convert the standard plenum casting to take a larger 75 mm (2.93 in) throttle disc.

Ultimately, as already mentioned, it is the maximum airflow capacity of the standard production injection inlet manifold that limits peak power. The twin plenum version was good enough to flow sufficient air for the 300+ bhp Group A racing engines, and since those days more development work has been invested in making this intake system flow still more. After the fitting of a larger throttle disc the incoming air enters the plenum chamber. In the plenum chamber base are eight flared steel trumpets of larger diameter in the twin plenum than the regular single plenum version. These trumpets have been shortened and replaced with still larger diameter versions in the quest for greater flow, particularly for bigger capacity Rover V8s. The manifold itself (on

183

ROVER V8

Example one: MGB V8 Roadster owned and built by Roger Parker produces 190 bhp at the rear wheels. Rover 3.5 litre precision built from a pre-SD1 engine...

...with early-type Federal injection inlet manifold, 10:1 compression ratio, standard camshaft and SD1 heads extensively modified by Automotive Performance Engineering.

Example two: the Triumph TR7 V8 race car of Mick Richards, 1991/2 Cox & Buckles TR Register Champion. It uses a Rover 3.9 litre built by Geoff Lee...

...producing 263 bhp at the flywheel, steel rods, forged pistons, Crane 248 camshaft, wet sump and heads modified by Automotive Engineering.

ROVER V8

which the plenum and base sit) with its eight individual runners to the inlet ports is especially difficult to work on, because the length and shape of the runners make them difficult to tackle with grinding and polishing tools. One process that could successfully port the manifold for increased airflow is "extrude honing", a relatively new process developed for this purpose in the USA. Basically it consists of a machine which forces an abrasive paste through alloy manifold runners under pressure, smoothing and enlarging as it goes. The abrasive texture of the paste and the pressure under which it is applied enables the process to be varied, depending on the amount of material to be removed and the finish of the surface. To my knowledge no machine has yet been imported into the UK, at least not for commercial use, and they are, I believe, designed for multiple runs, not one-off use, but this process has tremendous potential for modifying both inlet manifolds and alloy cylinder heads.

Useful Addresses

Bruce Crower
    15737 Lyons Valley Road
    Jamul
    California 92035
Rooster Racing
    2 The Crescent
    Walthamstow
    London E17 8AB
Kent Performance Cams Ltd
    Units 1 - 4
    Military Road
    Shorncliffe Industrial Estate
    Folkestone
    Kent CT20 3SP
Piper FM Ltd
    Bromley Green Road
    Ashford
    Kent
Real Steel
    Unit 9
    Tomo Industrial Estate
    Packet Boat Lane
    Cowley
    Uxbridge
    Middlesex UB8 2JP
J. E. Engineering Ltd
    Siskin Drive
    Coventry CV3 4FJ
Engine Components Ltd
    Unit C1
    Lincoln Park
    Borough Road
    Brackley
    Northants NN13 5BE
Torque Developments
    Unit 6
    Riverside Industrial Estate
    27 Thames Road
    Barking
    Essex EG11 0NZ

J. E. Developments
    Ashlea
    Oxford Road
    Ryton on Dunsmore
    Nr. Coventry
    CV8 3EA
MSD Ignition
    Autotronic Controls Corporation
    1490 Henry Brennan Dr.
    El Paso
    USA
Highpower Nitrous Oxide Systems
    T. M. C. (Automotives) Ltd
    Unit 2
    107 Rands Lane
    Armthorpe
    Doncaster DN3 3DR
Nitrous Oxide Systems
    5930 Lakeshore Drive
    Cypress
    CA 90630
    USA
Edelbrock Corp.
    2700 California Street
    Torrance
    CA 90503
Crane Cams
    530 Fentress Blvd
    Daytona Beach
    FL 32114
    USA
ExtrudeHone
    8800 Somerset Blvd
    Paramount
    CA 90723
Turbo Technics Ltd
    17 Galowhill Road
    Brackmills
    Northampton
    NN4 0EE

DPR
Watercombe Lane
Lynx West Trading Estate
Yeovil
Somerset
BA20 2HP

Roverpart International Ltd
Wayside Garage
Holt Road
Horsford
Norwich
Norfolk NR10 3EE

Rovercraft
Unit 1
Progress Estate
Parkwood
Maidstone
Kent

John Wolfe Racing
Wolfe House
Norse Road
Bedford MK41 0LF

F. G. Rallying
PO Box 61
Bromyard
Herefordshire HR7 4DP

Janspeed Engineering
Castle Road
Salisbury
Wiltshire SP1 3SQ

Oselli Engineering
Ferry Hinksey Road
Oxford OX2 0BY

K & N Filters (Europe) Ltd
Wilderspool Causeway
Warrington WA4 6QP

Automotive Performance Engineering
Unit 1
Amber Buildings
Meadow Lane
Alfreton
Derbyshire DE5 7EZ

Rovertec
Unit 8
Victoria Works
Saddington Road
Fleckney
Leicestershire LE8 0AX

Index